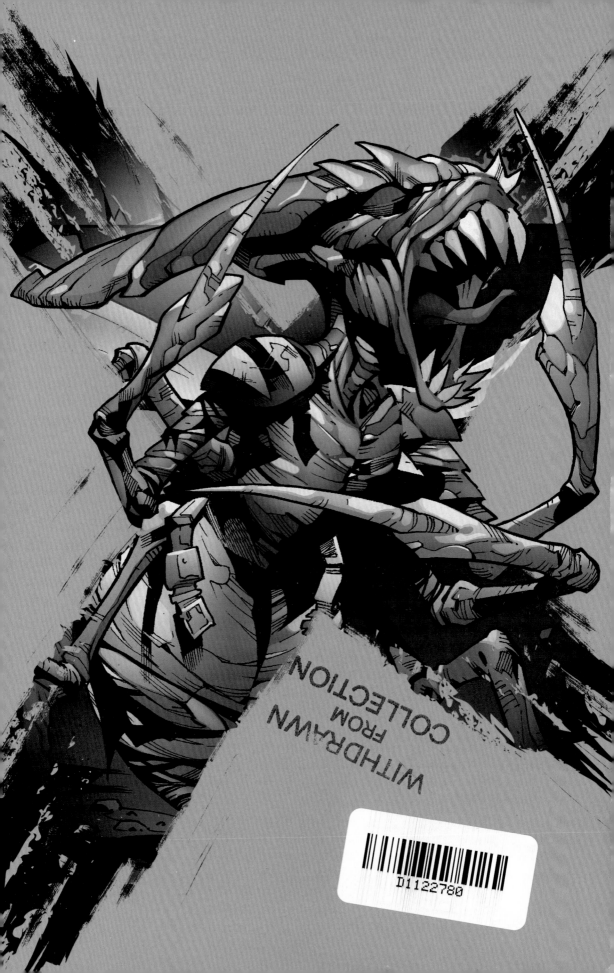

collection editor **JENNIFER GRÜNWALD**
assistant editor **CAITLIN O'CONNELL**
associate managing editor **KATERI WOODY**
editor, special projects **MARK D. BEAZLEY**
vp production & special projects **JEFF YOUNGQUIST**
svp print, sales & marketing **DAVID GABRIEL**
book designer **JAY BOWEN** with **ADAM DEL RE**

editor in chief **AXEL ALONSO**
chief creative officer **JOE QUESADA**
president **DAN BUCKLEY**
executive producer **ALAN FINE**

ALL-NEW WOLVERINE VOL. 4: IMMUNE. Contains material originally published in magazine form as ALL-NEW WOLVERINE #19-24. First printing 2017. ISBN# 978-1-302-90935-2. Published by MARVEL WORLDWIDE, INC., a subsidiary of MARVEL ENTERTAINMENT, LLC. OFFICE OF PUBLICATION: 135 West 50th Street, New York, NY 10020. Copyright © 2017 MARVEL No similarity between any of the names, characters, persons, and/or institutions in this magazine with those of any living or dead person or institution is intended, and any such similarity which may exist is purely coincidental. **Printed in Canada.** DAN BUCKLEY, President, Marvel Entertainment; JOE QUESADA, Chief Creative Officer; TOM BREVOORT, SVP of Publishing; DAVID BOGART, SVP of Business Affairs & Operations, Publishing & Partnership; C.B. CEBULSKI, VP of Brand Management & Development, Asia; DAVID GABRIEL, SVP of Sales & Marketing, Publishing; JEFF YOUNGQUIST, VP of Production & Special Projects; DAN CARR, Executive Director of Publishing Technology; ALEX MORALES, Director of Publishing Operations; SUSAN CRESPI, Production Manager; STAN LEE, Chairman Emeritus. For information regarding advertising in Marvel Comics or on Marvel.com, please contact Vit DeBellis, Integrated Sales Manager, at vdebellis@marvel.com. For Marvel subscription inquiries, please call 888-511-5480. **Manufactured between 10/6/2017 and 11/7/2017 by SOLISCO PRINTERS, SCOTT, QC, CANADA.**

10 9 8 7 6 5 4 3 2 1

X-23 WAS CREATED TO BE A WEAPON.

For a time, that's all she was. But Laura Kinney escaped that life with the help of the man she was cloned from, the man who became her mentor: THE WOLVERINE. Tragically, the original Wolverine has fallen, but Laura will live as his legacy, and fight for her better future. She is the...

ALL-NEW WOLVERINE

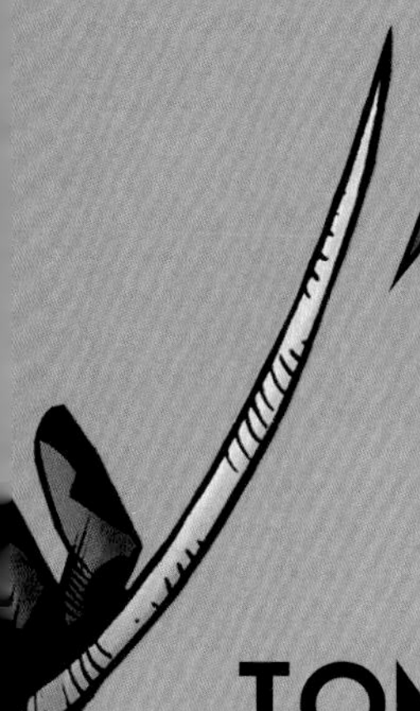

Laura is free. The threat of the Trigger Scent — which endangered everyone she loved, including her preteen clone, Gabby — can no longer affect her. Laura and Gabby are done hiding...and ready to bring the fight to the bad guys.

writer
TOM TAYLOR

penciler
LEONARD KIRK

inkers
CORY HAMSCHER (#19-22)
& **LEONARD KIRK** (#22-24)
WITH **MARC DEERING** (#20)
& **TERRY PALLOT** (#20-21)

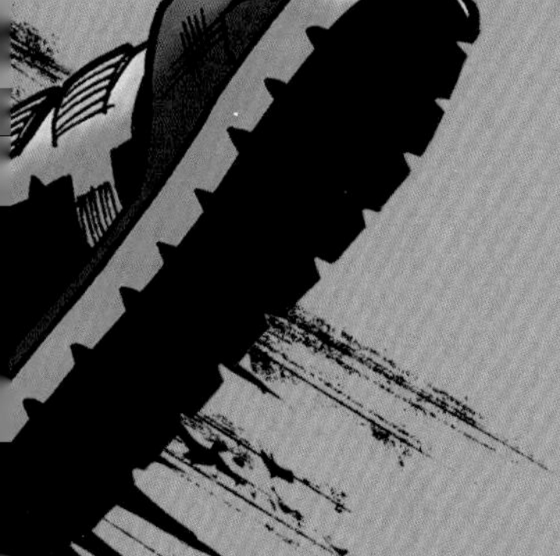

color artists
MICHAEL GARLAND (#19-24)
& **ERICK ARCINIEGA** (#22-24)
WITH **CHRIS SOTOMAYOR** (#20)

letterer
VC'S CORY PETIT (#19-21, #23-24) & **JOE SABINO** (#22)

cover art
ADAM KUBERT & **FRANK MARTIN** (#19-20),
LEINIL FRANCIS YU & **ROMULO FAJARDO JR.** (#21-22),
LEINIL FRANCIS YU & **DAVID CURIEL** (#23)
AND **LEINIL FRANCIS YU** (#24)

assistant editor
CHRISTINA HARRINGTON

editor
MARK PANICCIA

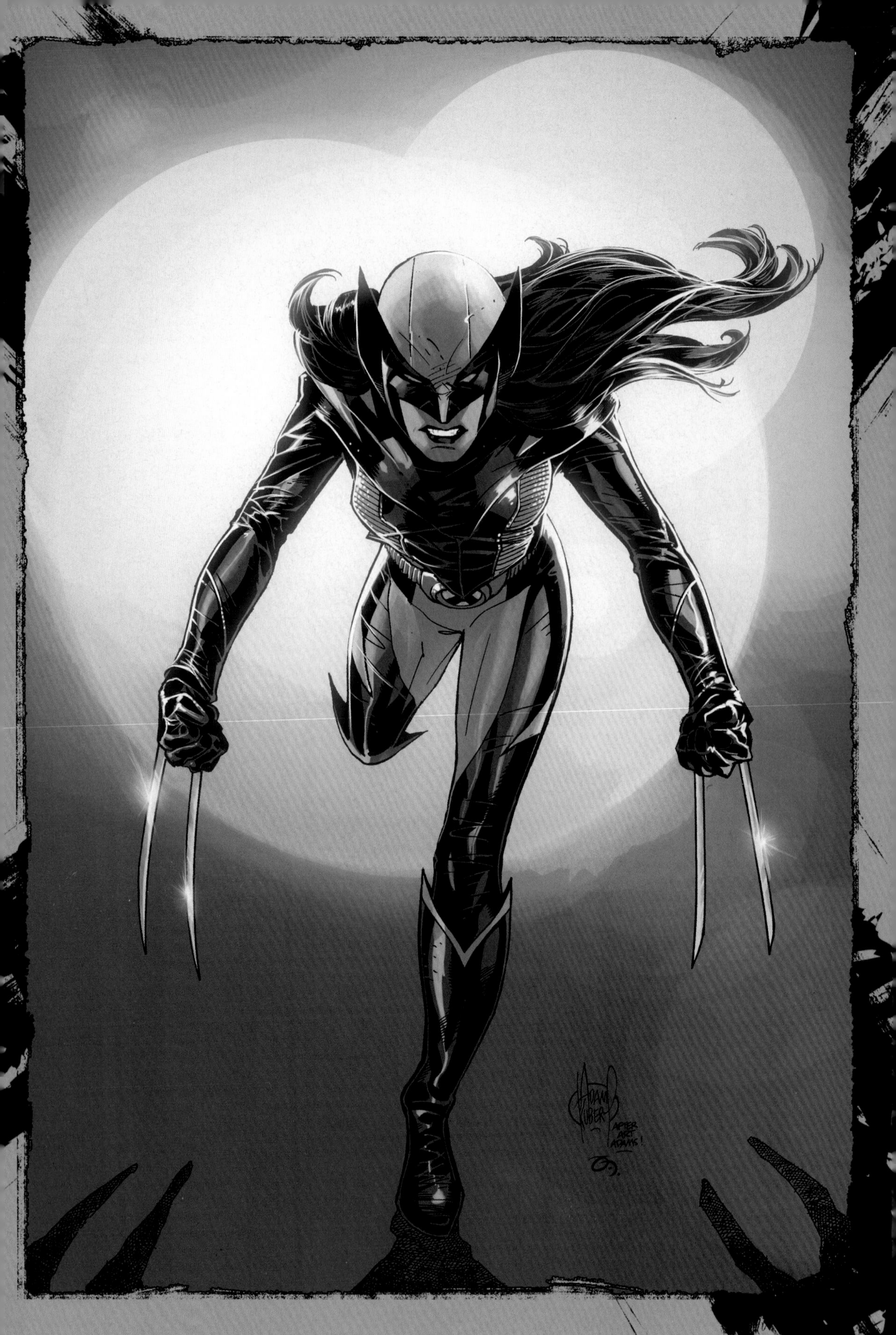
AFTER ART ADAMS!

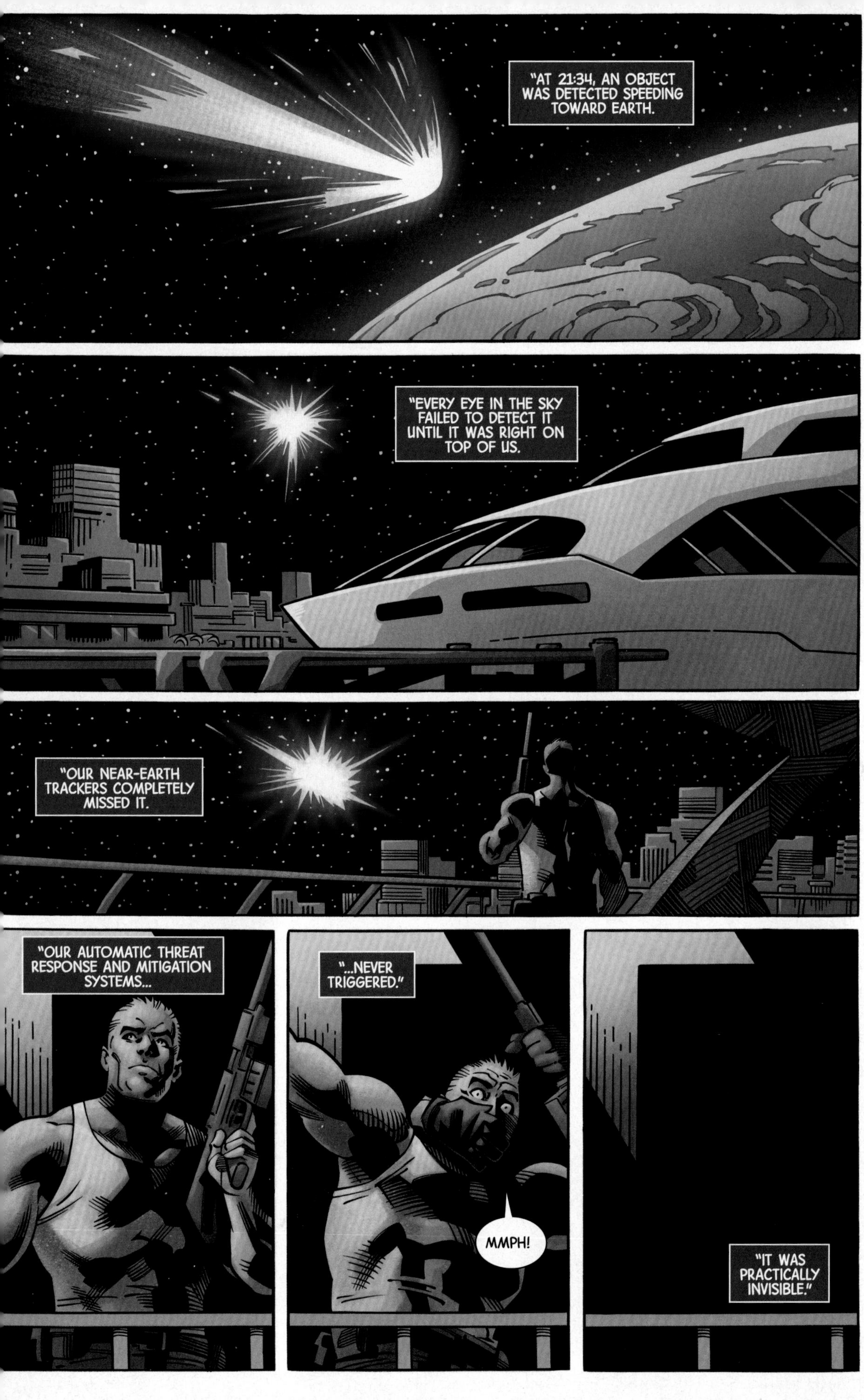
"AT 21:34, AN OBJECT WAS DETECTED SPEEDING TOWARD EARTH.
"EVERY EYE IN THE SKY FAILED TO DETECT IT UNTIL IT WAS RIGHT ON TOP OF US.
"OUR NEAR-EARTH TRACKERS COMPLETELY MISSED IT.
"OUR AUTOMATIC THREAT RESPONSE AND MITIGATION SYSTEMS...
"...NEVER TRIGGERED."
MMPH!
"IT WAS PRACTICALLY INVISIBLE."

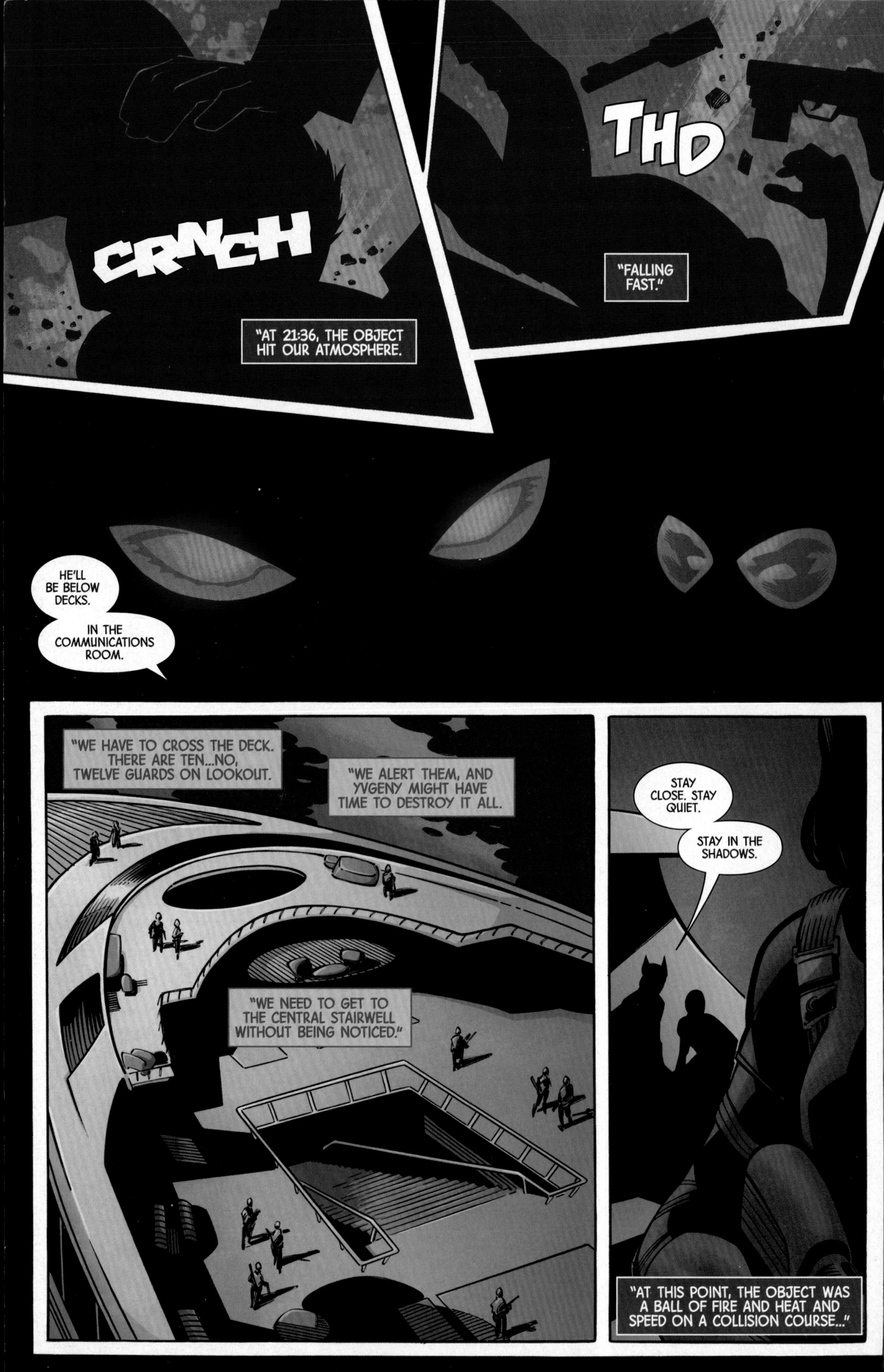
CRNCH
"AT 21:36, THE OBJECT HIT OUR ATMOSPHERE.
THD
"FALLING FAST."
HE'LL BE BELOW DECKS.
IN THE COMMUNICATIONS ROOM.
"WE HAVE TO CROSS THE DECK. THERE ARE TEN...NO, TWELVE GUARDS ON LOOKOUT.
"WE ALERT THEM, AND YVGENY MIGHT HAVE TIME TO DESTROY IT ALL.
"WE NEED TO GET TO THE CENTRAL STAIRWELL WITHOUT BEING NOTICED."
STAY CLOSE. STAY QUIET.
STAY IN THE SHADOWS.
"AT THIS POINT, THE OBJECT WAS A BALL OF FIRE AND HEAT AND SPEED ON A COLLISION COURSE..."

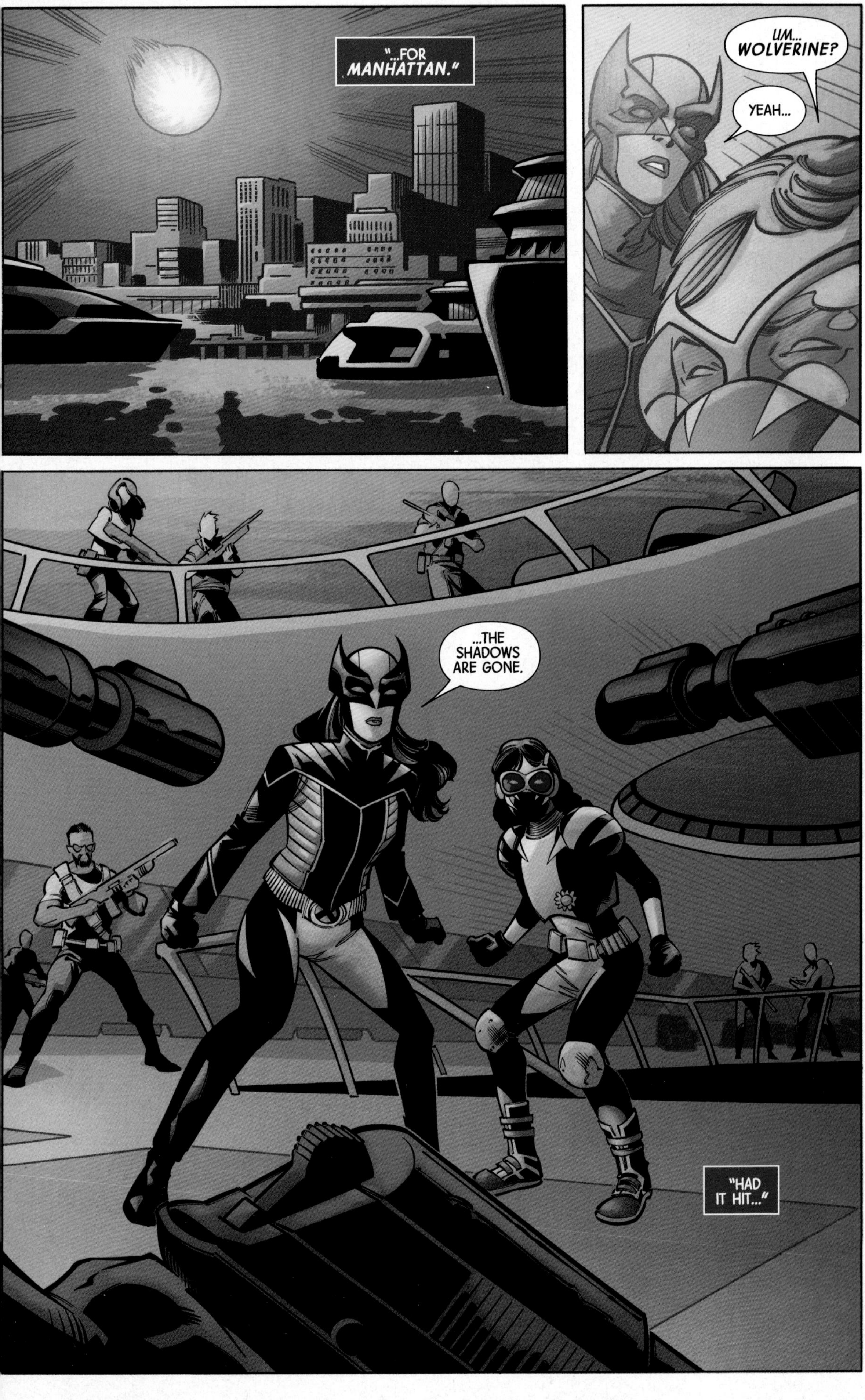
"...FOR MANHATTAN."
UM... WOLVERINE?
YEAH...
...THE SHADOWS ARE GONE.
"HAD IT HIT..."

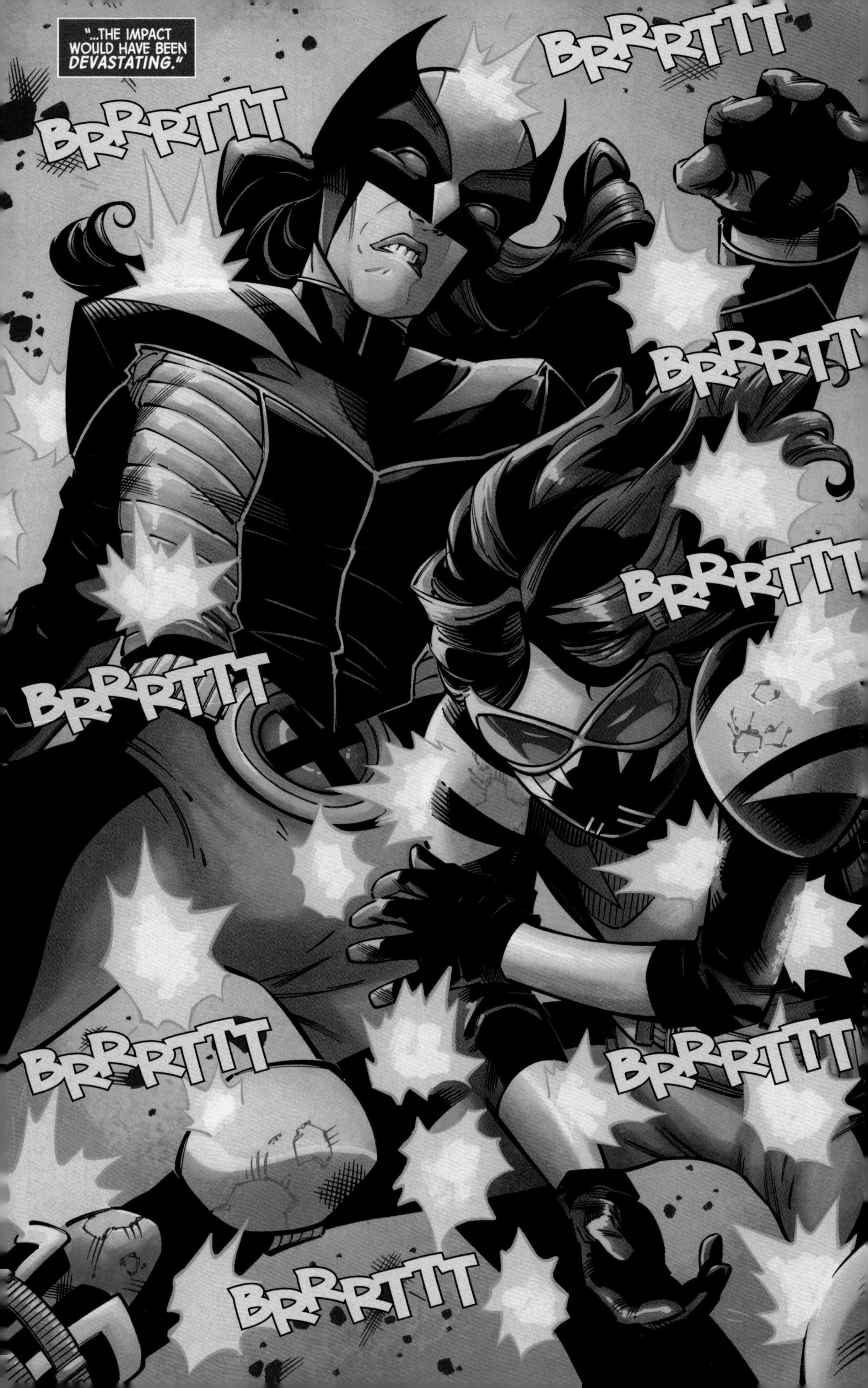
"...THE IMPACT WOULD HAVE BEEN DEVASTATING."
BRRRTTT
BRRRTTT
BRRRTT
BRRRTTT
BRRRTTT
BRRRTTT
BRRRTTT
BRRRTTT

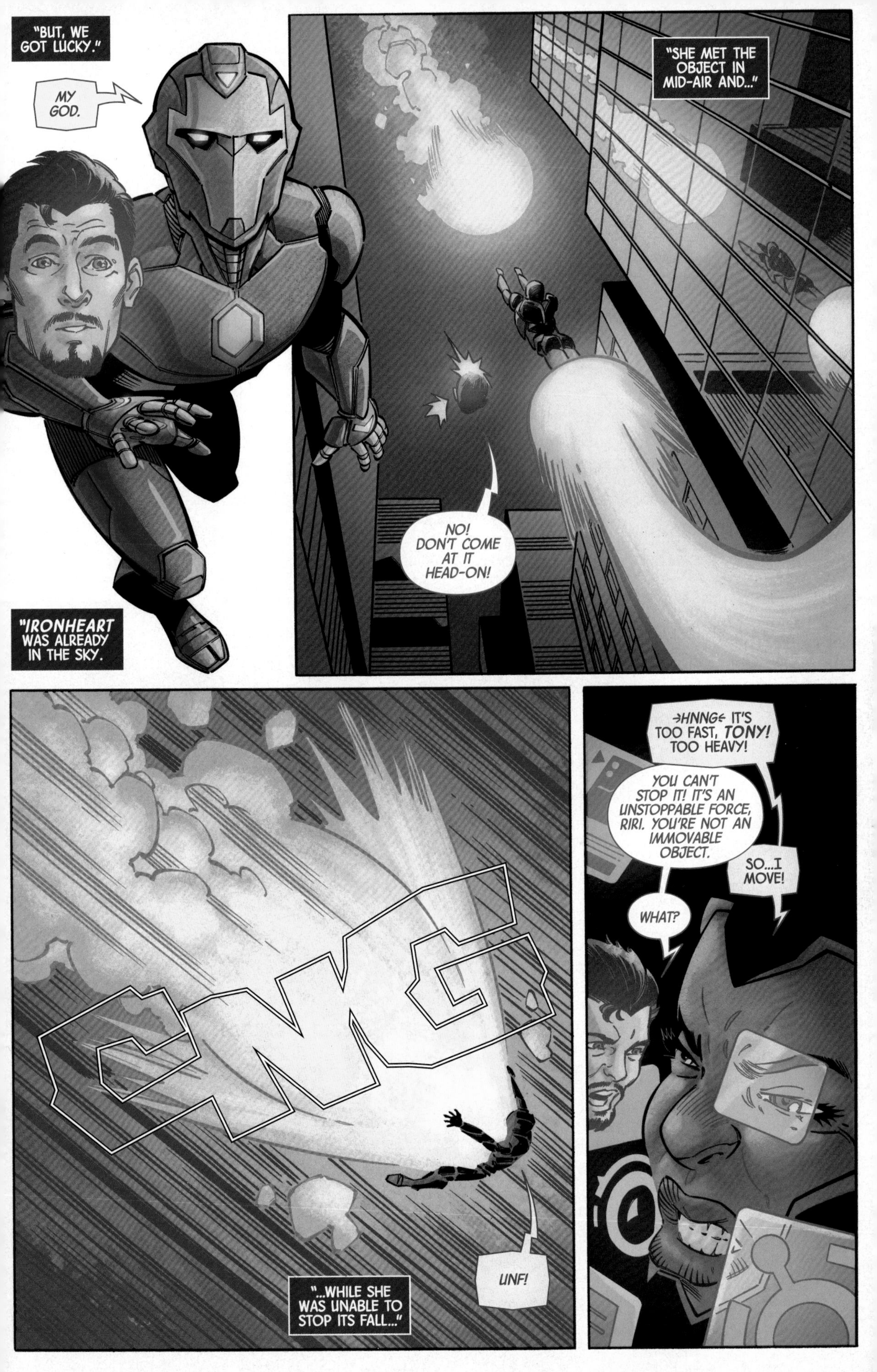
"BUT, WE GOT LUCKY."
MY GOD.
"IRONHEART WAS ALREADY IN THE SKY.
"SHE MET THE OBJECT IN MID-AIR AND..."
NO! DON'T COME AT IT HEAD-ON!
CWG
UNF!
"...WHILE SHE WAS UNABLE TO STOP ITS FALL..."
→HNNG← IT'S TOO FAST, TONY! TOO HEAVY!
YOU CAN'T STOP IT! IT'S AN UNSTOPPABLE FORCE, RIRI. YOU'RE NOT AN IMMOVABLE OBJECT.
SO...I MOVE!
WHAT?

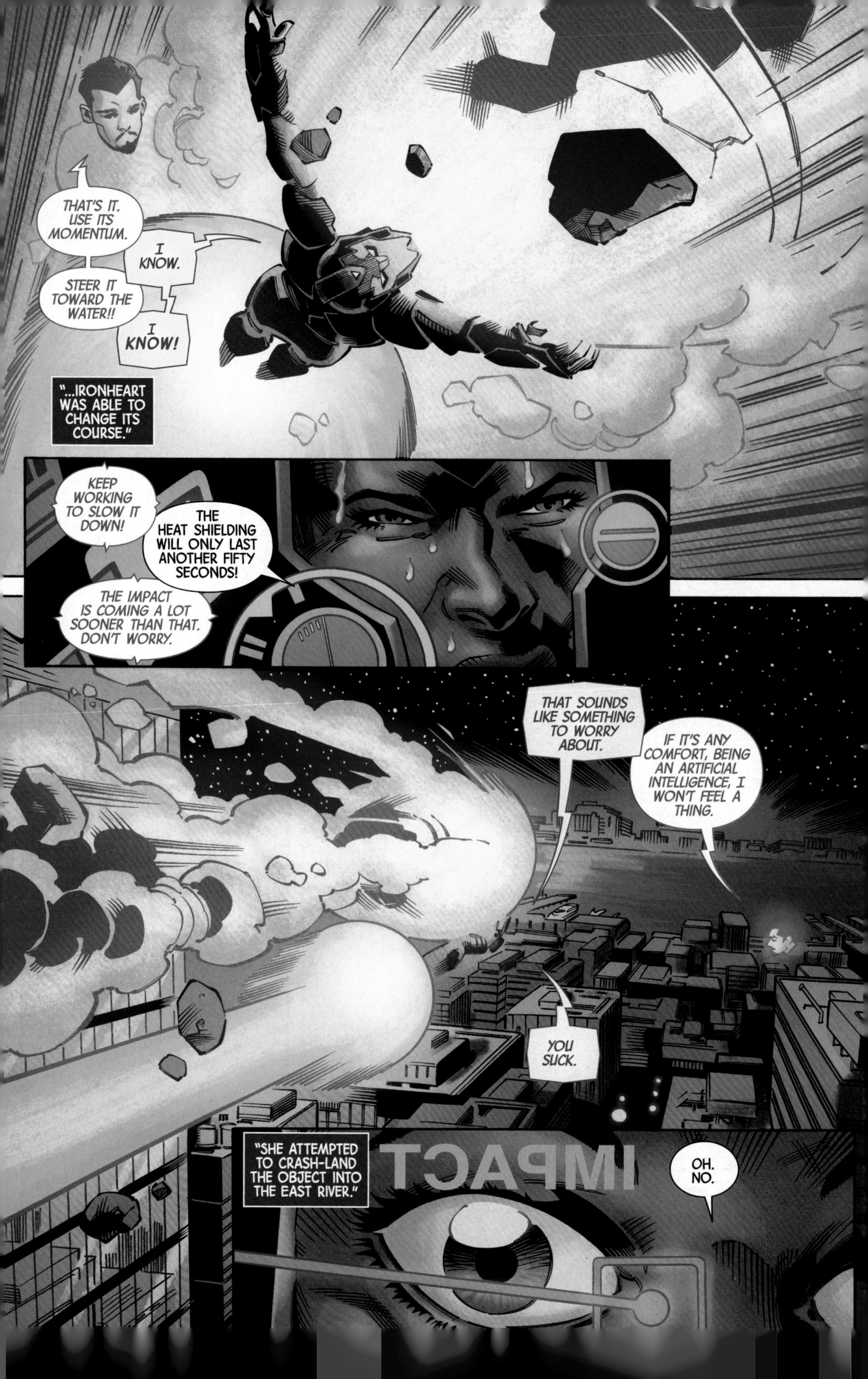
THAT'S IT. USE ITS MOMENTUM.
I KNOW.
STEER IT TOWARD THE WATER!!
I KNOW!
"...IRONHEART WAS ABLE TO CHANGE ITS COURSE."
KEEP WORKING TO SLOW IT DOWN!
THE HEAT SHIELDING WILL ONLY LAST ANOTHER FIFTY SECONDS!
THE IMPACT IS COMING A LOT SOONER THAN THAT. DON'T WORRY.
THAT SOUNDS LIKE SOMETHING TO WORRY ABOUT.
IF IT'S ANY COMFORT, BEING AN ARTIFICIAL INTELLIGENCE, I WON'T FEEL A THING.
YOU SUCK.
"SHE ATTEMPTED TO CRASH-LAND THE OBJECT INTO THE EAST RIVER."
IMPACT
OH. NO.

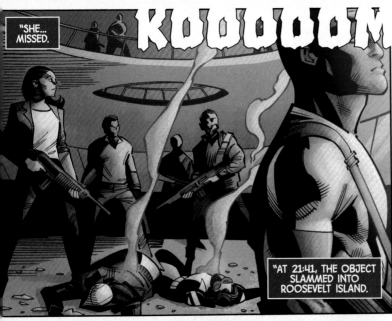

"SHE... MISSED.

KBOOOOM

"AT 21:41, THE OBJECT SLAMMED INTO ROOSEVELT ISLAND.

"THE DAMAGE COULD HAVE BEEN--*SHOULD* HAVE BEEN--FAR WORSE."

DID YOU HEAR THAT?

THE WHOLE *CITY* HEARD THAT.

HUH...?

TNK

TNK

TNK

TNK

DON'T HOLD BACK, *GABBY*. YOU KNOW WHAT THESE PEOPLE ARE. WHAT THEY'VE DONE. GET TO THE COMMS ROOM. GET TO YVGENY.

DO WE STILL HAVE TO BE QUIET?

NO.

I THINK THAT SHIP'S SAILED.

SNIKT

SNIKT

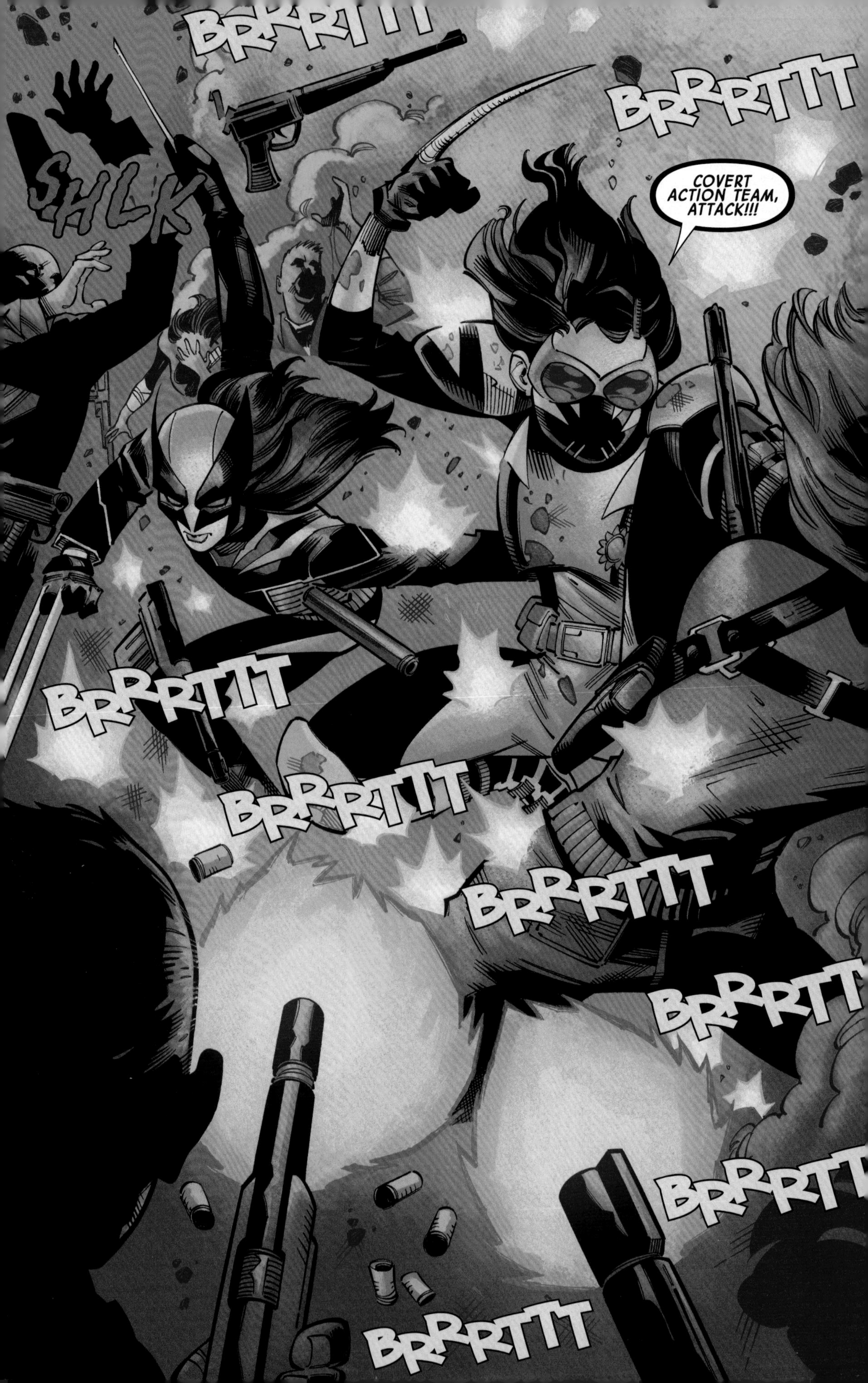
BRRRTTT
SHLK
BRRRTTT
COVERT ACTION TEAM, ATTACK!!!
BRRRTTT
BRRRTTT
BRRRTTT
BRRRTT
BRRRTT
BRRRTTT

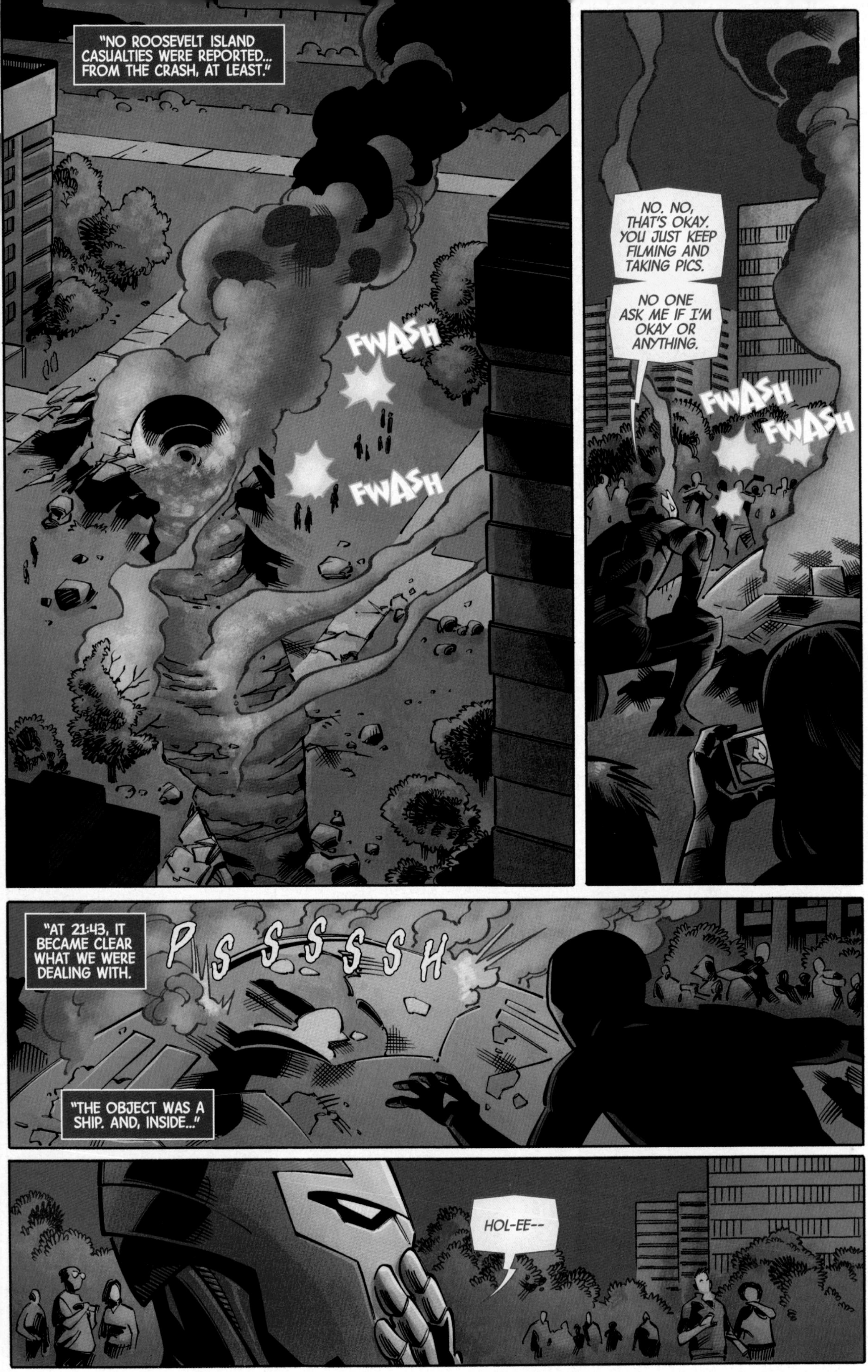
"NO ROOSEVELT ISLAND CASUALTIES WERE REPORTED... FROM THE CRASH, AT LEAST."
FWASH
FWASH
NO. NO, THAT'S OKAY. YOU JUST KEEP FILMING AND TAKING PICS.
NO ONE ASK ME IF I'M OKAY OR ANYTHING.
FWASH
FWASH
"AT 21:43, IT BECAME CLEAR WHAT WE WERE DEALING WITH.
PSSSSSH
"THE OBJECT WAS A SHIP. AND, INSIDE..."
HOL-EE--

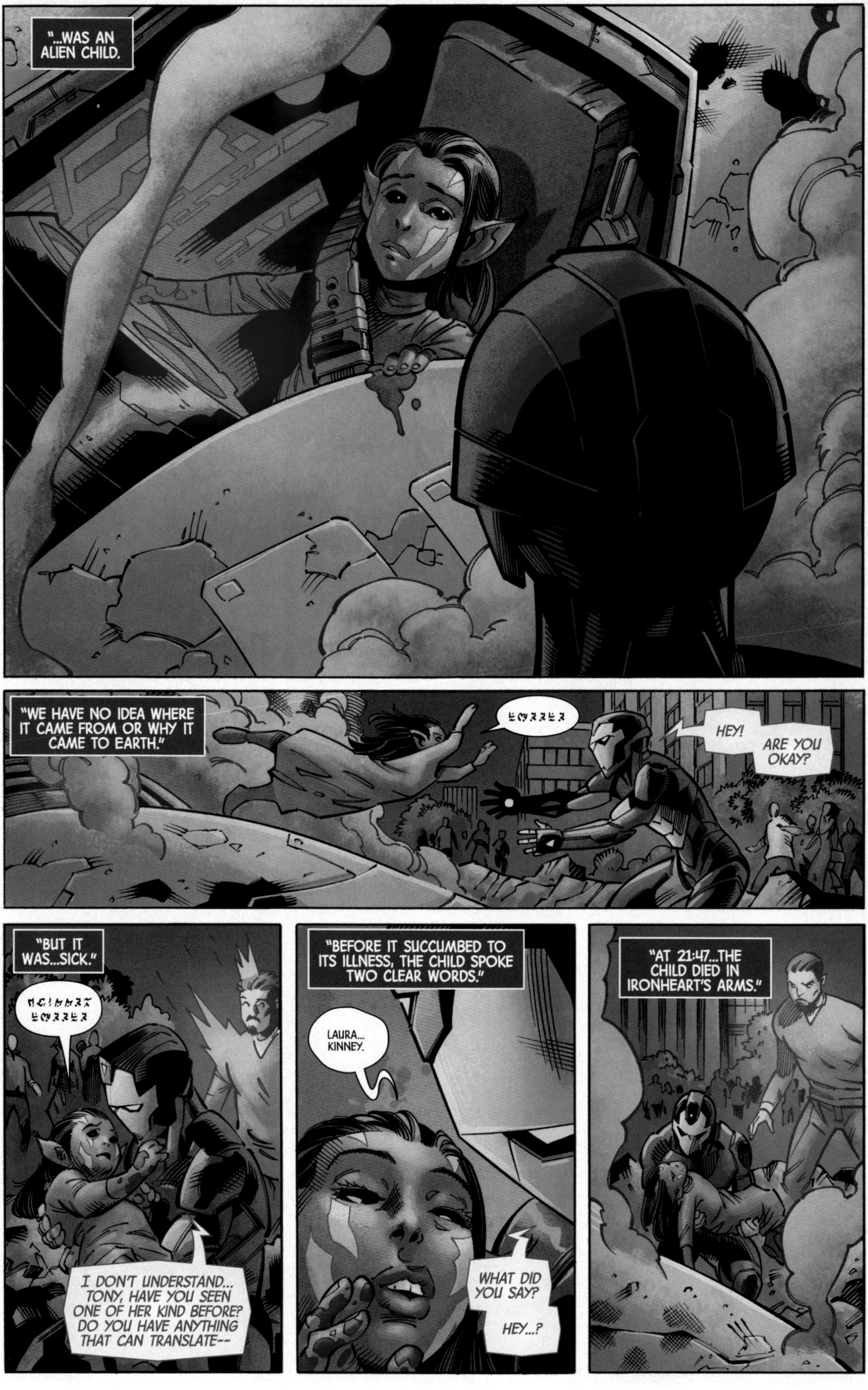

"...WAS AN ALIEN CHILD.
"WE HAVE NO IDEA WHERE IT CAME FROM OR WHY IT CAME TO EARTH."
HEY!
ARE YOU OKAY?
"BUT IT WAS...SICK."
I DON'T UNDERSTAND... TONY, HAVE YOU SEEN ONE OF HER KIND BEFORE? DO YOU HAVE ANYTHING THAT CAN TRANSLATE--
"BEFORE IT SUCCUMBED TO ITS ILLNESS, THE CHILD SPOKE TWO CLEAR WORDS."
LAURA... KINNEY.
WHAT DID YOU SAY?
HEY...?
"AT 21:47...THE CHILD DIED IN IRONHEART'S ARMS."

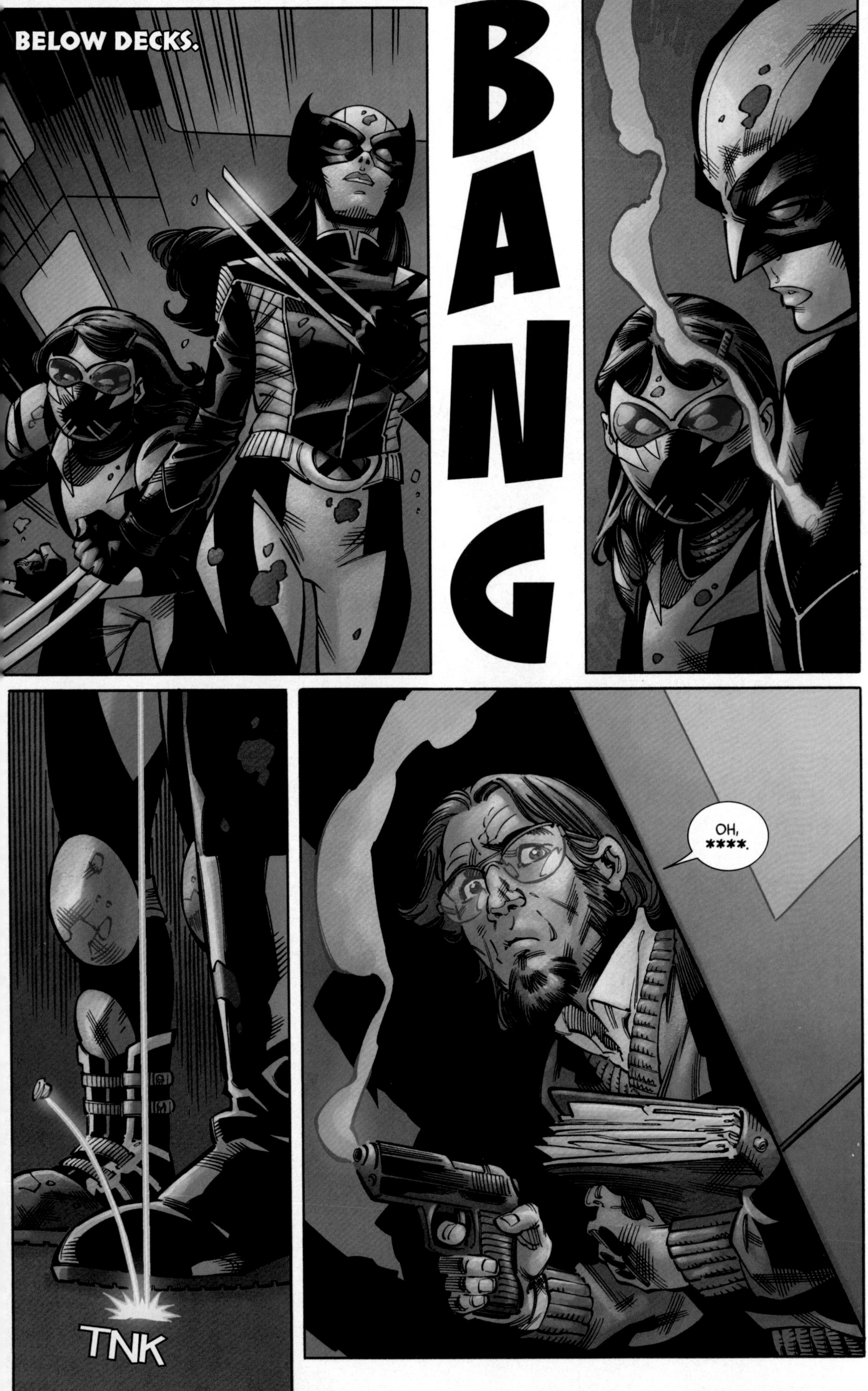
BELOW DECKS.
BANG
TNK
OH, ****.

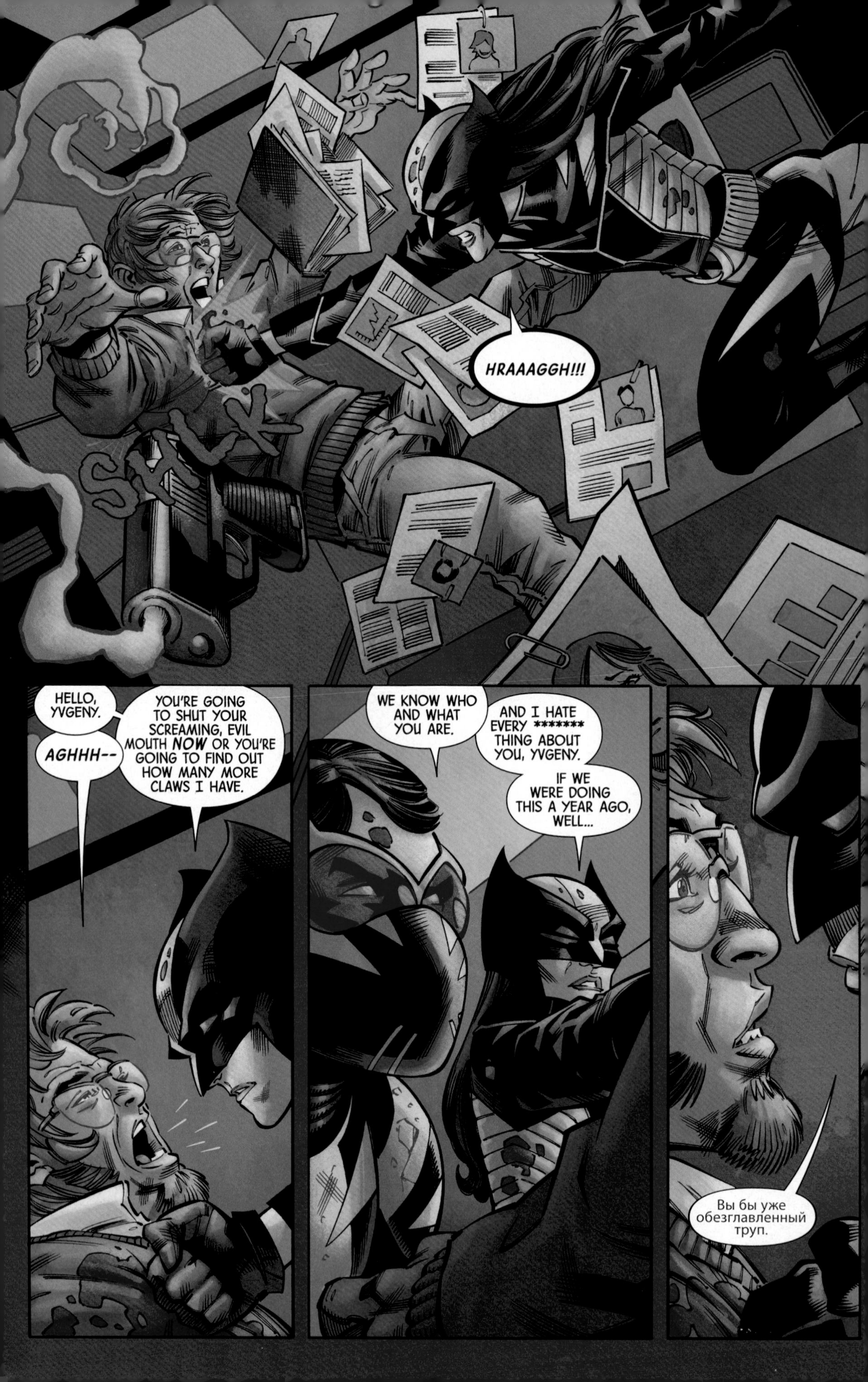

SHLK
HRAAAGGH!!!
HELLO, YVGENY.
AGHHH--
YOU'RE GOING TO SHUT YOUR SCREAMING, EVIL MOUTH NOW OR YOU'RE GOING TO FIND OUT HOW MANY MORE CLAWS I HAVE.
WE KNOW WHO AND WHAT YOU ARE.
AND I HATE EVERY ******* THING ABOUT YOU, YVGENY.
IF WE WERE DOING THIS A YEAR AGO, WELL...
Вы бы уже обезглавленный труп.

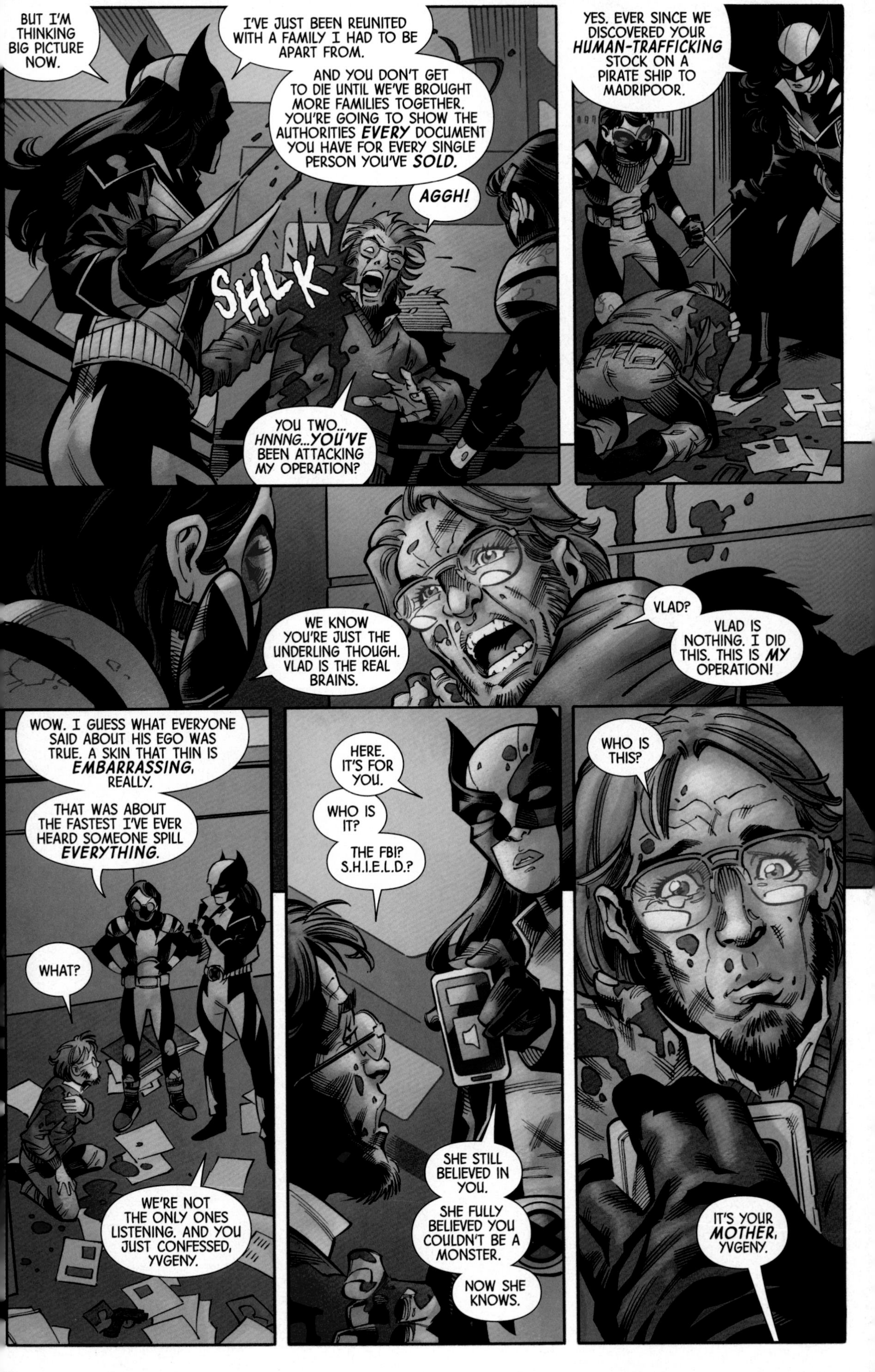
BUT I'M THINKING BIG PICTURE NOW.
I'VE JUST BEEN REUNITED WITH A FAMILY I HAD TO BE APART FROM.
AND YOU DON'T GET TO DIE UNTIL WE'VE BROUGHT MORE FAMILIES TOGETHER. YOU'RE GOING TO SHOW THE AUTHORITIES **EVERY** DOCUMENT YOU HAVE FOR EVERY SINGLE PERSON YOU'VE **SOLD.**
AGGH!
SHLK
YOU TWO... HNNNG...**YOU'VE** BEEN ATTACKING MY OPERATION?
YES. EVER SINCE WE DISCOVERED YOUR **HUMAN-TRAFFICKING** STOCK ON A PIRATE SHIP TO MADRIPOOR.
WE KNOW YOU'RE JUST THE UNDERLING THOUGH. VLAD IS THE REAL BRAINS.
VLAD?
VLAD IS NOTHING. I DID THIS. THIS IS **MY** OPERATION!
WOW. I GUESS WHAT EVERYONE SAID ABOUT HIS EGO WAS TRUE. A SKIN THAT THIN IS **EMBARRASSING**, REALLY.
THAT WAS ABOUT THE FASTEST I'VE EVER HEARD SOMEONE SPILL **EVERYTHING**.
WHAT?
WE'RE NOT THE ONLY ONES LISTENING. AND YOU JUST CONFESSED, YVGENY.
HERE. IT'S FOR YOU.
WHO IS IT?
THE FBI? S.H.I.E.L.D.?
SHE STILL BELIEVED IN YOU.
SHE FULLY BELIEVED YOU COULDN'T BE A MONSTER.
NOW SHE KNOWS.
WHO IS THIS?
IT'S YOUR **MOTHER**, YVGENY.

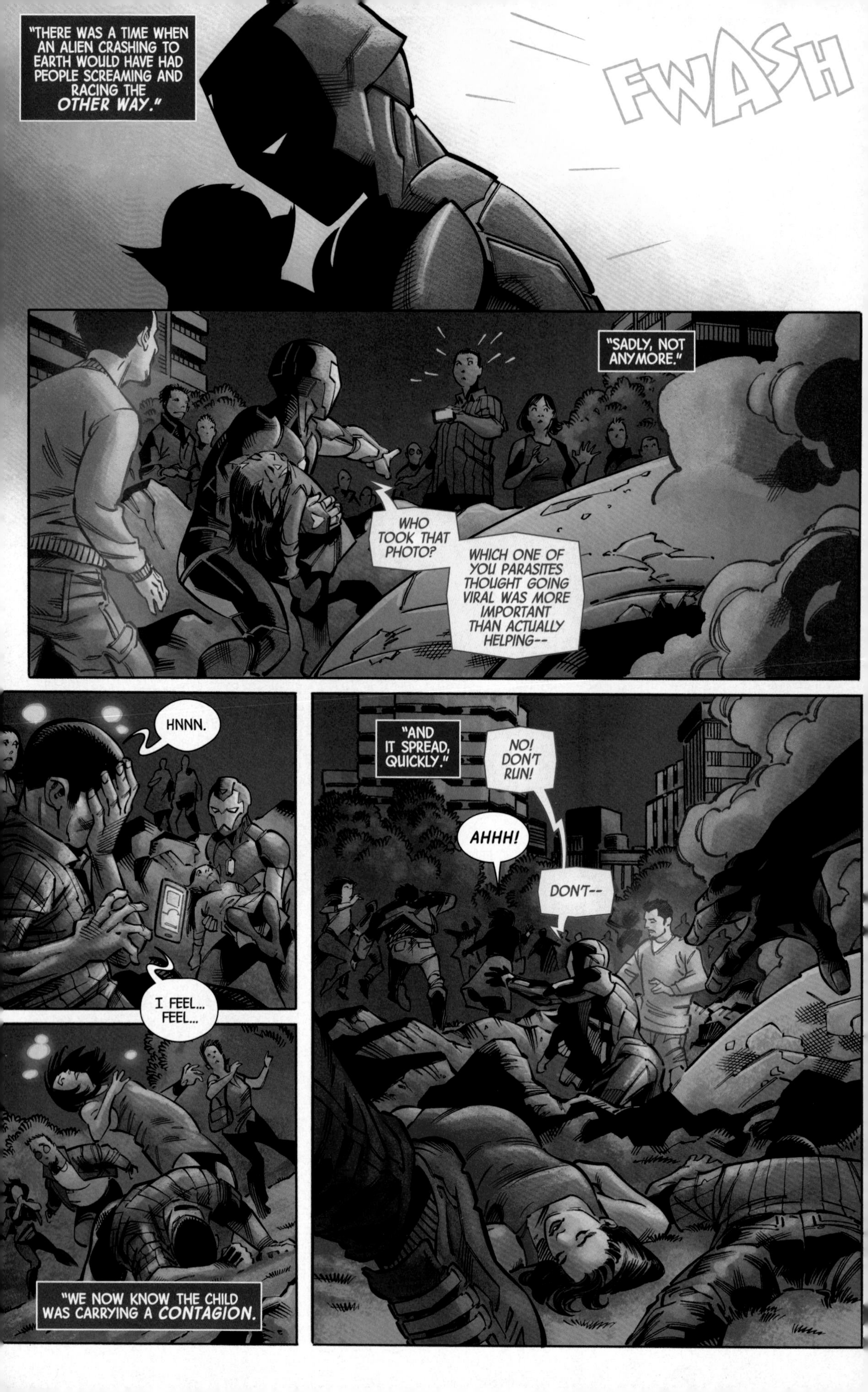
"THERE WAS A TIME WHEN AN ALIEN CRASHING TO EARTH WOULD HAVE HAD PEOPLE SCREAMING AND RACING THE OTHER WAY."
FWASH
"SADLY, NOT ANYMORE."
WHO TOOK THAT PHOTO?
WHICH ONE OF YOU PARASITES THOUGHT GOING VIRAL WAS MORE IMPORTANT THAN ACTUALLY HELPING--
HNNN.
I FEEL... FEEL...
"WE NOW KNOW THE CHILD WAS CARRYING A CONTAGION.
"AND IT SPREAD, QUICKLY."
NO! DON'T RUN!
AHHH!
DON'T--

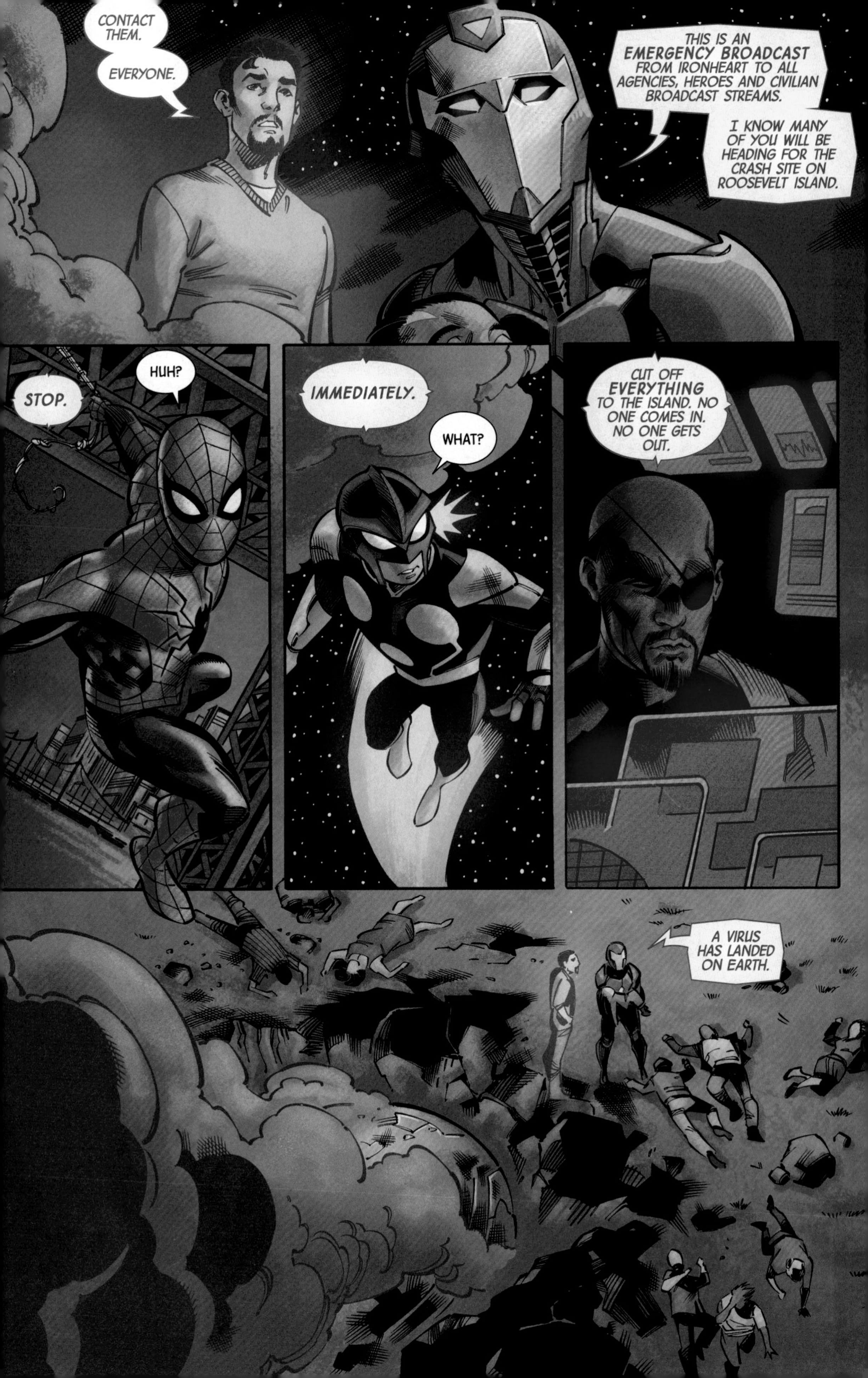
CONTACT THEM.
EVERYONE.
THIS IS AN EMERGENCY BROADCAST FROM IRONHEART TO ALL AGENCIES, HEROES AND CIVILIAN BROADCAST STREAMS.
I KNOW MANY OF YOU WILL BE HEADING FOR THE CRASH SITE ON ROOSEVELT ISLAND.
STOP.
HUH?
IMMEDIATELY.
WHAT?
CUT OFF EVERYTHING TO THE ISLAND. NO ONE COMES IN. NO ONE GETS OUT.
A VIRUS HAS LANDED ON EARTH.

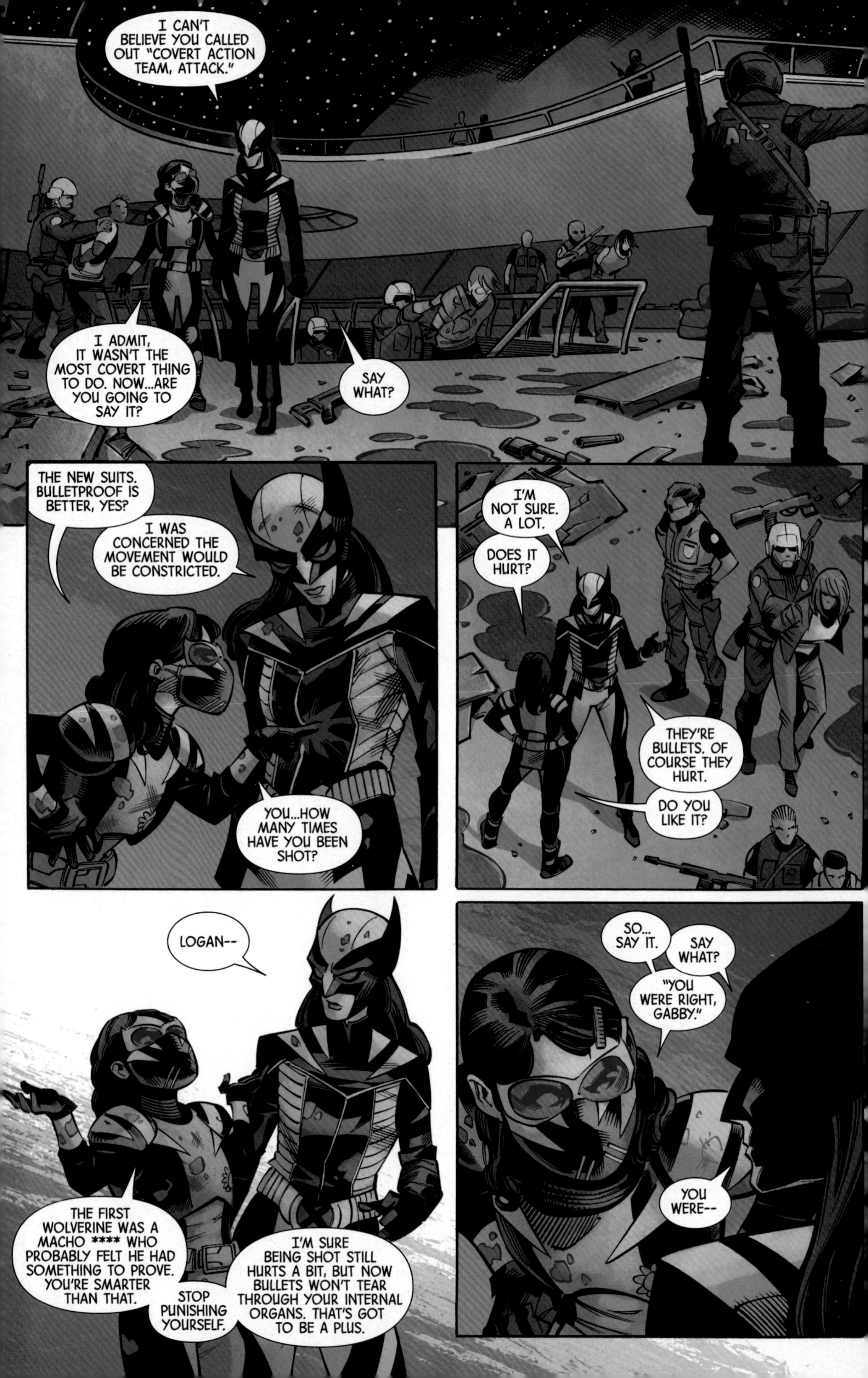
I CAN'T BELIEVE YOU CALLED OUT "COVERT ACTION TEAM, ATTACK."
I ADMIT, IT WASN'T THE MOST COVERT THING TO DO. NOW...ARE YOU GOING TO SAY IT?
SAY WHAT?
THE NEW SUITS. BULLETPROOF IS BETTER, YES?
I WAS CONCERNED THE MOVEMENT WOULD BE CONSTRICTED.
YOU...HOW MANY TIMES HAVE YOU BEEN SHOT?
I'M NOT SURE. A LOT.
DOES IT HURT?
THEY'RE BULLETS. OF COURSE THEY HURT.
DO YOU LIKE IT?
LOGAN--
THE FIRST WOLVERINE WAS A MACHO **** WHO PROBABLY FELT HE HAD SOMETHING TO PROVE. YOU'RE SMARTER THAN THAT.
STOP PUNISHING YOURSELF.
I'M SURE BEING SHOT STILL HURTS A BIT, BUT NOW BULLETS WON'T TEAR THROUGH YOUR INTERNAL ORGANS. THAT'S GOT TO BE A PLUS.
SO... SAY IT.
SAY WHAT?
"YOU WERE RIGHT, GABBY."
YOU WERE--

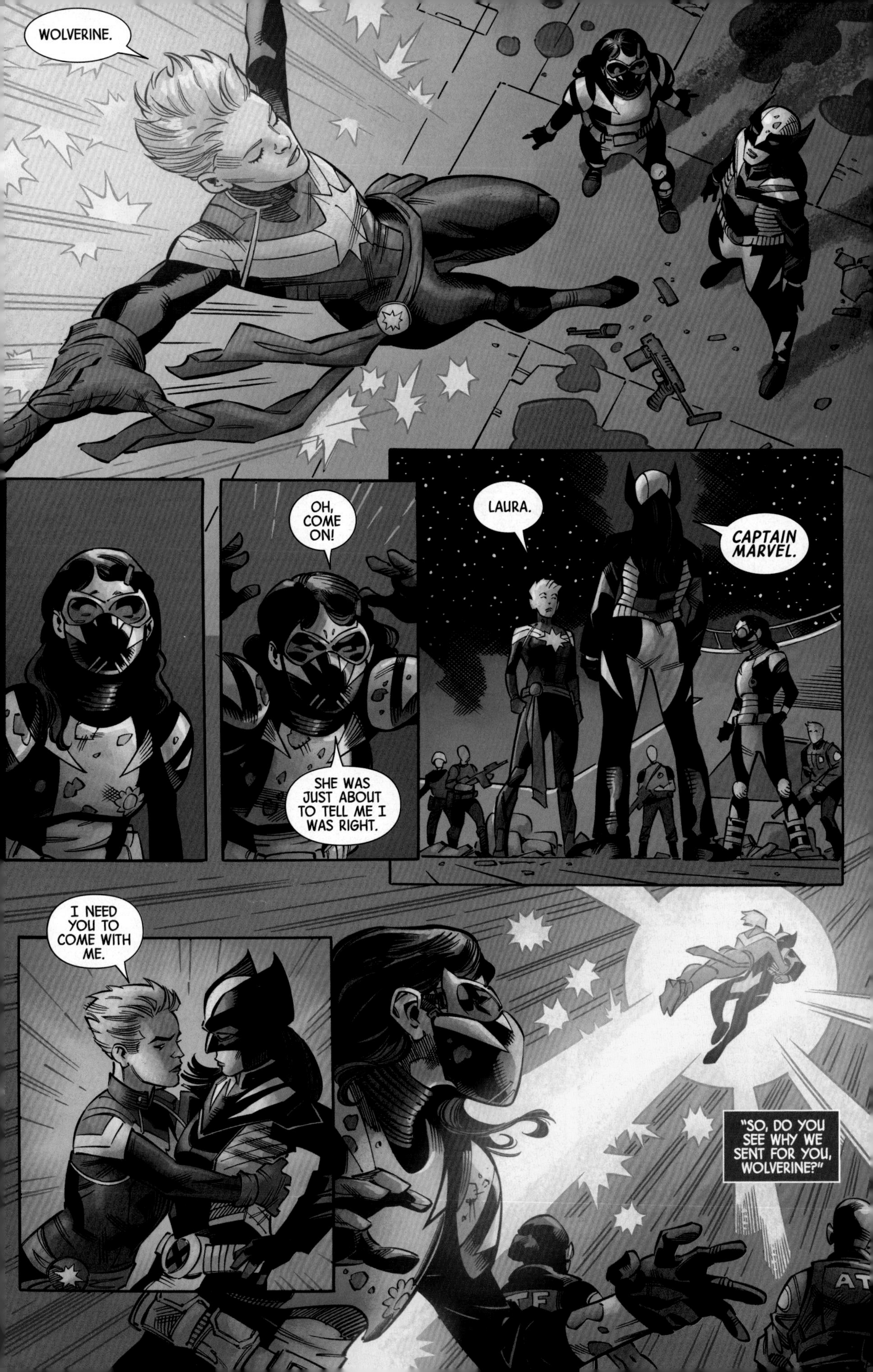
WOLVERINE.
OH, COME ON!
SHE WAS JUST ABOUT TO TELL ME I WAS RIGHT.
LAURA.
CAPTAIN MARVEL.
I NEED YOU TO COME WITH ME.
"SO, DO YOU SEE WHY WE SENT FOR YOU, WOLVERINE?"

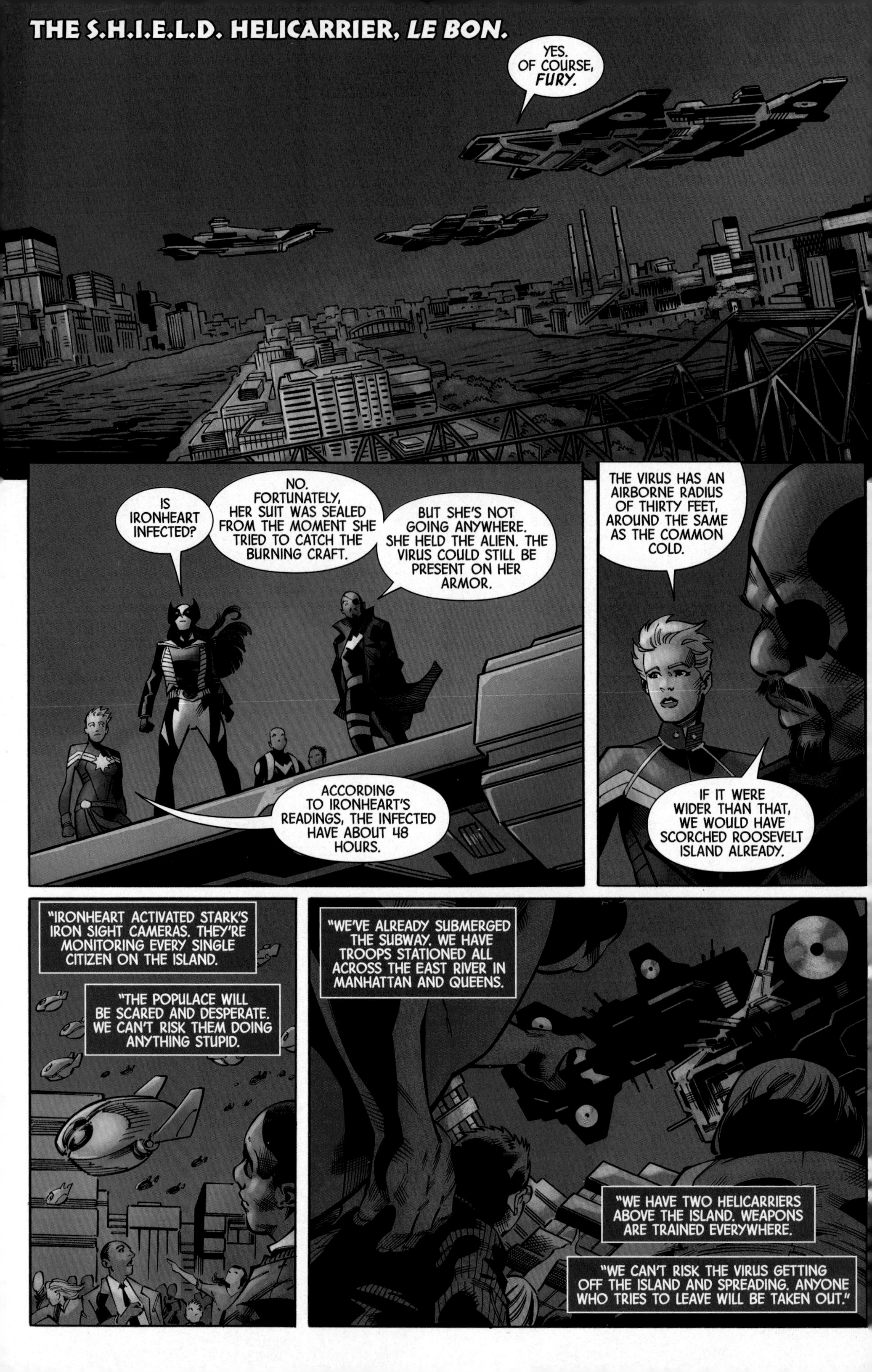
THE S.H.I.E.L.D. HELICARRIER, *LE BON.*
YES. OF COURSE, *FURY.*
IS IRONHEART INFECTED?
NO. FORTUNATELY, HER SUIT WAS SEALED FROM THE MOMENT SHE TRIED TO CATCH THE BURNING CRAFT.
BUT SHE'S NOT GOING ANYWHERE. SHE HELD THE ALIEN. THE VIRUS COULD STILL BE PRESENT ON HER ARMOR.
ACCORDING TO IRONHEART'S READINGS, THE INFECTED HAVE ABOUT 48 HOURS.
THE VIRUS HAS AN AIRBORNE RADIUS OF THIRTY FEET, AROUND THE SAME AS THE COMMON COLD.
IF IT WERE WIDER THAN THAT, WE WOULD HAVE SCORCHED ROOSEVELT ISLAND ALREADY.
"IRONHEART ACTIVATED STARK'S IRON SIGHT CAMERAS. THEY'RE MONITORING EVERY SINGLE CITIZEN ON THE ISLAND.
"THE POPULACE WILL BE SCARED AND DESPERATE. WE CAN'T RISK THEM DOING ANYTHING STUPID.
"WE'VE ALREADY SUBMERGED THE SUBWAY. WE HAVE TROOPS STATIONED ALL ACROSS THE EAST RIVER IN MANHATTAN AND QUEENS.
"WE HAVE TWO HELICARRIERS ABOVE THE ISLAND. WEAPONS ARE TRAINED EVERYWHERE.
"WE CAN'T RISK THE VIRUS GETTING OFF THE ISLAND AND SPREADING. ANYONE WHO TRIES TO LEAVE WILL BE TAKEN OUT."

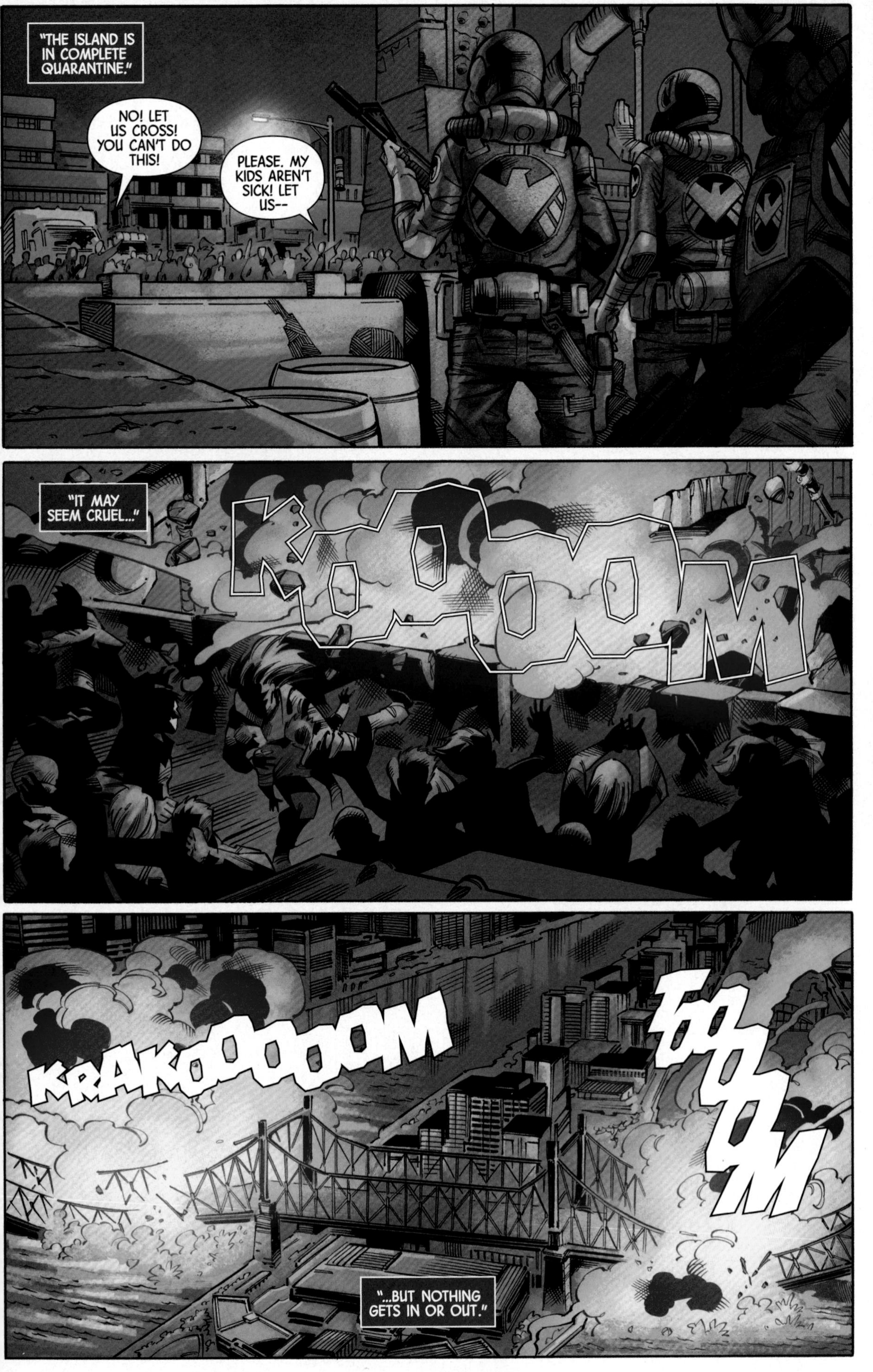
"THE ISLAND IS IN COMPLETE QUARANTINE."
NO! LET US CROSS! YOU CAN'T DO THIS!
PLEASE. MY KIDS AREN'T SICK! LET US--
"IT MAY SEEM CRUEL..."
KOOOOM
KRAKOOOOOM
BOOOM
"...BUT NOTHING GETS IN OR OUT."

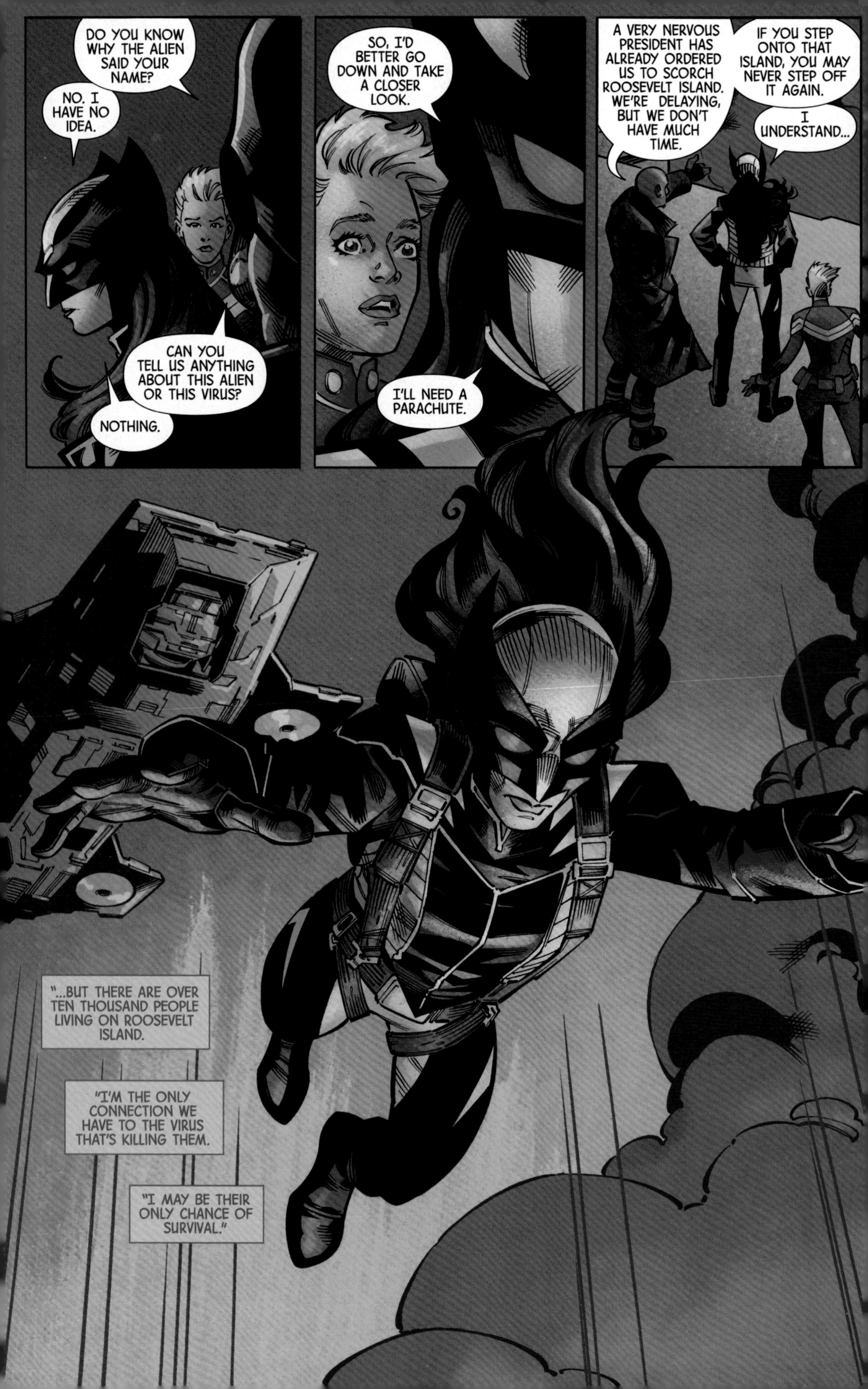
DO YOU KNOW WHY THE ALIEN SAID YOUR NAME?
NO. I HAVE NO IDEA.
CAN YOU TELL US ANYTHING ABOUT THIS ALIEN OR THIS VIRUS?
NOTHING.
SO, I'D BETTER GO DOWN AND TAKE A CLOSER LOOK.
I'LL NEED A PARACHUTE.
A VERY NERVOUS PRESIDENT HAS ALREADY ORDERED US TO SCORCH ROOSEVELT ISLAND. WE'RE DELAYING, BUT WE DON'T HAVE MUCH TIME.
IF YOU STEP ONTO THAT ISLAND, YOU MAY NEVER STEP OFF IT AGAIN.
I UNDERSTAND...
"...BUT THERE ARE OVER TEN THOUSAND PEOPLE LIVING ON ROOSEVELT ISLAND.
"I'M THE ONLY CONNECTION WE HAVE TO THE VIRUS THAT'S KILLING THEM.
"I MAY BE THEIR ONLY CHANCE OF SURVIVAL."

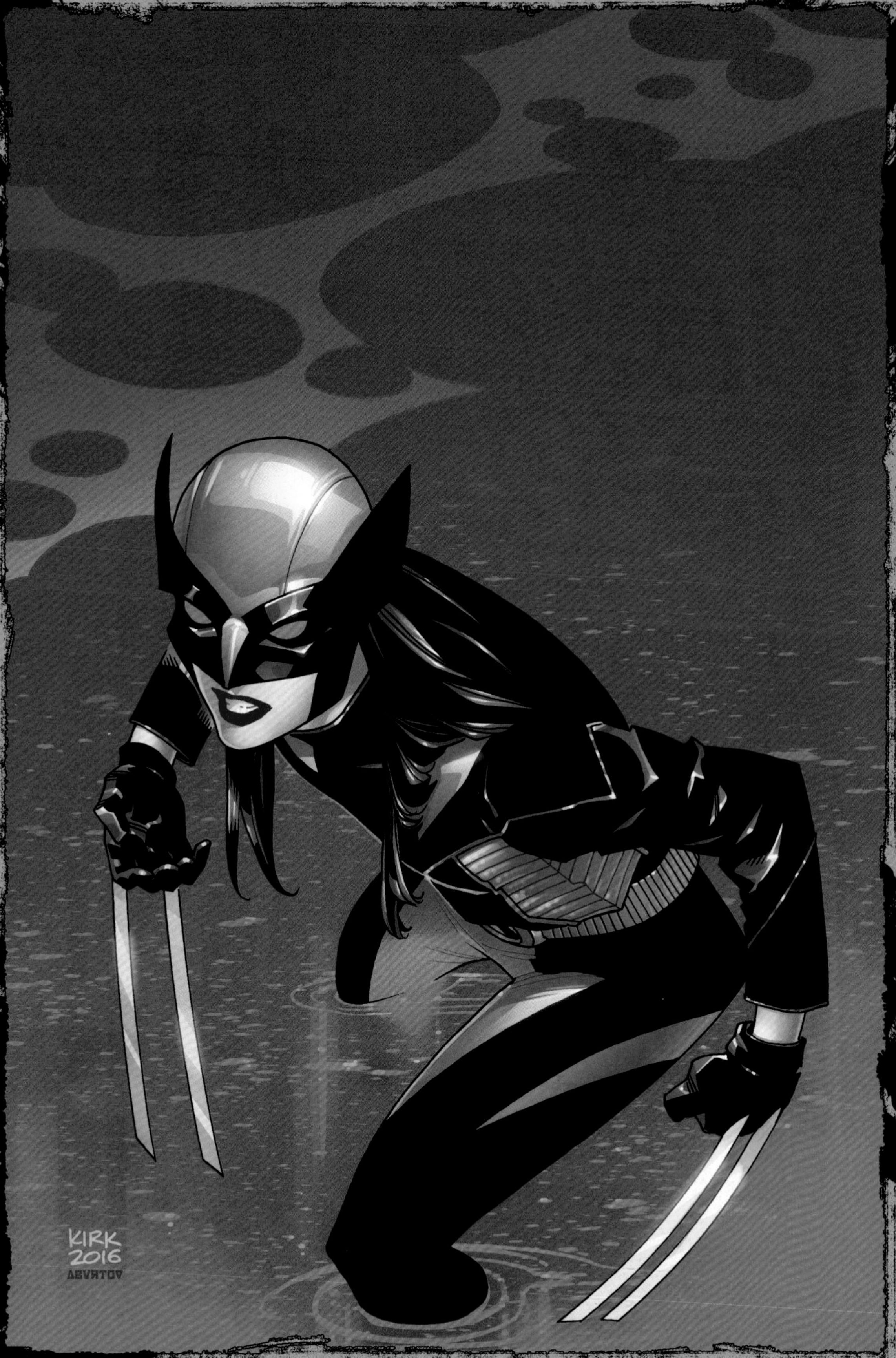
KIRK
2016
ABURTOV

#19 variant by

LEONARD KIRK & **JESUS ABURTOV**

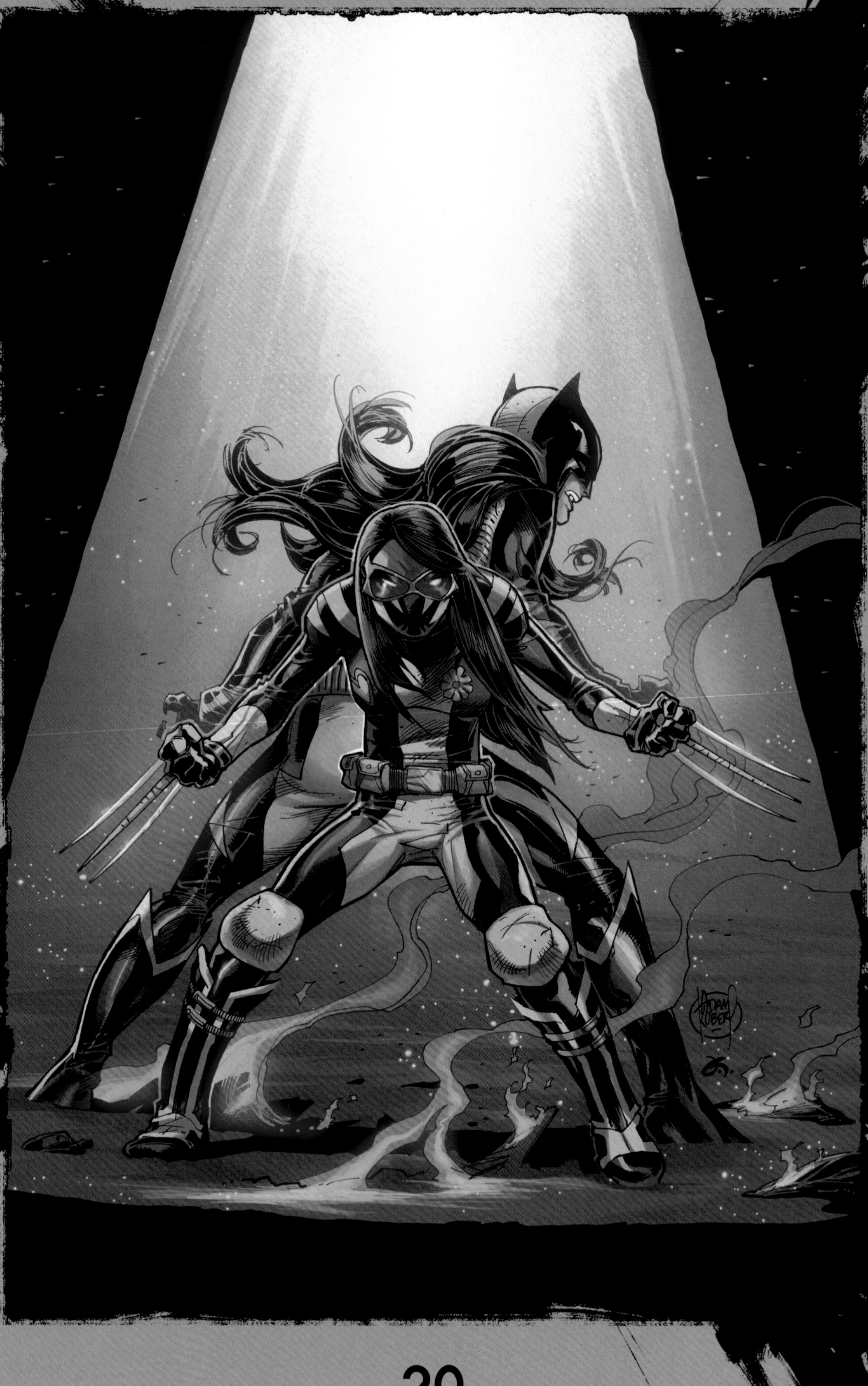

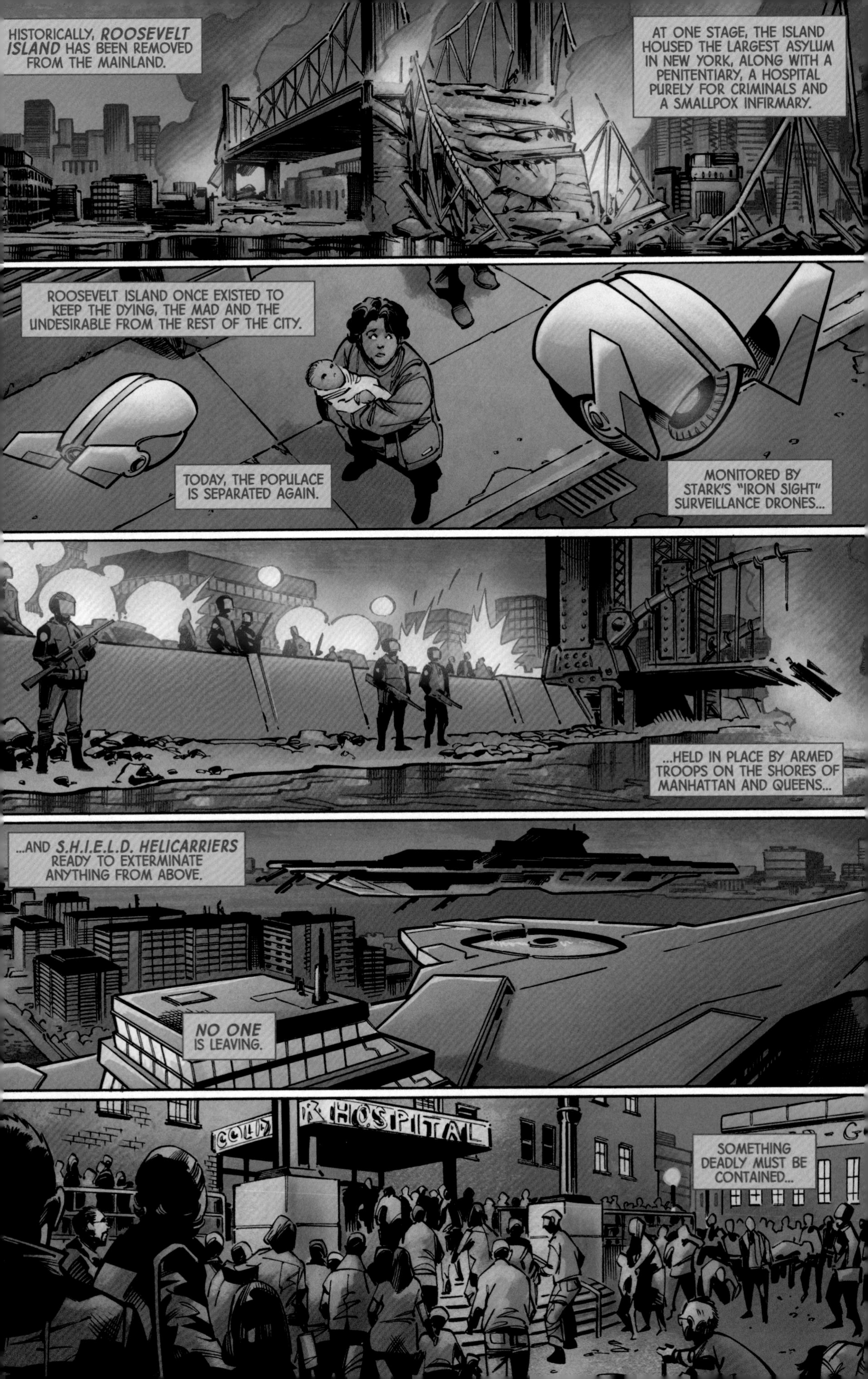
HISTORICALLY, ROOSEVELT ISLAND HAS BEEN REMOVED FROM THE MAINLAND.
AT ONE STAGE, THE ISLAND HOUSED THE LARGEST ASYLUM IN NEW YORK, ALONG WITH A PENITENTIARY, A HOSPITAL PURELY FOR CRIMINALS AND A SMALLPOX INFIRMARY.
ROOSEVELT ISLAND ONCE EXISTED TO KEEP THE DYING, THE MAD AND THE UNDESIRABLE FROM THE REST OF THE CITY.
TODAY, THE POPULACE IS SEPARATED AGAIN.
MONITORED BY STARK'S "IRON SIGHT" SURVEILLANCE DRONES...
...HELD IN PLACE BY ARMED TROOPS ON THE SHORES OF MANHATTAN AND QUEENS...
...AND S.H.I.E.L.D. HELICARRIERS READY TO EXTERMINATE ANYTHING FROM ABOVE.
NO ONE IS LEAVING.
HOSPITAL
SOMETHING DEADLY MUST BE CONTAINED...

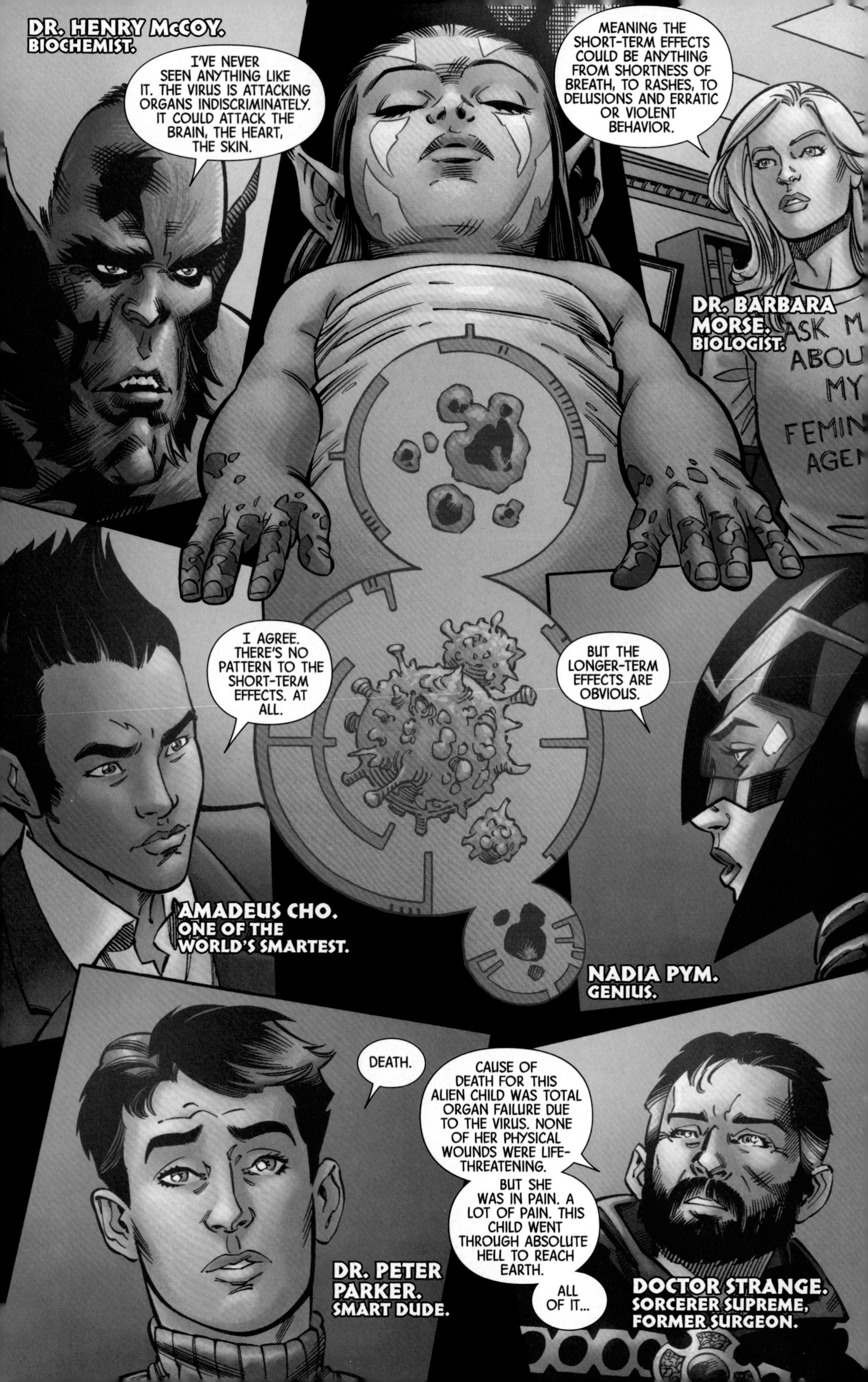
DR. HENRY McCOY. BIOCHEMIST.
I'VE NEVER SEEN ANYTHING LIKE IT. THE VIRUS IS ATTACKING ORGANS INDISCRIMINATELY. IT COULD ATTACK THE BRAIN, THE HEART, THE SKIN.
MEANING THE SHORT-TERM EFFECTS COULD BE ANYTHING FROM SHORTNESS OF BREATH, TO RASHES, TO DELUSIONS AND ERRATIC OR VIOLENT BEHAVIOR.
DR. BARBARA MORSE. BIOLOGIST.
I AGREE. THERE'S NO PATTERN TO THE SHORT-TERM EFFECTS. AT ALL.
BUT THE LONGER-TERM EFFECTS ARE OBVIOUS.
AMADEUS CHO. ONE OF THE WORLD'S SMARTEST.
NADIA PYM. GENIUS.
DEATH.
CAUSE OF DEATH FOR THIS ALIEN CHILD WAS TOTAL ORGAN FAILURE DUE TO THE VIRUS. NONE OF HER PHYSICAL WOUNDS WERE LIFE-THREATENING.
BUT SHE WAS IN PAIN. A LOT OF PAIN. THIS CHILD WENT THROUGH ABSOLUTE HELL TO REACH EARTH.
ALL OF IT...
DR. PETER PARKER. SMART DUDE.
DOCTOR STRANGE. SORCERER SUPREME, FORMER SURGEON.

...TO REACH YOU, WOLVERINE.

THE WOUNDS ON HER HANDS AND ARMS--

ARE DEFENSIVE.

YES.

THE INJURIES ON HER BACK WERE SUSTAINED RUNNING AWAY FROM AN ATTACKER.

HOW DO YOU--?

A LOT OF PEOPLE HAVE RUN FROM ME.

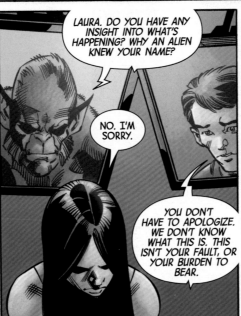

LAURA. DO YOU HAVE ANY INSIGHT INTO WHAT'S HAPPENING? WHY AN ALIEN KNEW YOUR NAME?

NO. I'M SORRY.

YOU DON'T HAVE TO APOLOGIZE. WE DON'T KNOW WHAT THIS IS. THIS ISN'T YOUR FAULT, OR YOUR BURDEN TO BEAR.

YEAH... I'M SORRY.

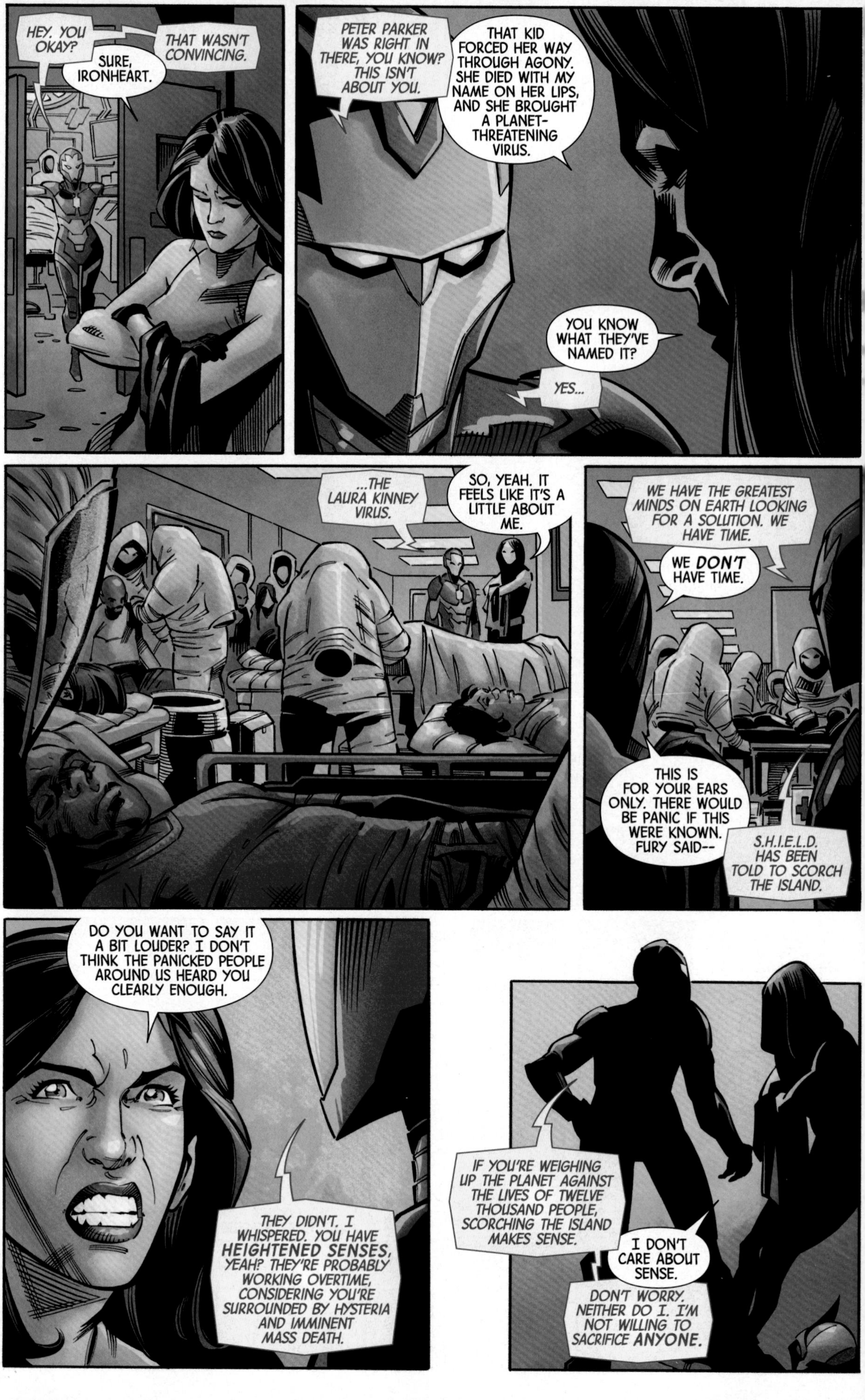
HEY. YOU OKAY?
SURE, IRONHEART.
THAT WASN'T CONVINCING.
PETER PARKER WAS RIGHT IN THERE, YOU KNOW? THIS ISN'T ABOUT YOU.
THAT KID FORCED HER WAY THROUGH AGONY. SHE DIED WITH MY NAME ON HER LIPS, AND SHE BROUGHT A PLANET-THREATENING VIRUS.
YOU KNOW WHAT THEY'VE NAMED IT?
YES...
...THE LAURA KINNEY VIRUS.
SO, YEAH. IT FEELS LIKE IT'S A LITTLE ABOUT ME.
WE HAVE THE GREATEST MINDS ON EARTH LOOKING FOR A SOLUTION. WE HAVE TIME.
WE DON'T HAVE TIME.
THIS IS FOR YOUR EARS ONLY. THERE WOULD BE PANIC IF THIS WERE KNOWN. FURY SAID--
S.H.I.E.L.D. HAS BEEN TOLD TO SCORCH THE ISLAND.
DO YOU WANT TO SAY IT A BIT LOUDER? I DON'T THINK THE PANICKED PEOPLE AROUND US HEARD YOU CLEARLY ENOUGH.
THEY DIDN'T. I WHISPERED. YOU HAVE HEIGHTENED SENSES, YEAH? THEY'RE PROBABLY WORKING OVERTIME, CONSIDERING YOU'RE SURROUNDED BY HYSTERIA AND IMMINENT MASS DEATH.
IF YOU'RE WEIGHING UP THE PLANET AGAINST THE LIVES OF TWELVE THOUSAND PEOPLE, SCORCHING THE ISLAND MAKES SENSE.
I DON'T CARE ABOUT SENSE.
DON'T WORRY. NEITHER DO I. I'M NOT WILLING TO SACRIFICE ANYONE.

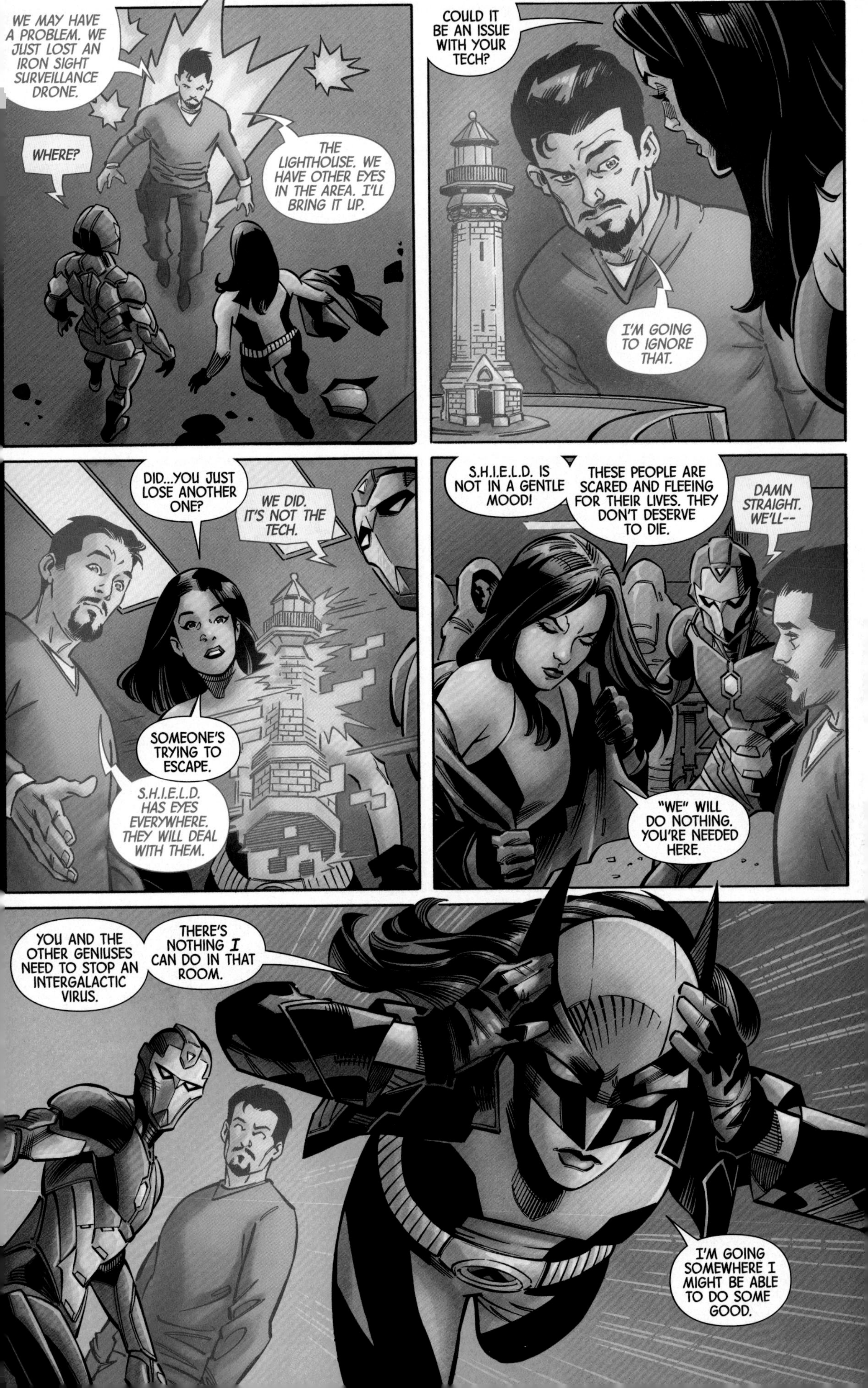
WE MAY HAVE A PROBLEM. WE JUST LOST AN IRON SIGHT SURVEILLANCE DRONE.
WHERE?
THE LIGHTHOUSE. WE HAVE OTHER EYES IN THE AREA. I'LL BRING IT UP.
COULD IT BE AN ISSUE WITH YOUR TECH?
I'M GOING TO IGNORE THAT.
DID...YOU JUST LOSE ANOTHER ONE?
WE DID. IT'S NOT THE TECH.
SOMEONE'S TRYING TO ESCAPE.
S.H.I.E.L.D. HAS EYES EVERYWHERE. THEY WILL DEAL WITH THEM.
S.H.I.E.L.D. IS NOT IN A GENTLE MOOD!
THESE PEOPLE ARE SCARED AND FLEEING FOR THEIR LIVES. THEY DON'T DESERVE TO DIE.
DAMN STRAIGHT. WE'LL--
"WE" WILL DO NOTHING. YOU'RE NEEDED HERE.
YOU AND THE OTHER GENIUSES NEED TO STOP AN INTERGALACTIC VIRUS.
THERE'S NOTHING I CAN DO IN THAT ROOM.
I'M GOING SOMEWHERE I MIGHT BE ABLE TO DO SOME GOOD.

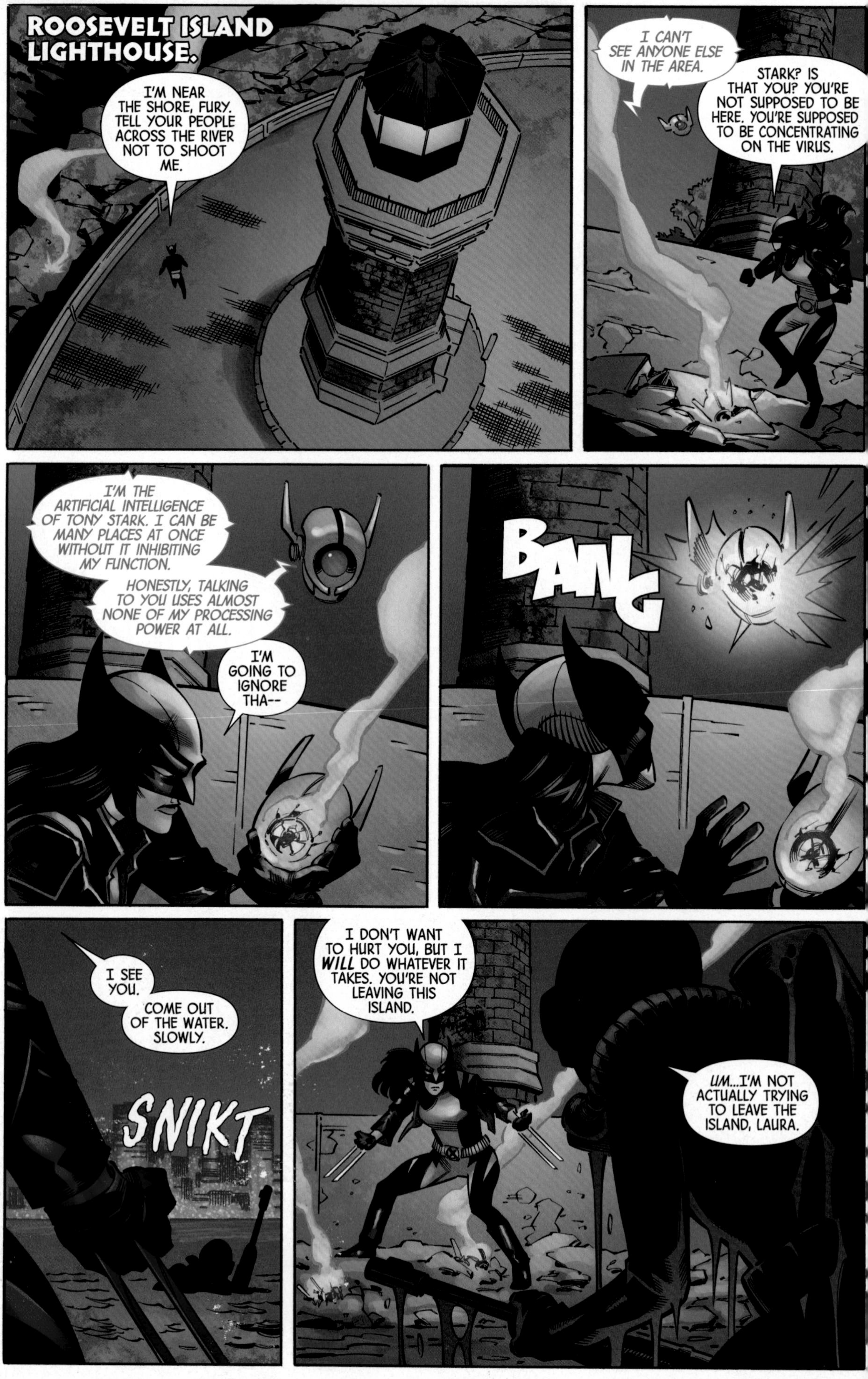
ROOSEVELT ISLAND LIGHTHOUSE.
I'M NEAR THE SHORE, FURY. TELL YOUR PEOPLE ACROSS THE RIVER NOT TO SHOOT ME.
I CAN'T SEE ANYONE ELSE IN THE AREA.
STARK? IS THAT YOU? YOU'RE NOT SUPPOSED TO BE HERE. YOU'RE SUPPOSED TO BE CONCENTRATING ON THE VIRUS.
I'M THE ARTIFICIAL INTELLIGENCE OF TONY STARK. I CAN BE MANY PLACES AT ONCE WITHOUT IT INHIBITING MY FUNCTION.
HONESTLY, TALKING TO YOU USES ALMOST NONE OF MY PROCESSING POWER AT ALL.
I'M GOING TO IGNORE THA--
BANG
I SEE YOU.
COME OUT OF THE WATER. SLOWLY.
SNIKT
I DON'T WANT TO HURT YOU, BUT I *WILL* DO WHATEVER IT TAKES. YOU'RE NOT LEAVING THIS ISLAND.
UM...I'M NOT ACTUALLY TRYING TO LEAVE THE ISLAND, LAURA.

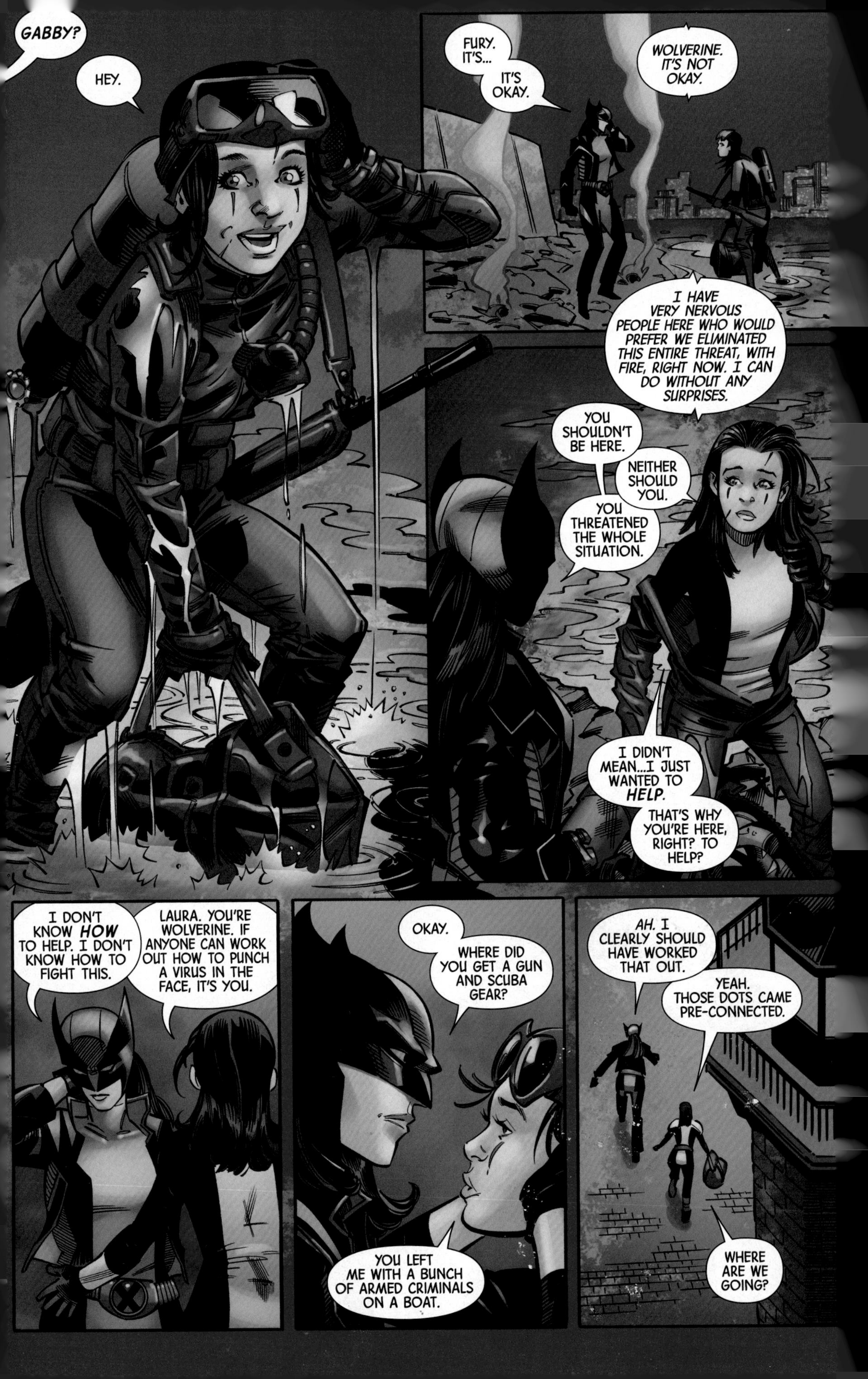
GABBY?
HEY.
FURY. IT'S... IT'S OKAY.
WOLVERINE. IT'S NOT OKAY.
I HAVE VERY NERVOUS PEOPLE HERE WHO WOULD PREFER WE ELIMINATED THIS ENTIRE THREAT, WITH FIRE, RIGHT NOW. I CAN DO WITHOUT ANY SURPRISES.
YOU SHOULDN'T BE HERE.
NEITHER SHOULD YOU.
YOU THREATENED THE WHOLE SITUATION.
I DIDN'T MEAN...I JUST WANTED TO HELP.
THAT'S WHY YOU'RE HERE, RIGHT? TO HELP?
I DON'T KNOW HOW TO HELP. I DON'T KNOW HOW TO FIGHT THIS.
LAURA. YOU'RE WOLVERINE. IF ANYONE CAN WORK OUT HOW TO PUNCH A VIRUS IN THE FACE, IT'S YOU.
OKAY.
WHERE DID YOU GET A GUN AND SCUBA GEAR?
YOU LEFT ME WITH A BUNCH OF ARMED CRIMINALS ON A BOAT.
AH. I CLEARLY SHOULD HAVE WORKED THAT OUT.
YEAH. THOSE DOTS CAME PRE-CONNECTED.
WHERE ARE WE GOING?

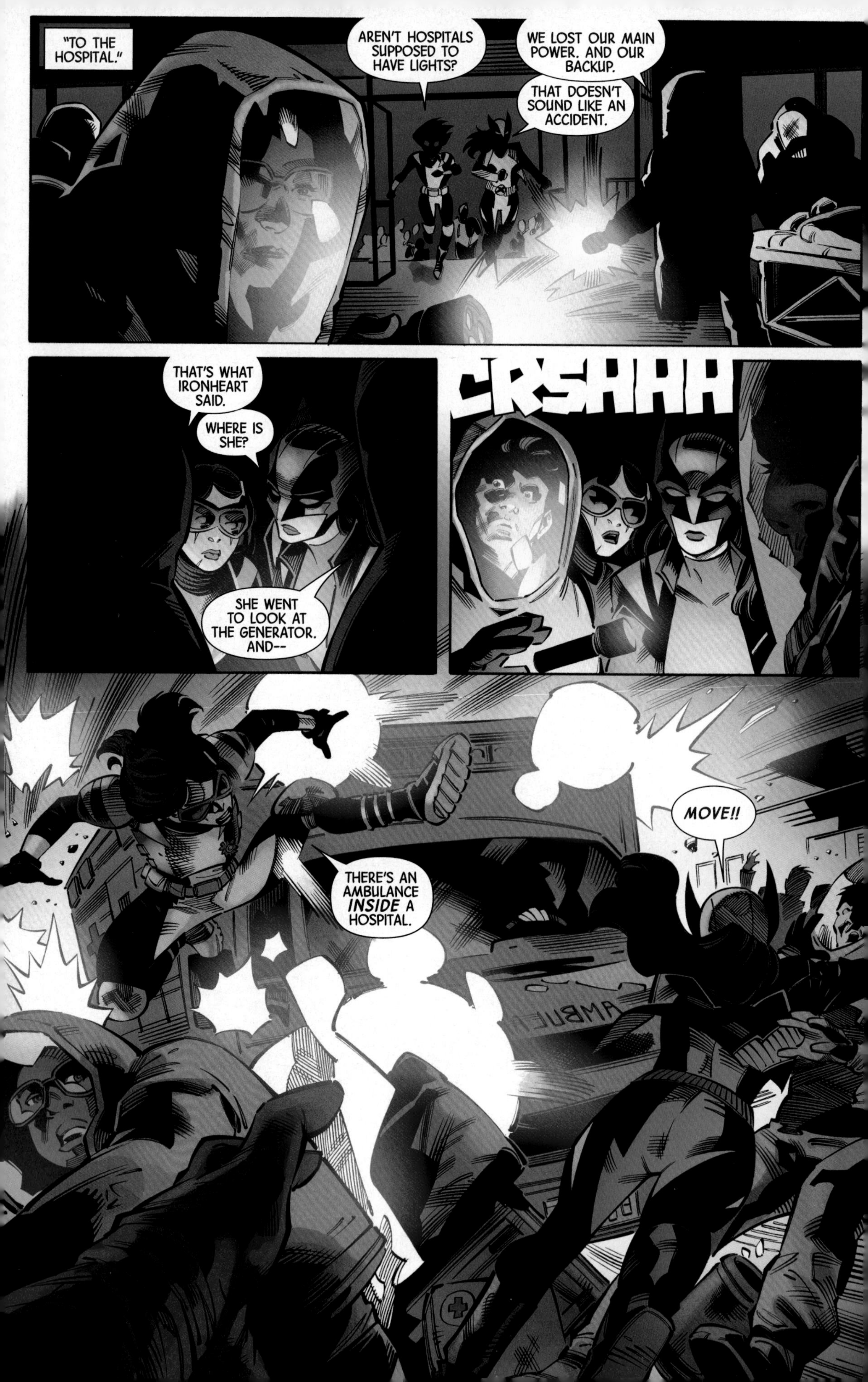

"TO THE HOSPITAL."
AREN'T HOSPITALS SUPPOSED TO HAVE LIGHTS?
WE LOST OUR MAIN POWER. AND OUR BACKUP.
THAT DOESN'T SOUND LIKE AN ACCIDENT.
THAT'S WHAT IRONHEART SAID.
WHERE IS SHE?
SHE WENT TO LOOK AT THE GENERATOR. AND--
CRSHHH
MOVE!!
THERE'S AN AMBULANCE *INSIDE* A HOSPITAL.

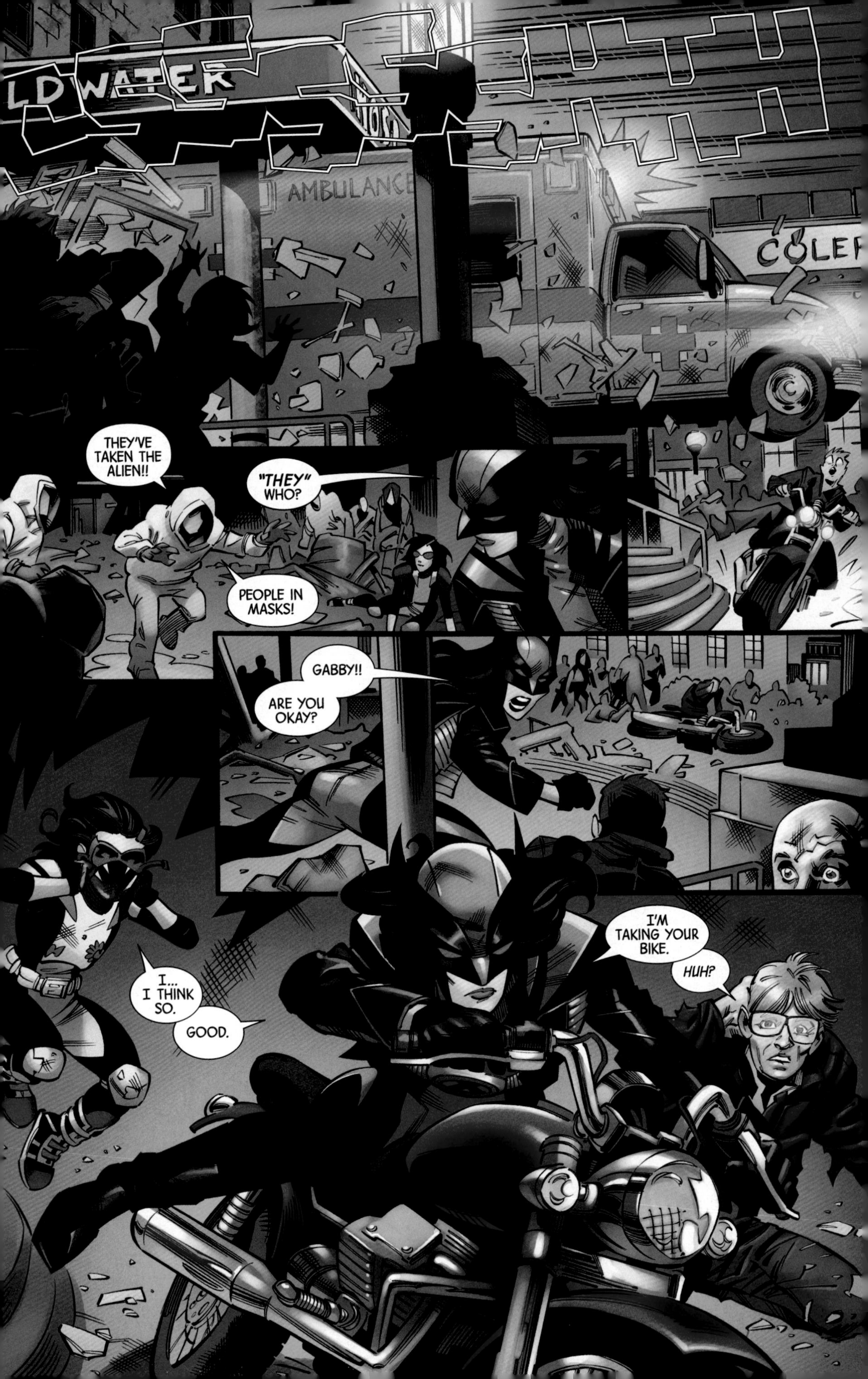

SHUTH
LDWATER
AMBULANCE
COLEF
THEY'VE TAKEN THE ALIEN!!
"THEY" WHO?
PEOPLE IN MASKS!
GABBY!!
ARE YOU OKAY?
I... I THINK SO.
GOOD.
I'M TAKING YOUR BIKE.
HUH?

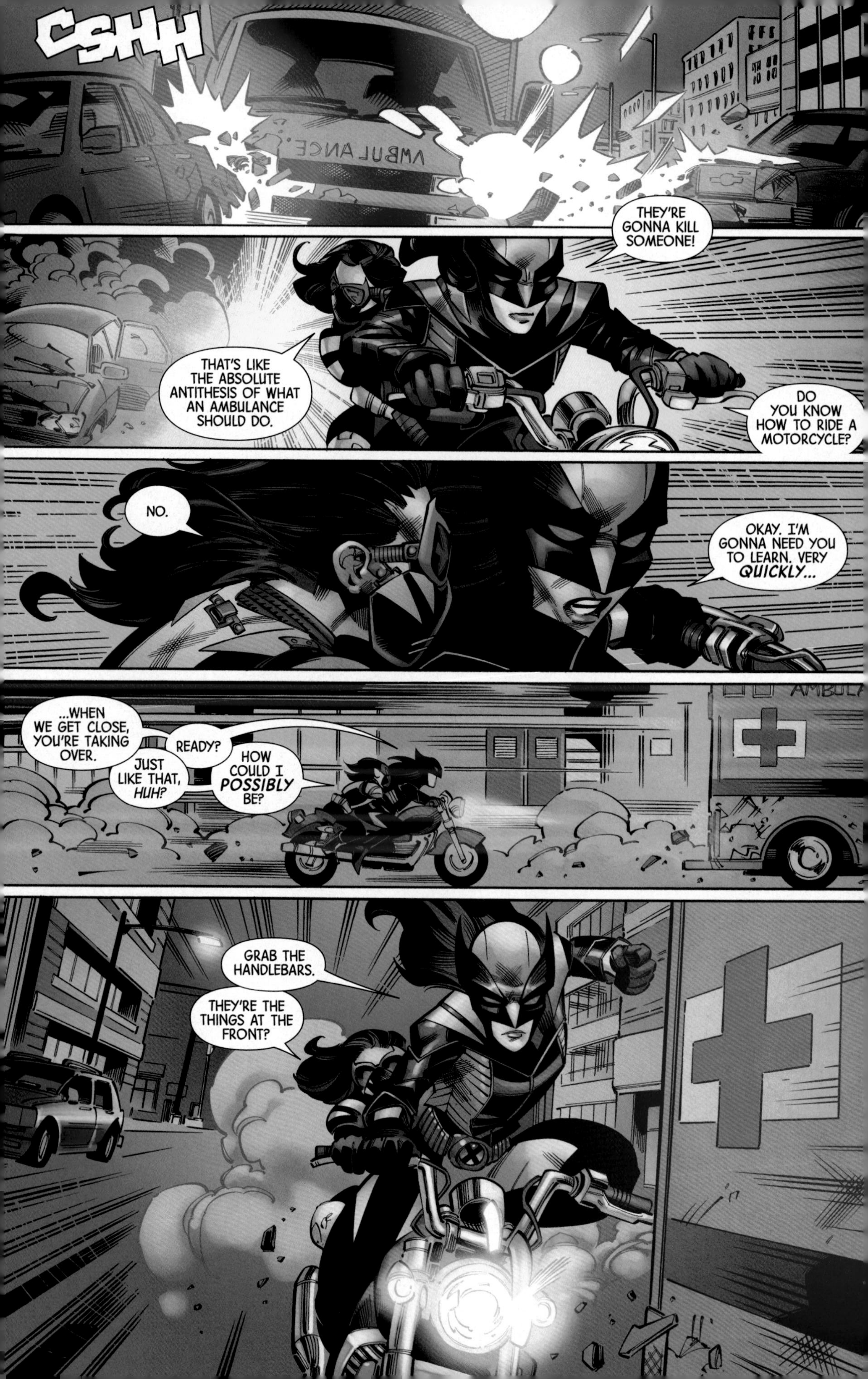
CSHH
AMBULANCE
THEY'RE GONNA KILL SOMEONE!
THAT'S LIKE THE ABSOLUTE ANTITHESIS OF WHAT AN AMBULANCE SHOULD DO.
DO YOU KNOW HOW TO RIDE A MOTORCYCLE?
NO.
OKAY. I'M GONNA NEED YOU TO LEARN. VERY *QUICKLY*...
...WHEN WE GET CLOSE, YOU'RE TAKING OVER.
JUST LIKE THAT, *HUH?*
READY?
HOW COULD I *POSSIBLY* BE?
GRAB THE HANDLEBARS.
THEY'RE THE THINGS AT THE FRONT?

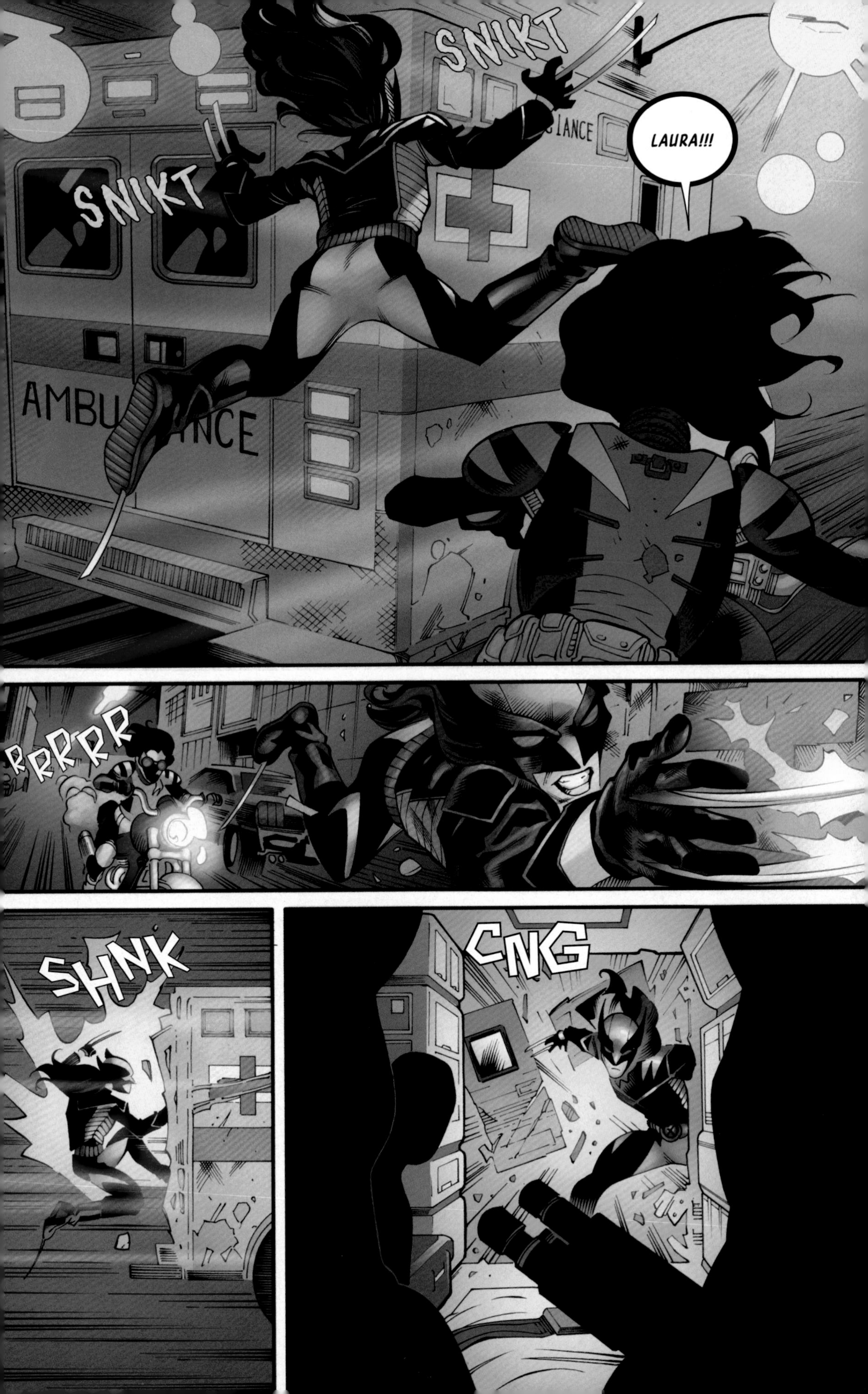
SNIKT
SNIKT
LAURA!!!
AMBULANCE
RRRRR
SHNK
CNG

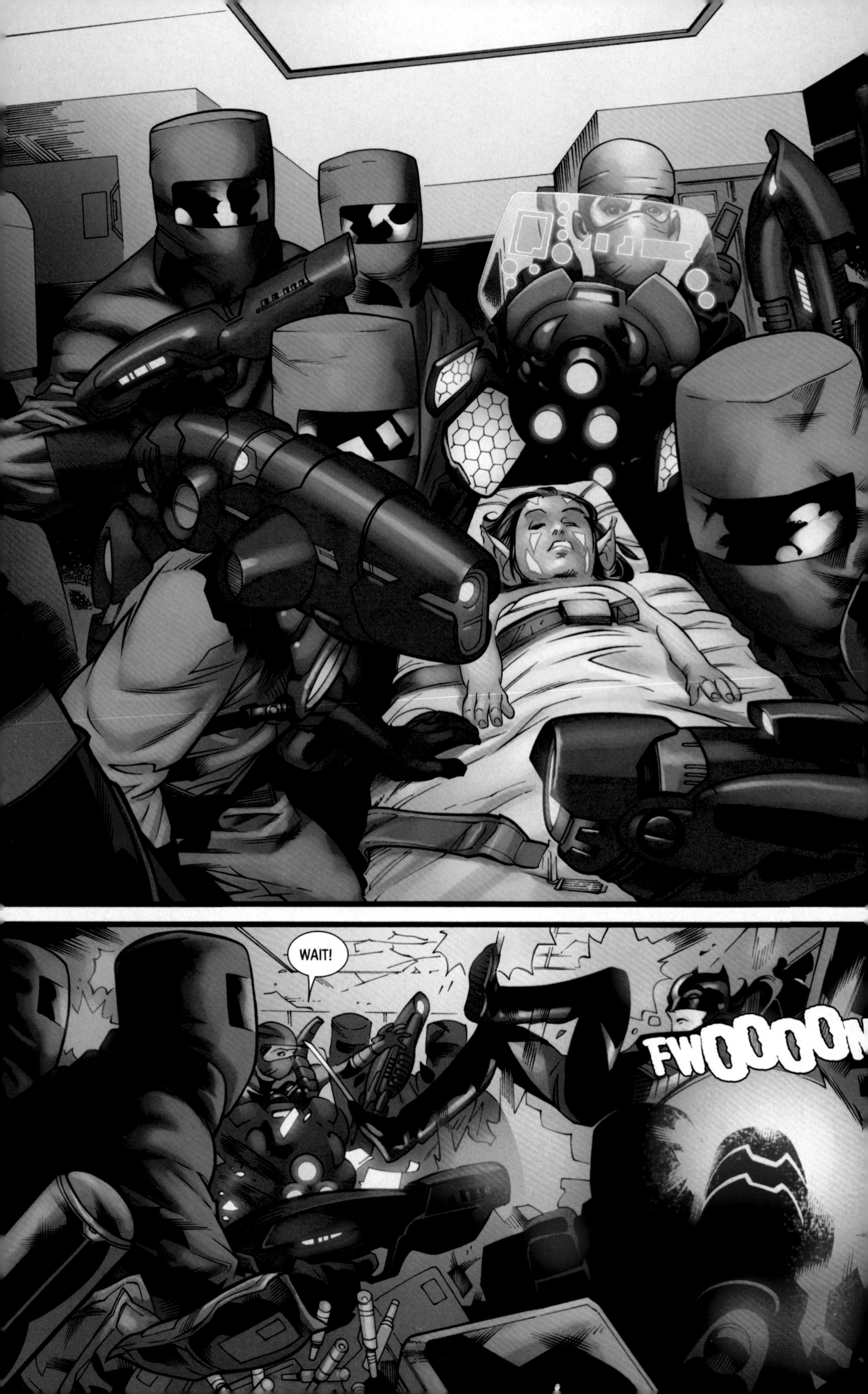
WAIT!
FWOOOOM

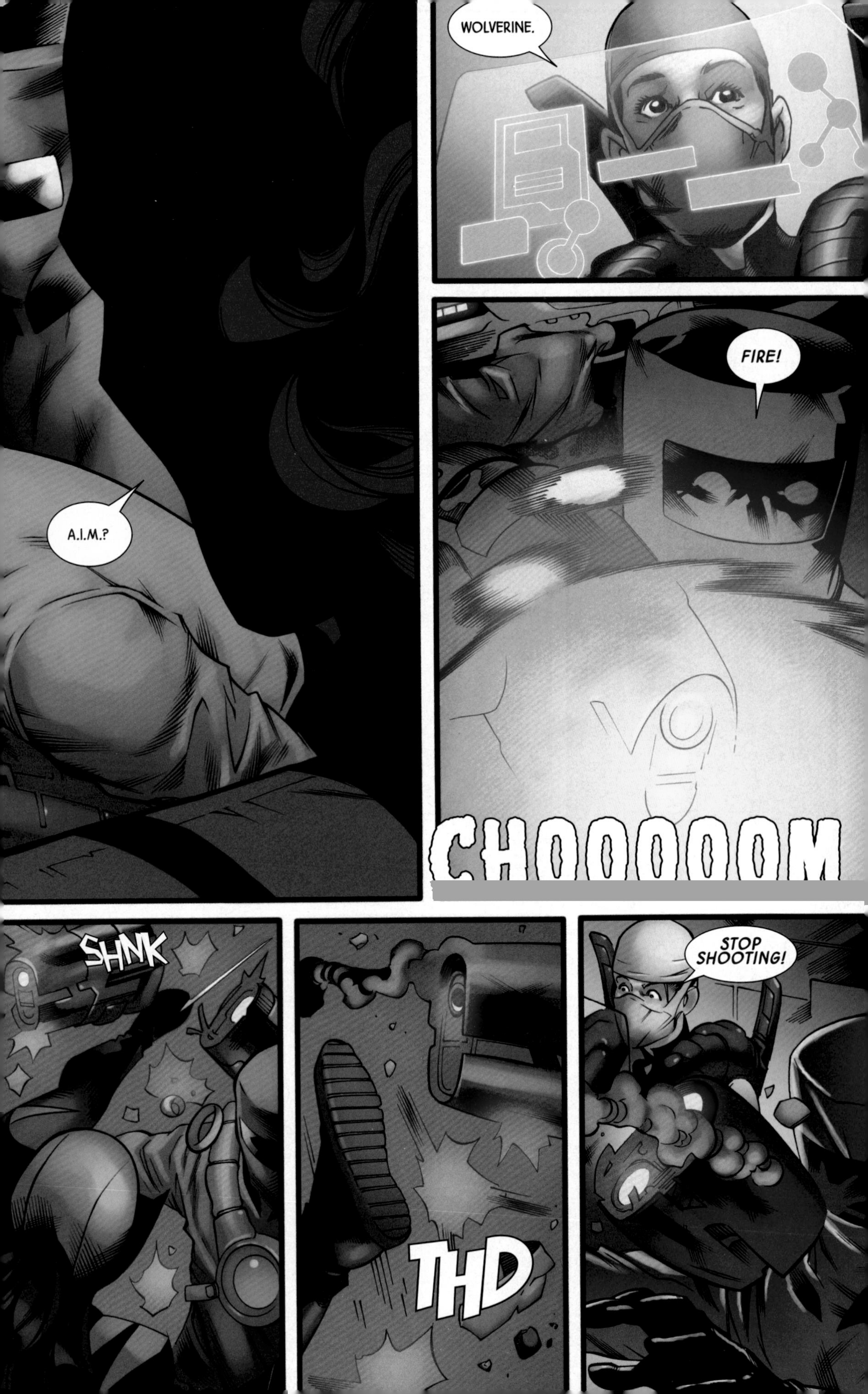
WOLVERINE.
A.I.M.?
FIRE!
CHOOOOOM
SHNK
THD
STOP SHOOTING!

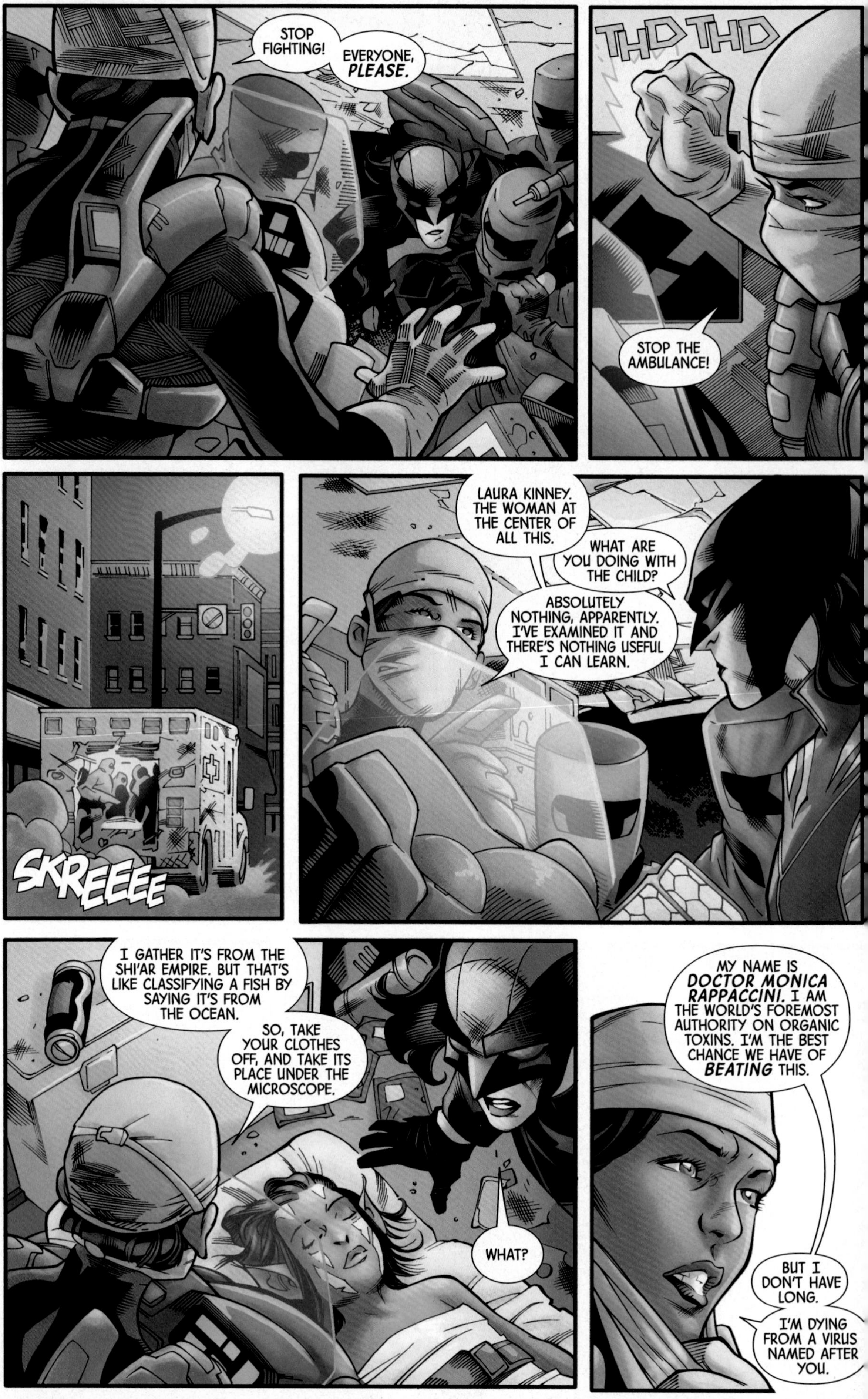

STOP FIGHTING!
EVERYONE, PLEASE.
THD THD
STOP THE AMBULANCE!
SKREEEEE
LAURA KINNEY. THE WOMAN AT THE CENTER OF ALL THIS.
WHAT ARE YOU DOING WITH THE CHILD?
ABSOLUTELY NOTHING, APPARENTLY. I'VE EXAMINED IT AND THERE'S NOTHING USEFUL I CAN LEARN.
I GATHER IT'S FROM THE SHI'AR EMPIRE. BUT THAT'S LIKE CLASSIFYING A FISH BY SAYING IT'S FROM THE OCEAN.
SO, TAKE YOUR CLOTHES OFF, AND TAKE ITS PLACE UNDER THE MICROSCOPE.
WHAT?
MY NAME IS DOCTOR MONICA RAPPACCINI. I AM THE WORLD'S FOREMOST AUTHORITY ON ORGANIC TOXINS. I'M THE BEST CHANCE WE HAVE OF BEATING THIS.
BUT I DON'T HAVE LONG.
I'M DYING FROM A VIRUS NAMED AFTER YOU.

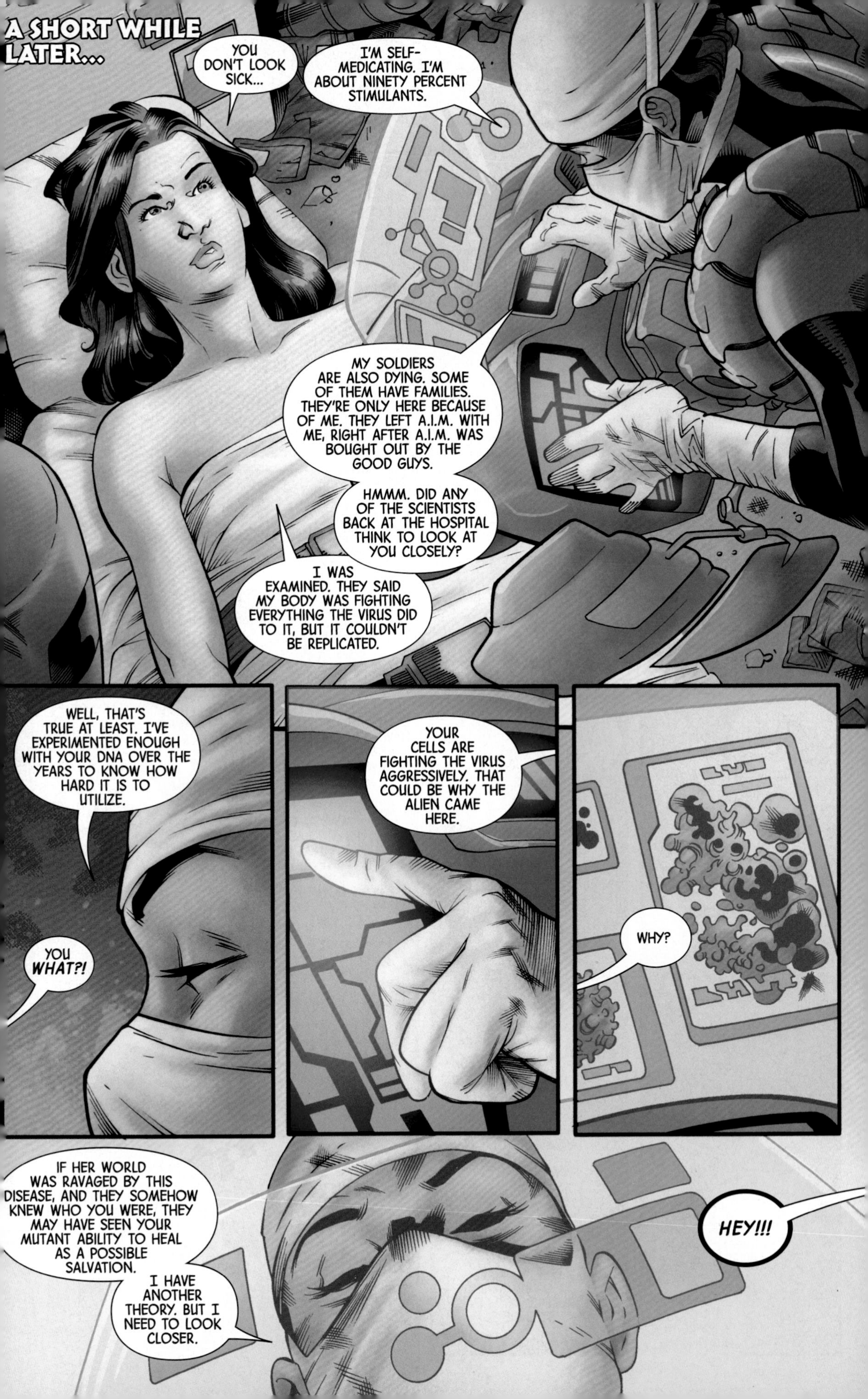
A SHORT WHILE LATER...
YOU DON'T LOOK SICK...
I'M SELF-MEDICATING. I'M ABOUT NINETY PERCENT STIMULANTS.
MY SOLDIERS ARE ALSO DYING. SOME OF THEM HAVE FAMILIES. THEY'RE ONLY HERE BECAUSE OF ME. THEY LEFT A.I.M. WITH ME, RIGHT AFTER A.I.M. WAS BOUGHT OUT BY THE GOOD GUYS.
HMMM. DID ANY OF THE SCIENTISTS BACK AT THE HOSPITAL THINK TO LOOK AT YOU CLOSELY?
I WAS EXAMINED. THEY SAID MY BODY WAS FIGHTING EVERYTHING THE VIRUS DID TO IT, BUT IT COULDN'T BE REPLICATED.
WELL, THAT'S TRUE AT LEAST. I'VE EXPERIMENTED ENOUGH WITH YOUR DNA OVER THE YEARS TO KNOW HOW HARD IT IS TO UTILIZE.
YOU *WHAT?!*
YOUR CELLS ARE FIGHTING THE VIRUS AGGRESSIVELY. THAT COULD BE WHY THE ALIEN CAME HERE.
WHY?
IF HER WORLD WAS RAVAGED BY THIS DISEASE, AND THEY SOMEHOW KNEW WHO YOU WERE, THEY MAY HAVE SEEN YOUR MUTANT ABILITY TO HEAL AS A POSSIBLE SALVATION.
I HAVE ANOTHER THEORY. BUT I NEED TO LOOK CLOSER.
HEY!!!

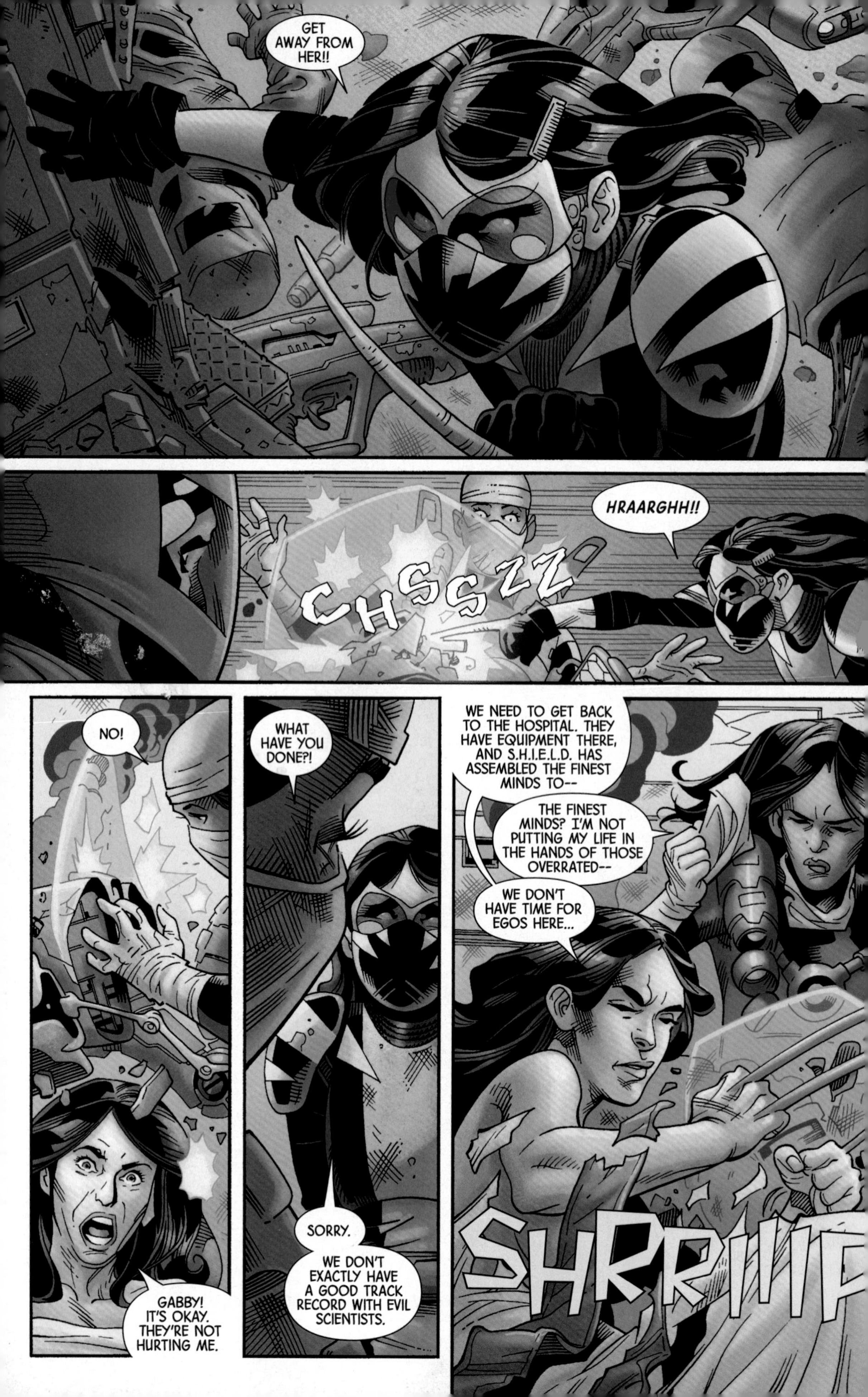
GET AWAY FROM HER!!
HRAARGHH!!
CHSSZZ
NO!
GABBY! IT'S OKAY. THEY'RE NOT HURTING ME.
WHAT HAVE YOU DONE?!
SORRY.
WE DON'T EXACTLY HAVE A GOOD TRACK RECORD WITH EVIL SCIENTISTS.
WE NEED TO GET BACK TO THE HOSPITAL. THEY HAVE EQUIPMENT THERE, AND S.H.I.E.L.D. HAS ASSEMBLED THE FINEST MINDS TO--
THE FINEST MINDS? I'M NOT PUTTING MY LIFE IN THE HANDS OF THOSE OVERRATED--
WE DON'T HAVE TIME FOR EGOS HERE...
SHRIIIIP

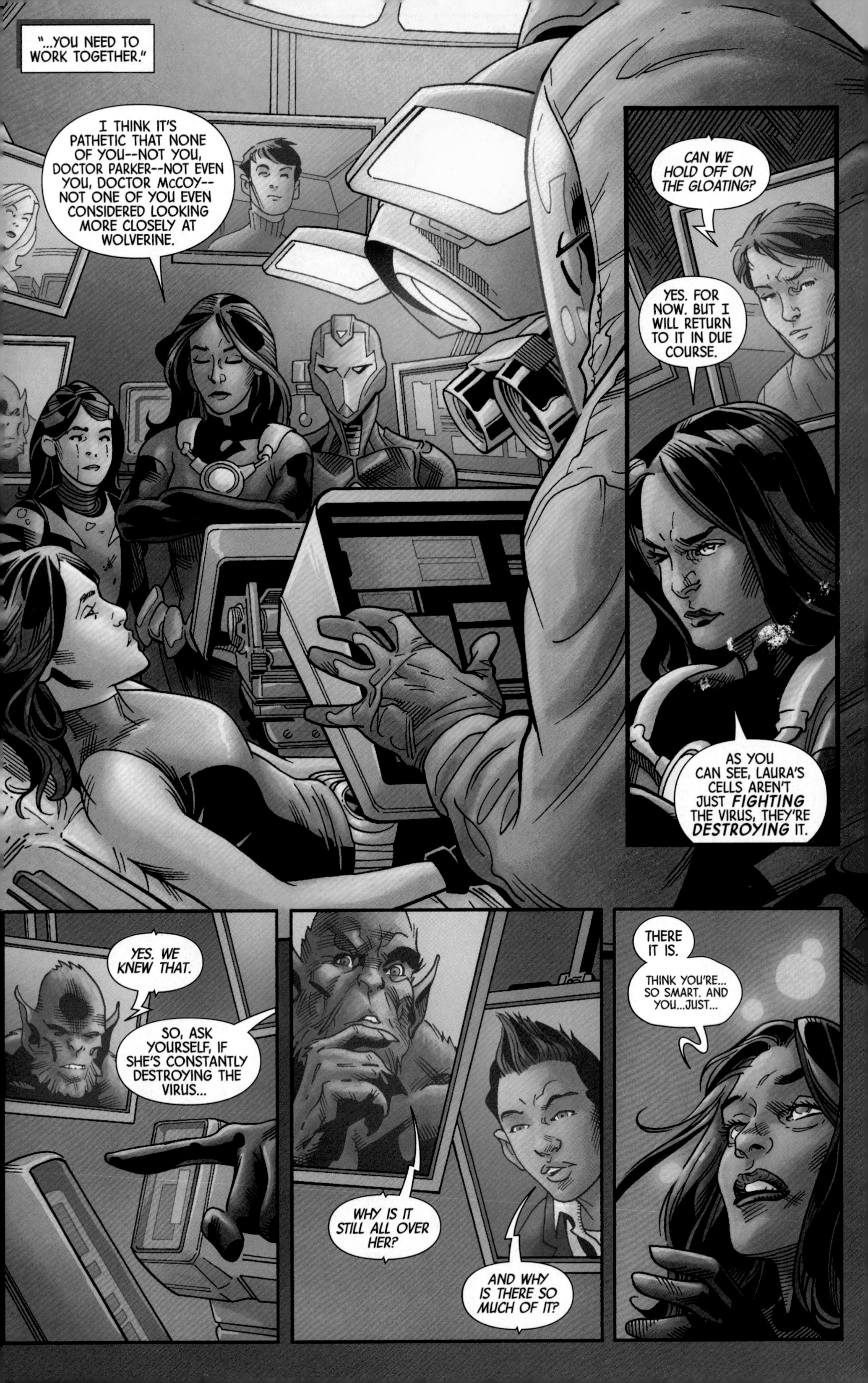
"...YOU NEED TO WORK TOGETHER."
I THINK IT'S PATHETIC THAT NONE OF YOU--NOT YOU, DOCTOR PARKER--NOT EVEN YOU, DOCTOR McCOY--NOT ONE OF YOU EVEN CONSIDERED LOOKING MORE CLOSELY AT WOLVERINE.
CAN WE HOLD OFF ON THE GLOATING?
YES. FOR NOW. BUT I WILL RETURN TO IT IN DUE COURSE.
AS YOU CAN SEE, LAURA'S CELLS AREN'T JUST FIGHTING THE VIRUS, THEY'RE DESTROYING IT.
YES. WE KNEW THAT.
SO, ASK YOURSELF, IF SHE'S CONSTANTLY DESTROYING THE VIRUS...
WHY IS IT STILL ALL OVER HER?
AND WHY IS THERE SO MUCH OF IT?
THERE IT IS.
THINK YOU'RE... SO SMART. AND YOU...JUST...

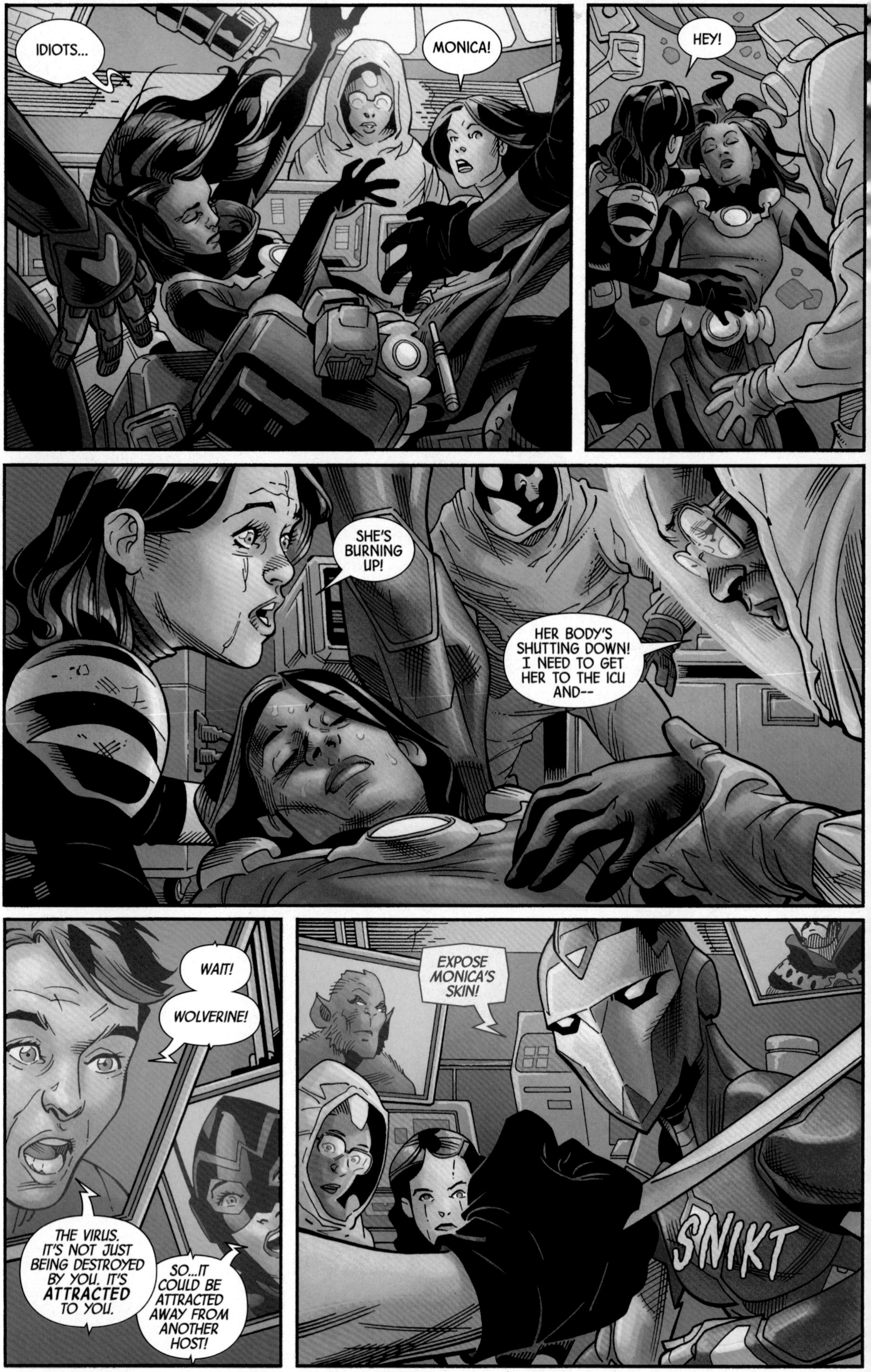

IDIOTS...
MONICA!
HEY!
SHE'S BURNING UP!
HER BODY'S SHUTTING DOWN! I NEED TO GET HER TO THE ICU AND--
WAIT!
WOLVERINE!
THE VIRUS. IT'S NOT JUST BEING DESTROYED BY YOU. IT'S **ATTRACTED** TO YOU.
SO...IT COULD BE ATTRACTED AWAY FROM ANOTHER HOST!
EXPOSE MONICA'S SKIN!
SNIKT

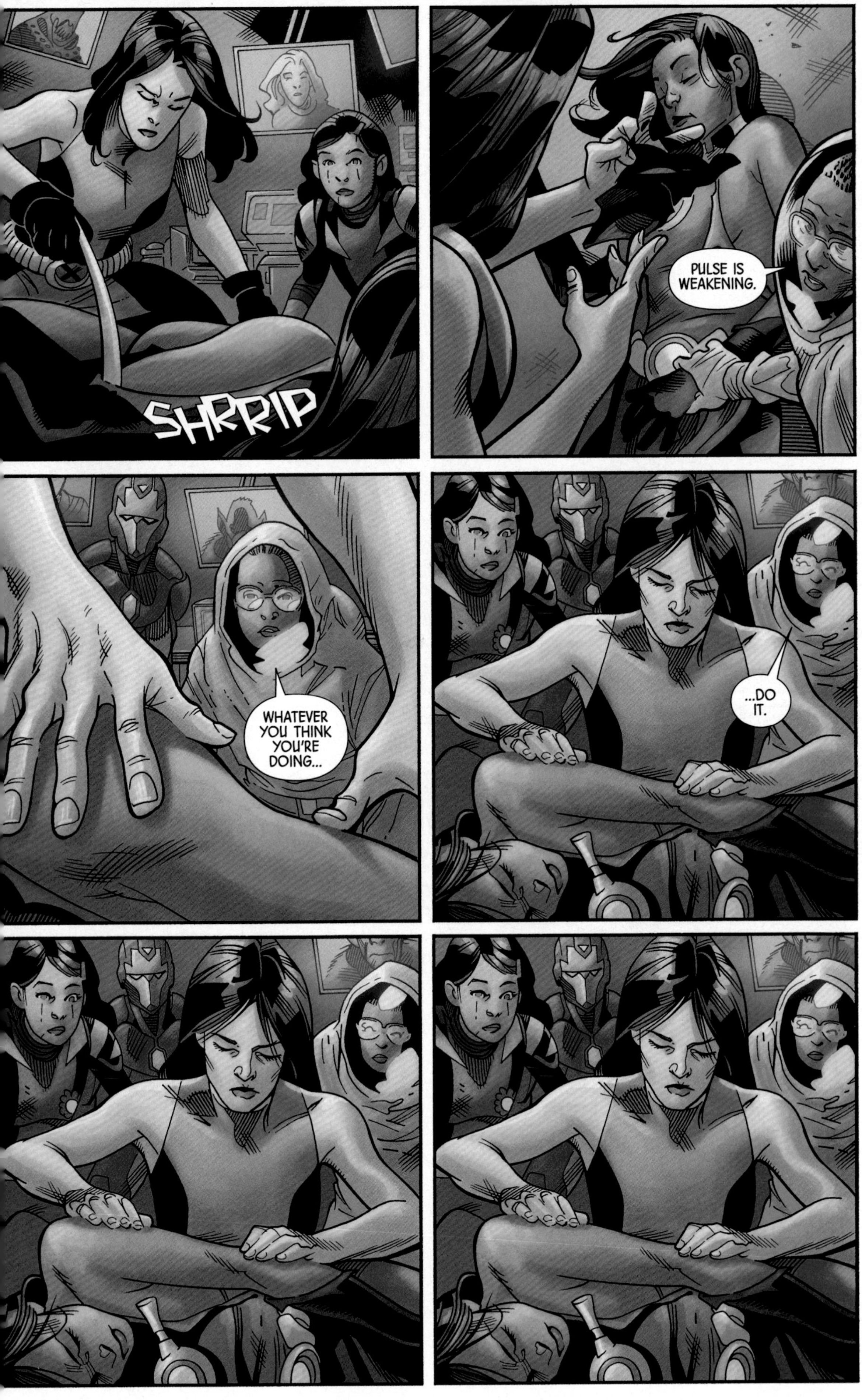
SHRRIP
PULSE IS WEAKENING.
WHATEVER YOU THINK YOU'RE DOING...
...DO IT.

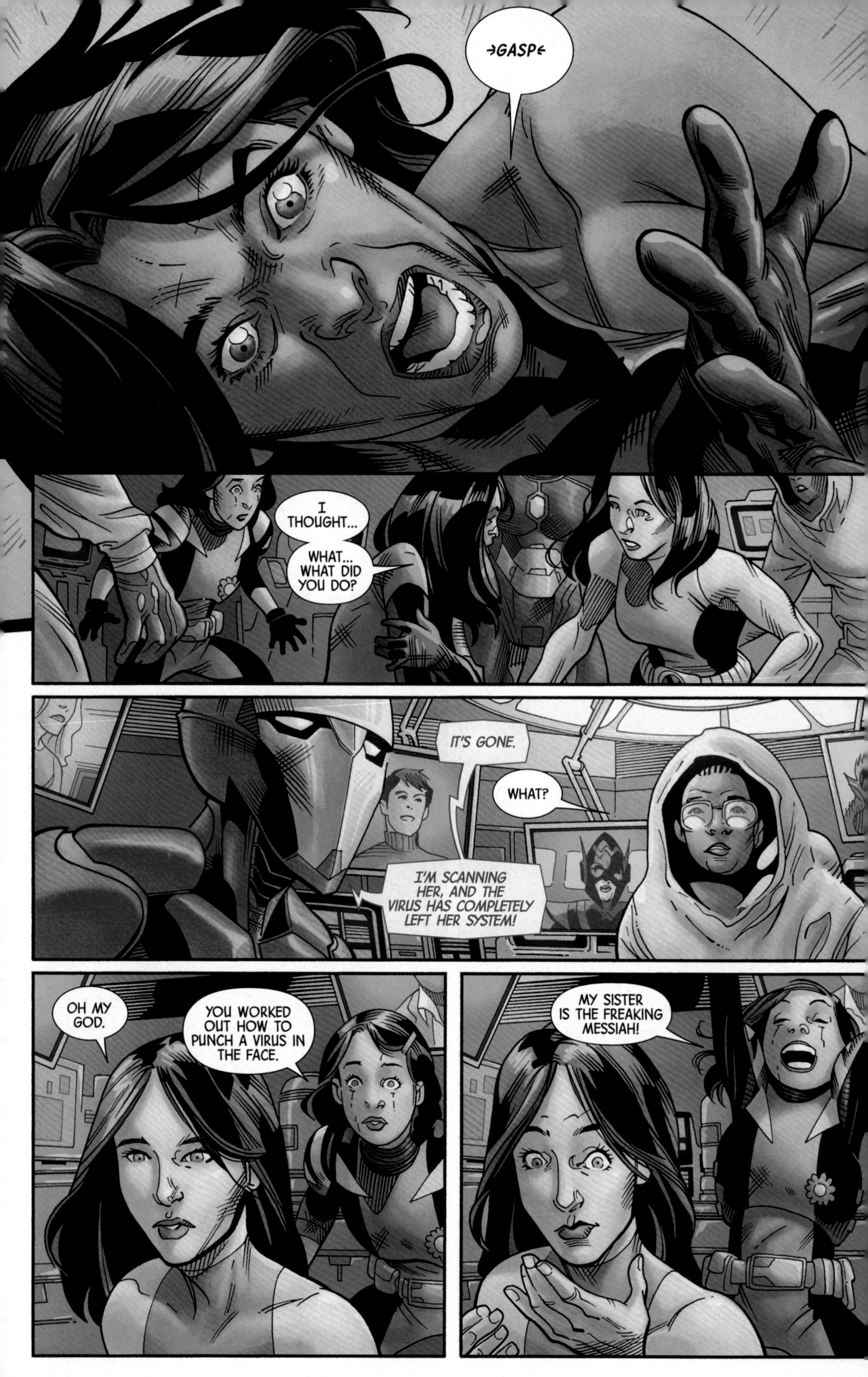
→GASP←
I THOUGHT...
WHAT... WHAT DID YOU DO?
IT'S GONE.
WHAT?
I'M SCANNING HER, AND THE VIRUS HAS COMPLETELY LEFT HER SYSTEM!
OH MY GOD.
YOU WORKED OUT HOW TO PUNCH A VIRUS IN THE FACE.
MY SISTER IS THE FREAKING MESSIAH!

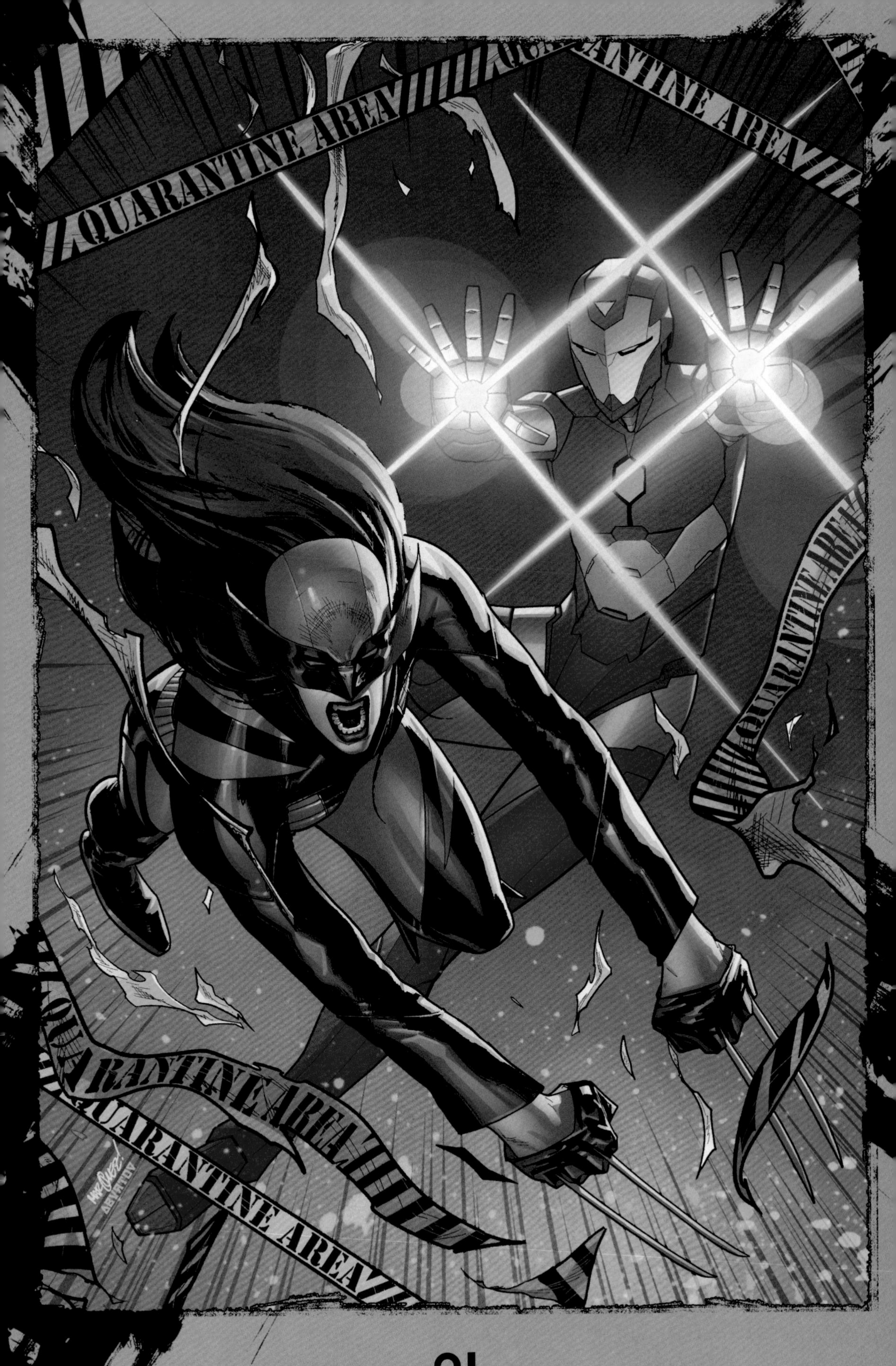
QUARANTINE AREA
QUARANTINE AREA
QUARANTINE AREA
QUARANTINE AREA

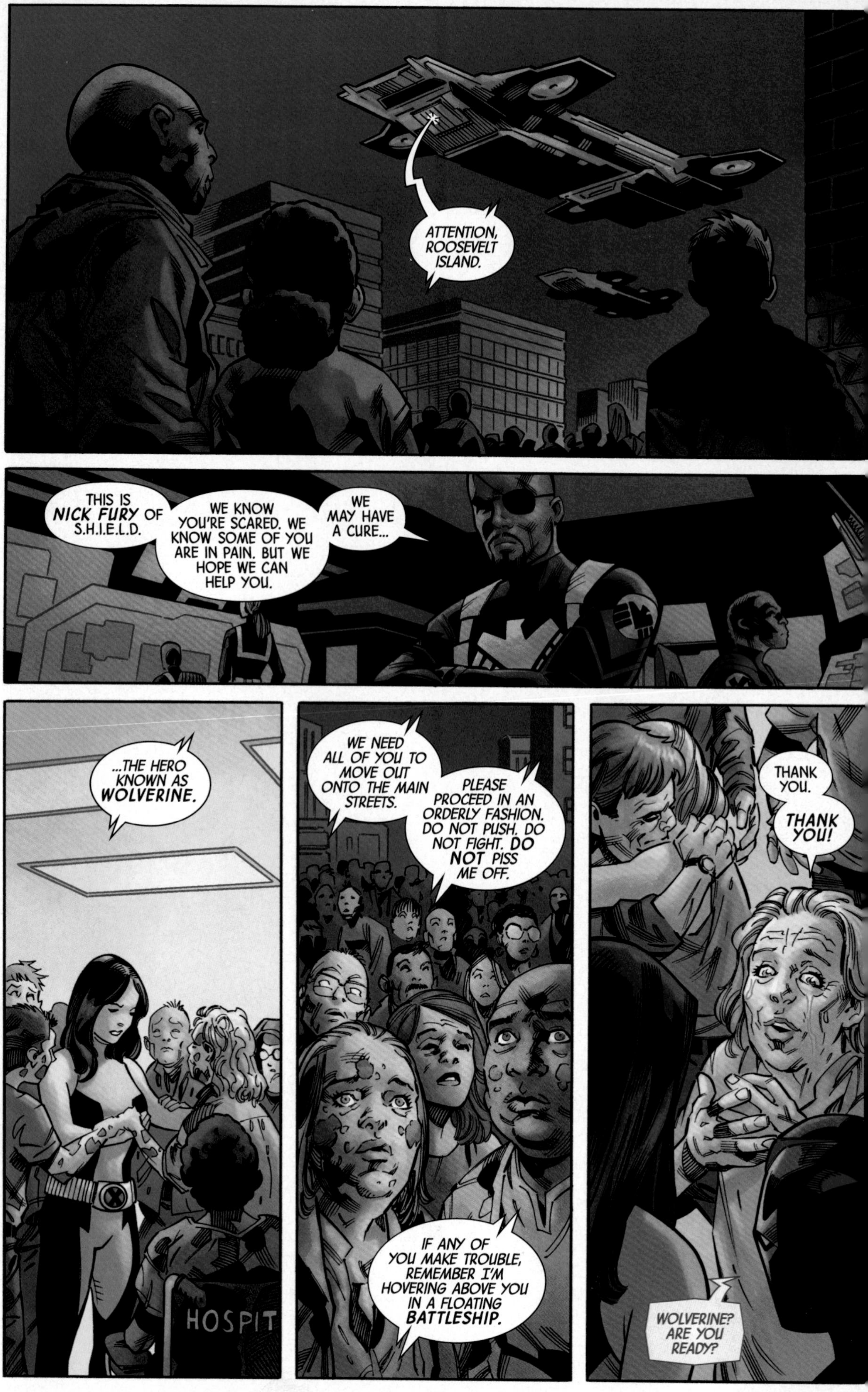
ATTENTION, ROOSEVELT ISLAND.
THIS IS NICK FURY OF S.H.I.E.L.D.
WE KNOW YOU'RE SCARED. WE KNOW SOME OF YOU ARE IN PAIN. BUT WE HOPE WE CAN HELP YOU.
WE MAY HAVE A CURE...
...THE HERO KNOWN AS WOLVERINE.
HOSPIT
WE NEED ALL OF YOU TO MOVE OUT ONTO THE MAIN STREETS.
PLEASE PROCEED IN AN ORDERLY FASHION. DO NOT PUSH. DO NOT FIGHT. DO NOT PISS ME OFF.
IF ANY OF YOU MAKE TROUBLE, REMEMBER I'M HOVERING ABOVE YOU IN A FLOATING BATTLESHIP.
THANK YOU.
THANK YOU!
WOLVERINE? ARE YOU READY?

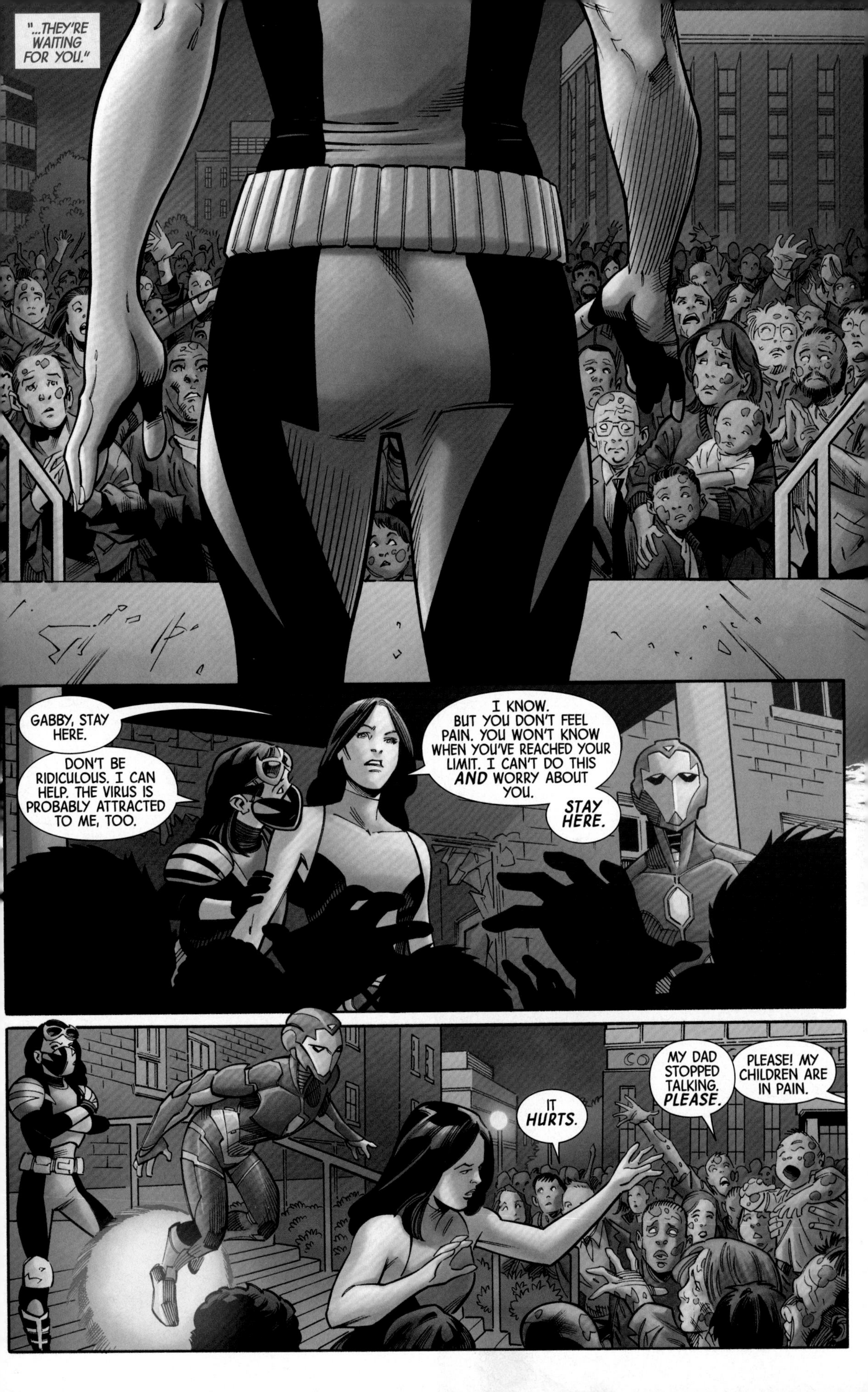
"...THEY'RE WAITING FOR YOU."
GABBY, STAY HERE.
DON'T BE RIDICULOUS. I CAN HELP. THE VIRUS IS PROBABLY ATTRACTED TO ME, TOO.
I KNOW. BUT YOU DON'T FEEL PAIN. YOU WON'T KNOW WHEN YOU'VE REACHED YOUR LIMIT. I CAN'T DO THIS AND WORRY ABOUT YOU.
STAY HERE.
IT HURTS.
MY DAD STOPPED TALKING. PLEASE.
PLEASE! MY CHILDREN ARE IN PAIN.

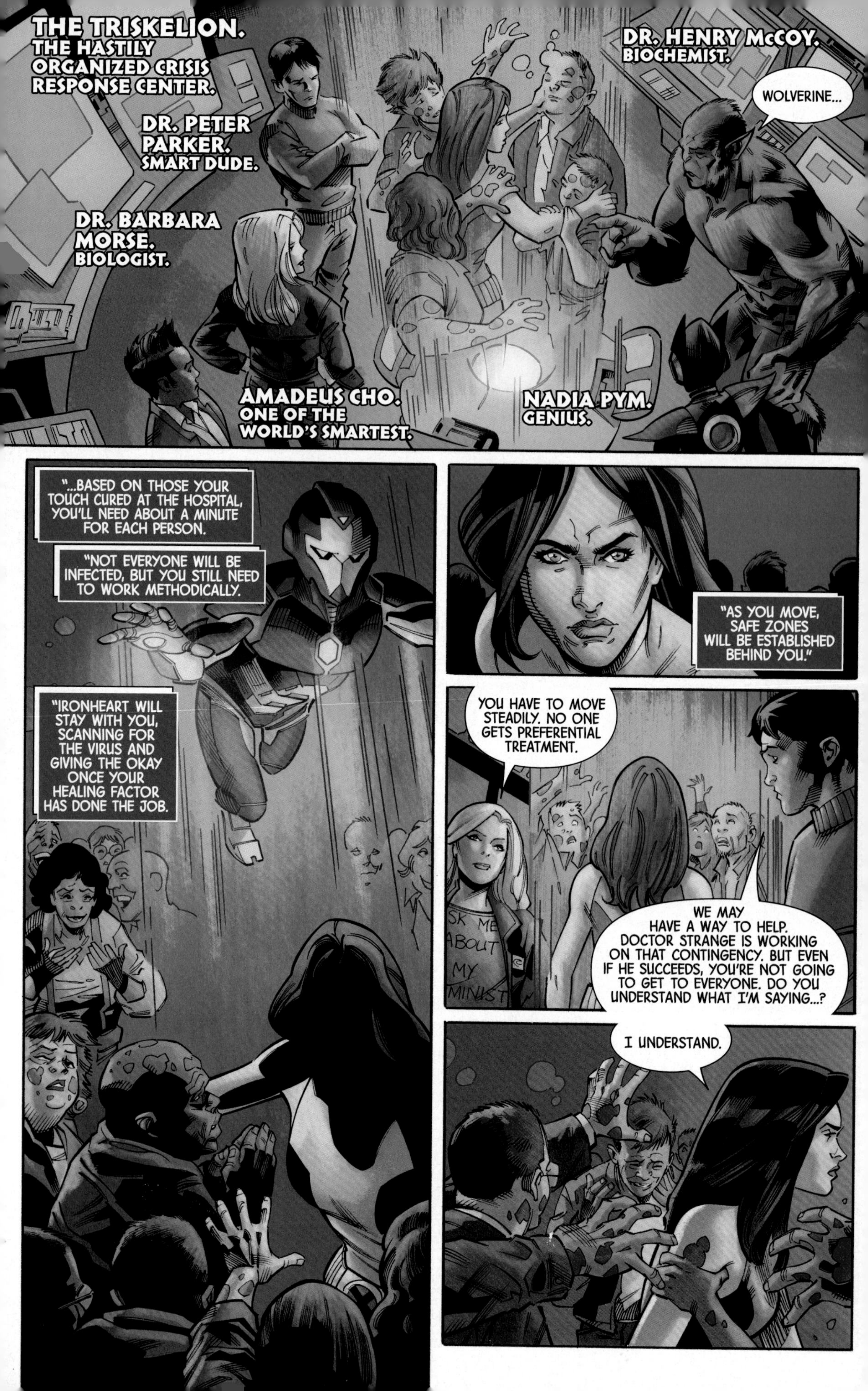
THE TRISKELION. THE HASTILY ORGANIZED CRISIS RESPONSE CENTER.
DR. PETER PARKER. SMART DUDE.
DR. BARBARA MORSE. BIOLOGIST.
AMADEUS CHO. ONE OF THE WORLD'S SMARTEST.
NADIA PYM. GENIUS.
DR. HENRY McCOY. BIOCHEMIST.
WOLVERINE...
"...BASED ON THOSE YOUR TOUCH CURED AT THE HOSPITAL, YOU'LL NEED ABOUT A MINUTE FOR EACH PERSON.
"NOT EVERYONE WILL BE INFECTED, BUT YOU STILL NEED TO WORK METHODICALLY.
"IRONHEART WILL STAY WITH YOU, SCANNING FOR THE VIRUS AND GIVING THE OKAY ONCE YOUR HEALING FACTOR HAS DONE THE JOB.
"AS YOU MOVE, SAFE ZONES WILL BE ESTABLISHED BEHIND YOU."
YOU HAVE TO MOVE STEADILY. NO ONE GETS PREFERENTIAL TREATMENT.
WE MAY HAVE A WAY TO HELP. DOCTOR STRANGE IS WORKING ON THAT CONTINGENCY. BUT EVEN IF HE SUCCEEDS, YOU'RE NOT GOING TO GET TO EVERYONE. DO YOU UNDERSTAND WHAT I'M SAYING...?
I UNDERSTAND.

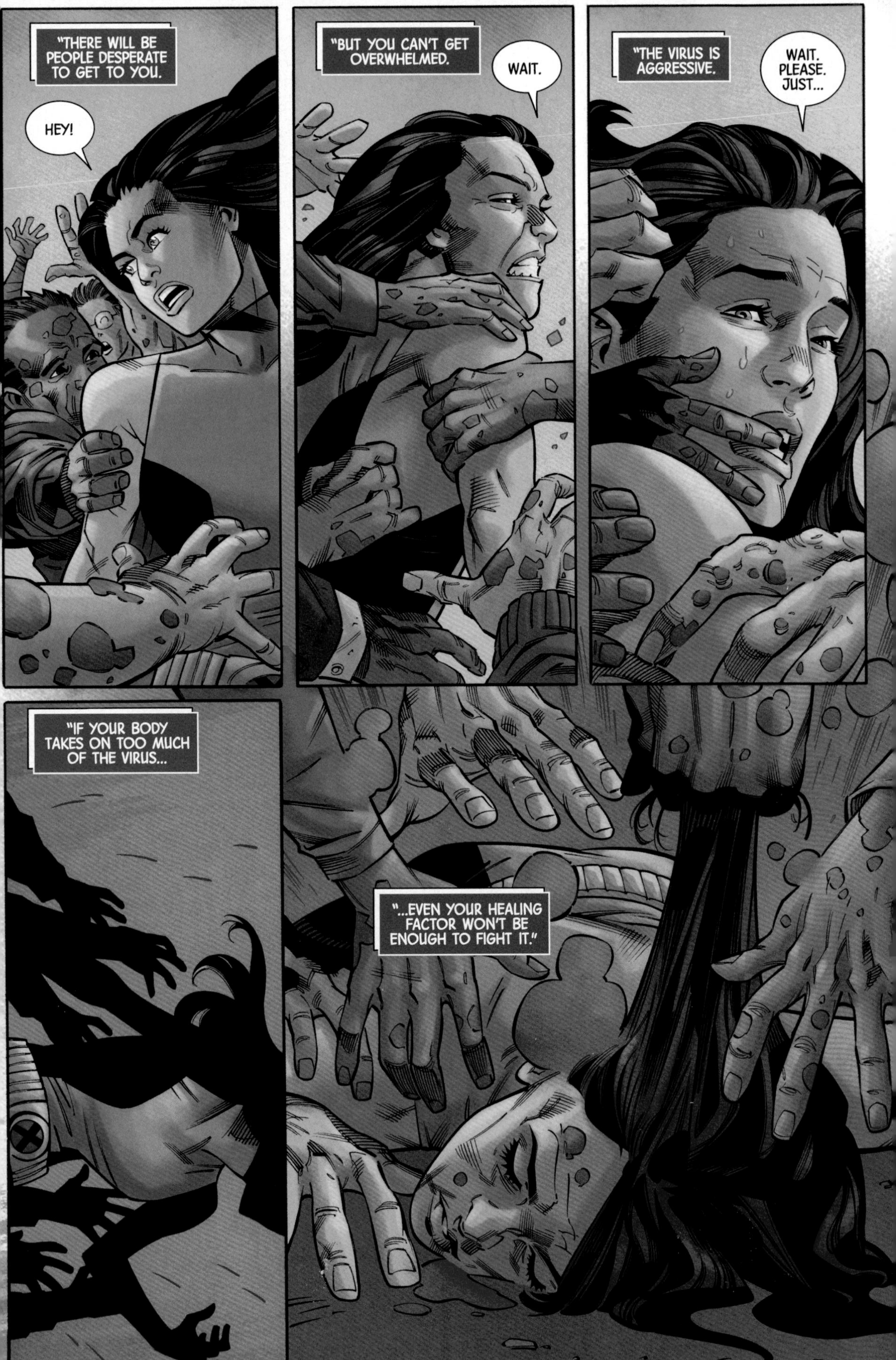
"THERE WILL BE PEOPLE DESPERATE TO GET TO YOU.
HEY!
"BUT YOU CAN'T GET OVERWHELMED.
WAIT.
"THE VIRUS IS AGGRESSIVE.
WAIT. PLEASE. JUST...
"IF YOUR BODY TAKES ON TOO MUCH OF THE VIRUS...
"...EVEN YOUR HEALING FACTOR WON'T BE ENOUGH TO FIGHT IT."

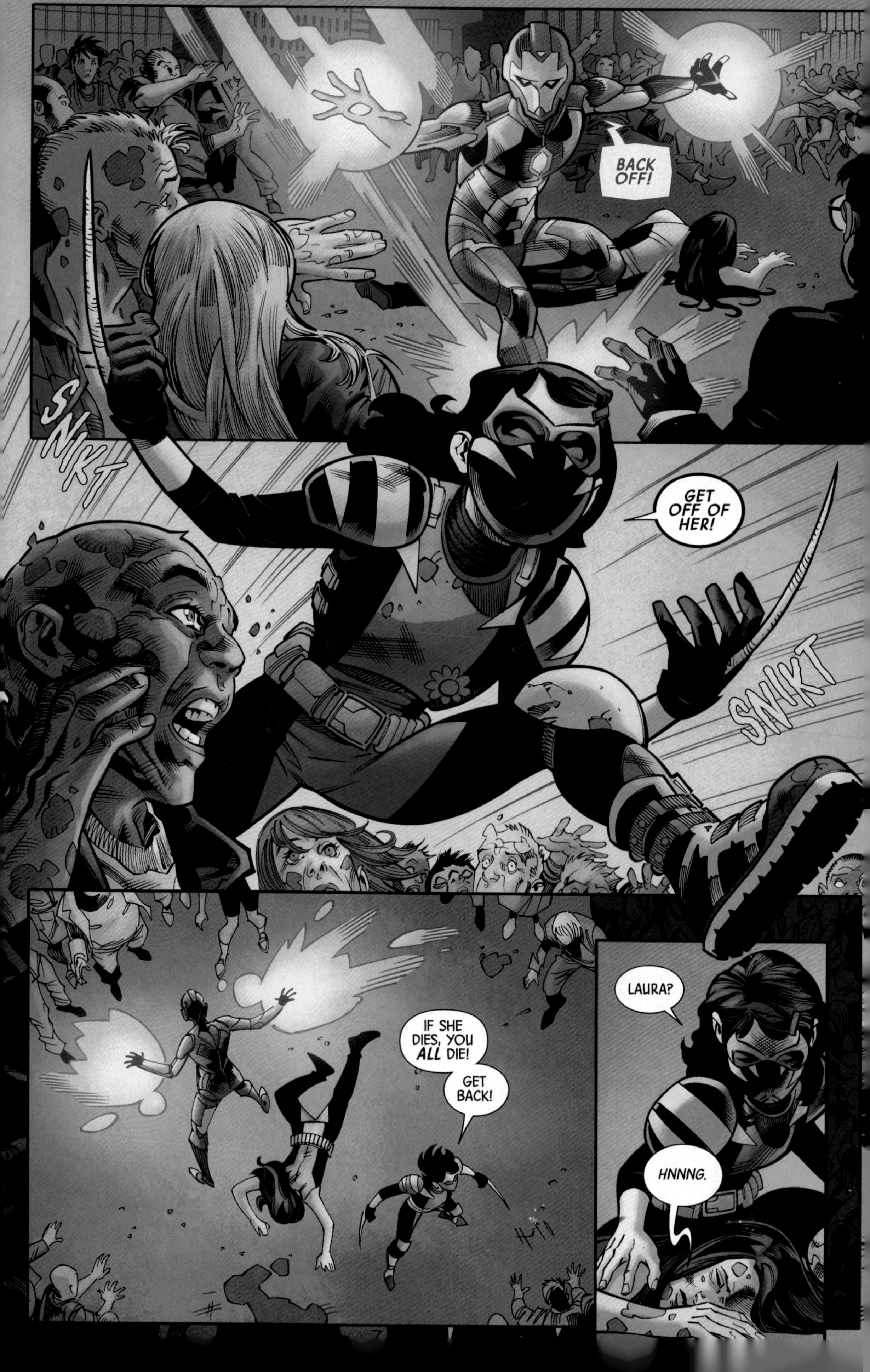
BACK OFF!
SNIKT
GET OFF OF HER!
SNIKT
IF SHE DIES, YOU ALL DIE!
GET BACK!
LAURA?
HNNNG.

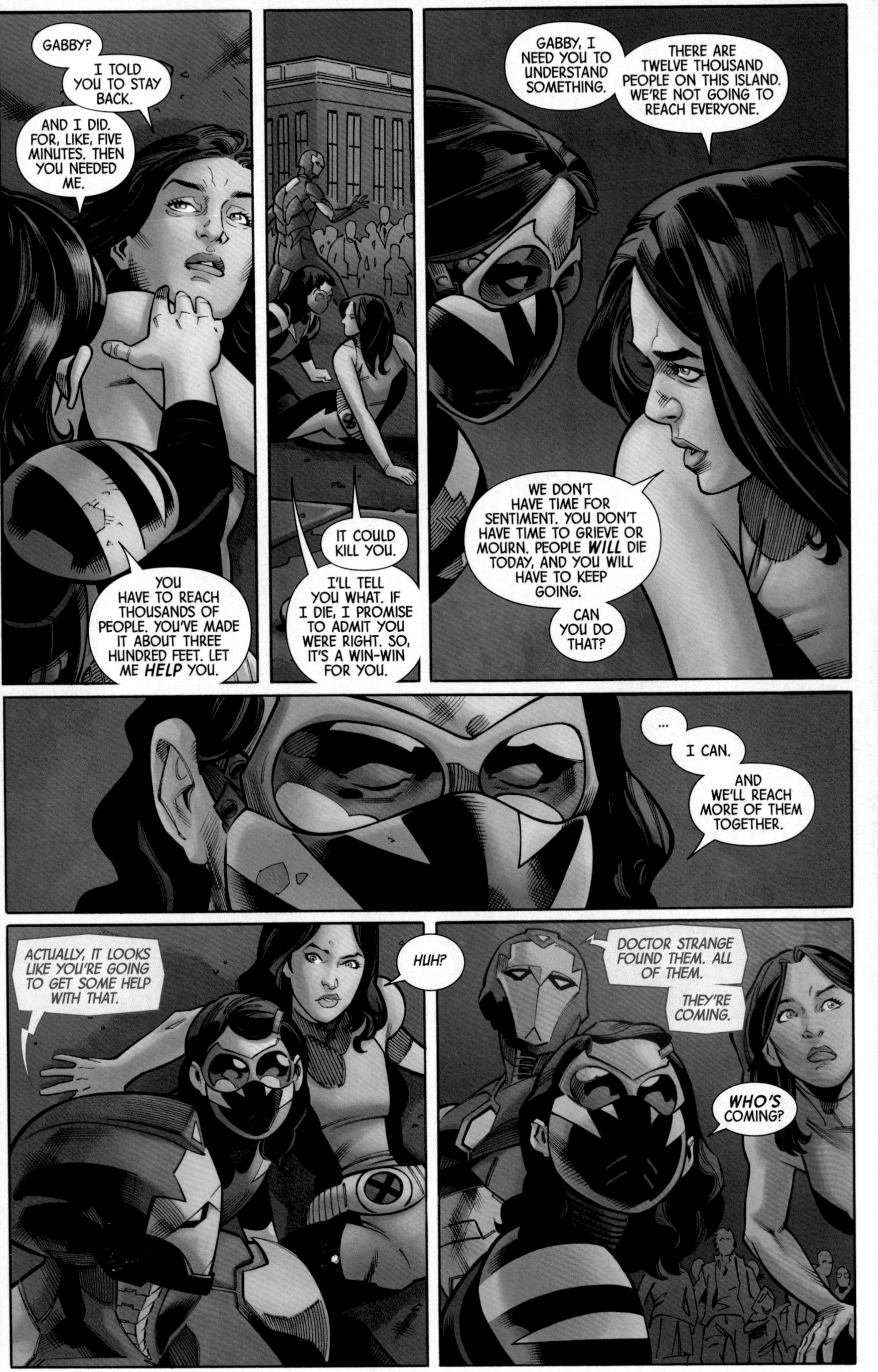
GABBY?
I TOLD YOU TO STAY BACK.
AND I DID. FOR, LIKE, FIVE MINUTES. THEN YOU NEEDED ME.
YOU HAVE TO REACH THOUSANDS OF PEOPLE. YOU'VE MADE IT ABOUT THREE HUNDRED FEET. LET ME HELP YOU.
IT COULD KILL YOU.
I'LL TELL YOU WHAT. IF I DIE, I PROMISE TO ADMIT YOU WERE RIGHT. SO, IT'S A WIN-WIN FOR YOU.
GABBY, I NEED YOU TO UNDERSTAND SOMETHING.
THERE ARE TWELVE THOUSAND PEOPLE ON THIS ISLAND. WE'RE NOT GOING TO REACH EVERYONE.
WE DON'T HAVE TIME FOR SENTIMENT. YOU DON'T HAVE TIME TO GRIEVE OR MOURN. PEOPLE WILL DIE TODAY, AND YOU WILL HAVE TO KEEP GOING.
CAN YOU DO THAT?
...
I CAN.
AND WE'LL REACH MORE OF THEM TOGETHER.
ACTUALLY, IT LOOKS LIKE YOU'RE GOING TO GET SOME HELP WITH THAT.
HUH?
DOCTOR STRANGE FOUND THEM. ALL OF THEM.
THEY'RE COMING.
WHO'S COMING?

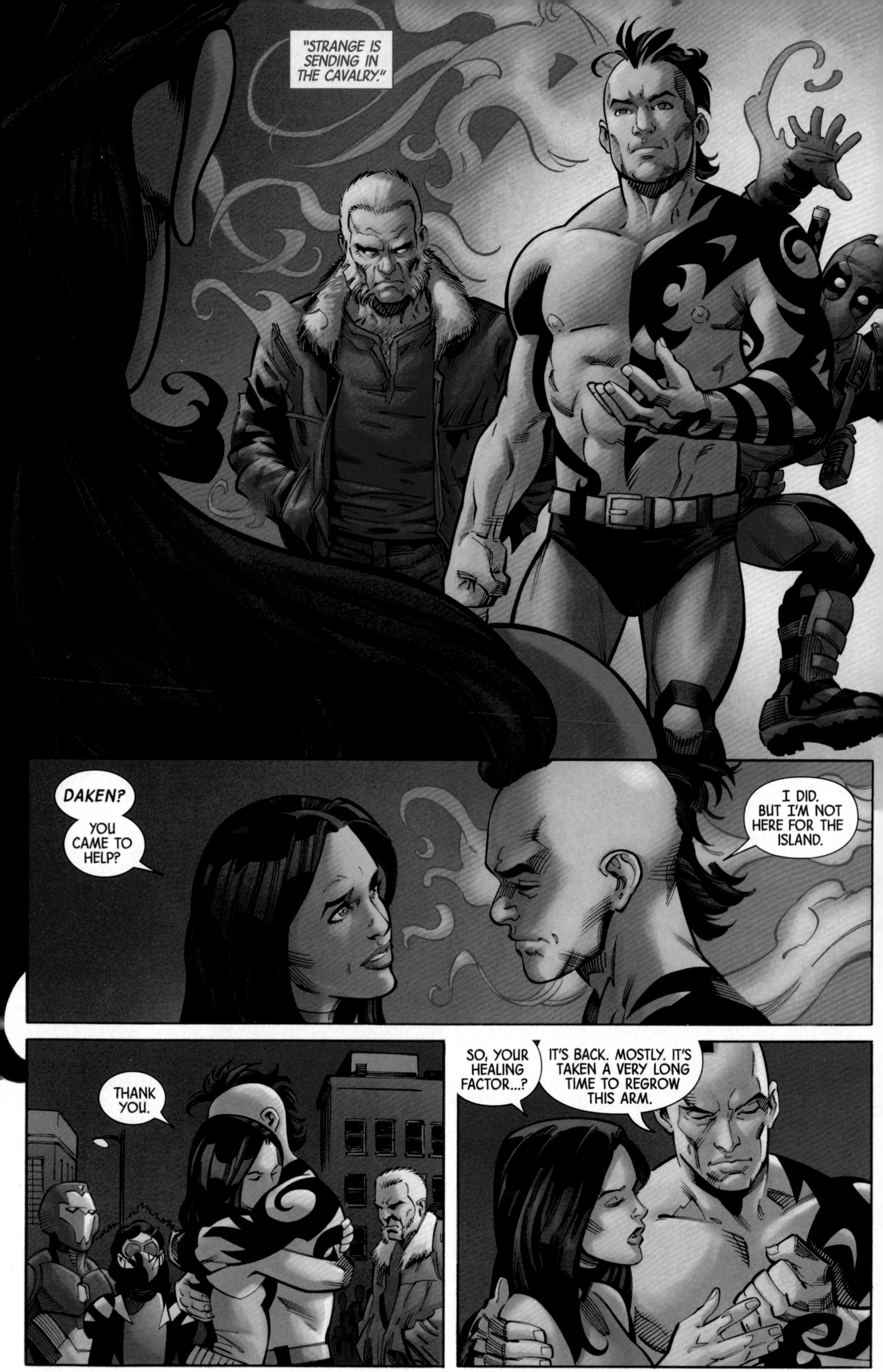
"STRANGE IS SENDING IN THE CAVALRY."
DAKEN?
YOU CAME TO HELP?
I DID. BUT I'M NOT HERE FOR THE ISLAND.
THANK YOU.
SO, YOUR HEALING FACTOR...?
IT'S BACK. MOSTLY. IT'S TAKEN A VERY LONG TIME TO REGROW THIS ARM.

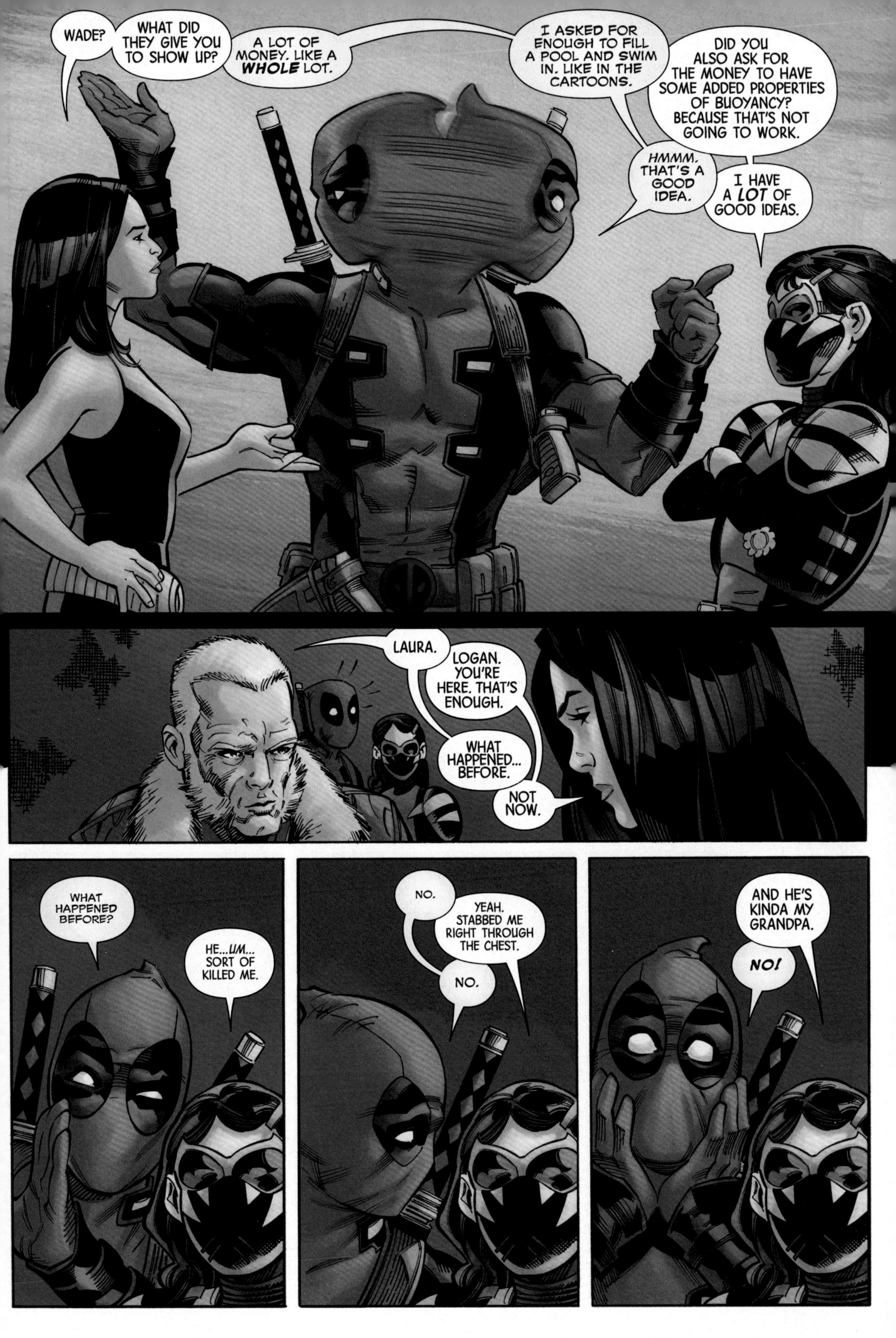
WADE?
WHAT DID THEY GIVE YOU TO SHOW UP?
A LOT OF MONEY. LIKE A *WHOLE* LOT.
I ASKED FOR ENOUGH TO FILL A POOL AND SWIM IN. LIKE IN THE CARTOONS.
DID YOU ALSO ASK FOR THE MONEY TO HAVE SOME ADDED PROPERTIES OF BUOYANCY? BECAUSE THAT'S NOT GOING TO WORK.
HMMM. THAT'S A GOOD IDEA.
I HAVE A *LOT* OF GOOD IDEAS.
LAURA.
LOGAN. YOU'RE HERE. THAT'S ENOUGH.
WHAT HAPPENED... BEFORE.
NOT NOW.
WHAT HAPPENED BEFORE?
HE...*UM*... SORT OF KILLED ME.
NO.
YEAH. STABBED ME RIGHT THROUGH THE CHEST.
NO.
AND HE'S KINDA MY GRANDPA.
NO!

WE NEED SKIN-TO-SKIN CONTACT WITH THE INFECTED FOR THIS TO WORK.

UM... I'M SORRY ABOUT THIS, KID.

YOU MIGHT WANT TO LOOK SOMEWHERE ELSE.

WHY WOULD I LOOK SOMEWHERE ELSE?

BECAUSE MY BODY LOOKS LIKE THE WAX FIGURES OF CHURCHILL AND HITLER MELTED TOGETHER INTO A PERFECTLY FUSED ARTISTIC REPRESENTATION OF THEIR ANIMOSITY.

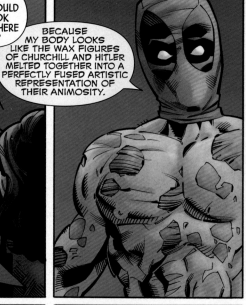

ARE YOU TALKING ABOUT THE *SCARS?*

MEH. I THOUGHT YOU WERE GONNA HAVE, LIKE, SIX NIPPLES OR SOMETHING. LIKE YOU WERE CROSSBRED WITH A CAT.

WHY WOULD YOU THINK THAT?

I THINK A LOT OF WEIRD THINGS.

IT'S OKAY. I HAVE SCARS, TOO.

SEE.

THEY DON'T REALLY BUG ME.

THEY SHOULDN'T. I THINK THEY'RE *DELIGHTFUL.*

THANK YOU.

SO ARE YOURS.

WE'RE BEST FRIENDS NOW.

AGREED.

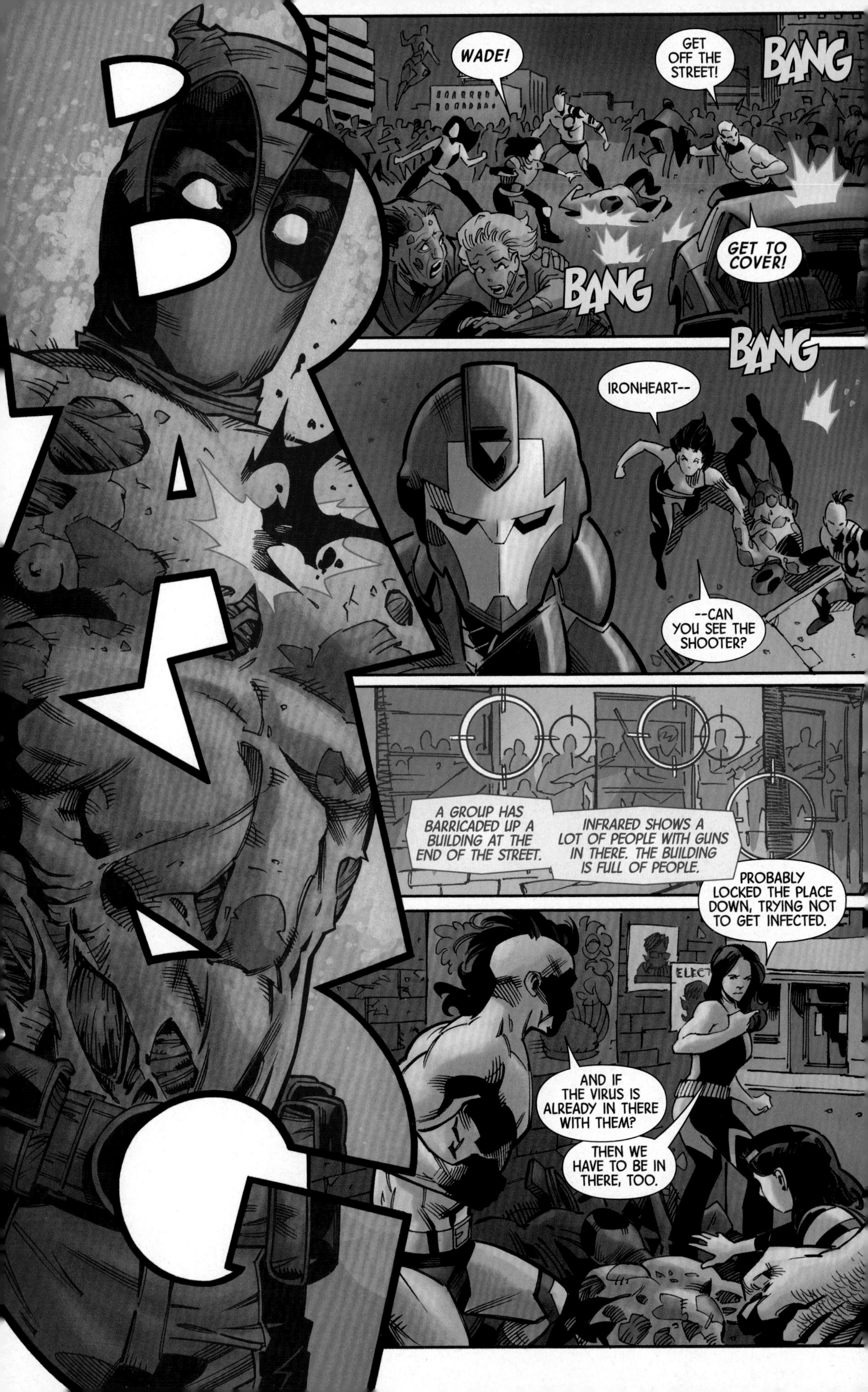
WADE!
GET OFF THE STREET!
BANG
BANG
GET TO COVER!
BANG
IRONHEART--
--CAN YOU SEE THE SHOOTER?
A GROUP HAS BARRICADED UP A BUILDING AT THE END OF THE STREET.
INFRARED SHOWS A LOT OF PEOPLE WITH GUNS IN THERE. THE BUILDING IS FULL OF PEOPLE.
PROBABLY LOCKED THE PLACE DOWN, TRYING NOT TO GET INFECTED.
AND IF THE VIRUS IS ALREADY IN THERE WITH THEM?
THEN WE HAVE TO BE IN THERE, TOO.

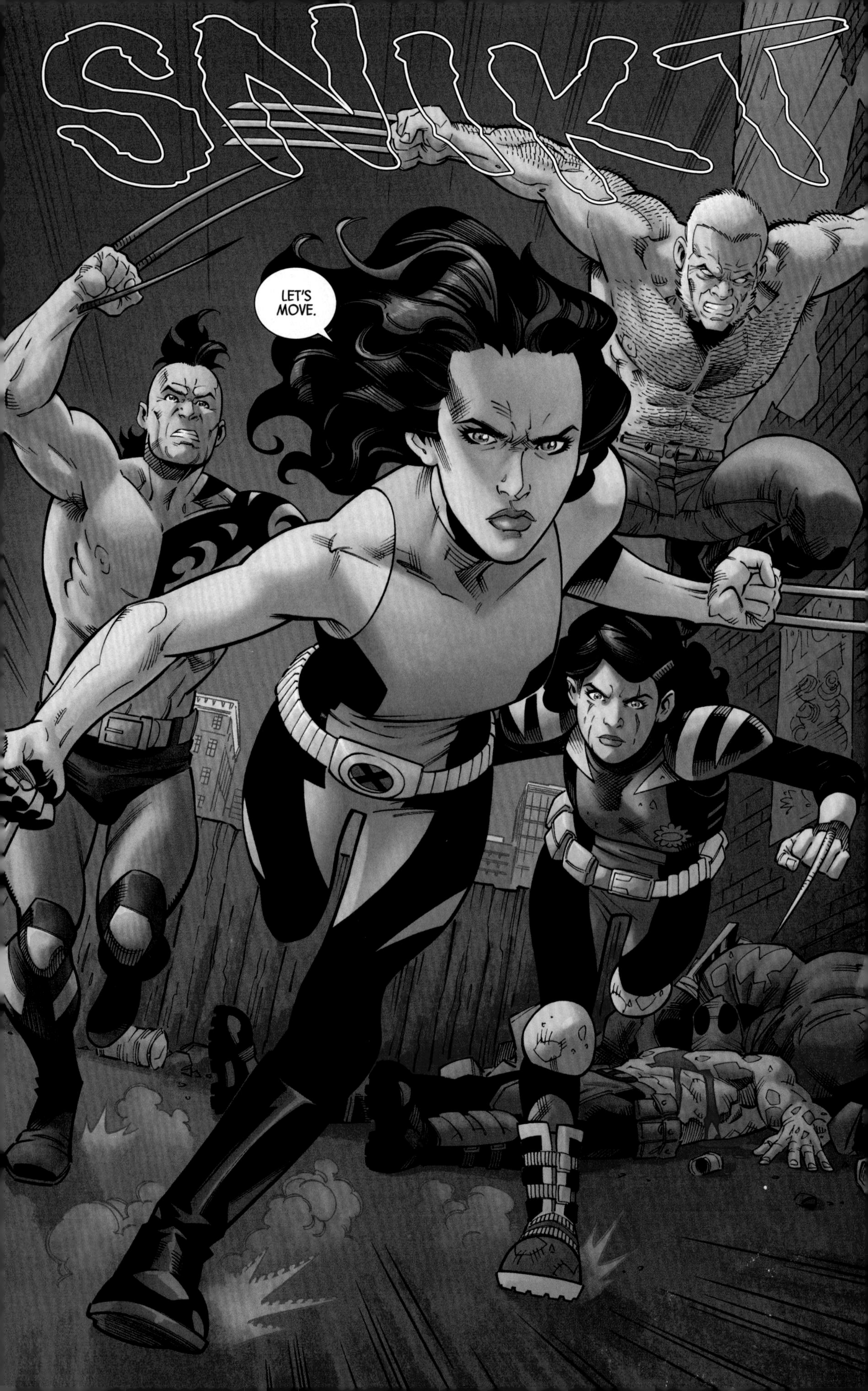
SNIKT
LET'S MOVE.

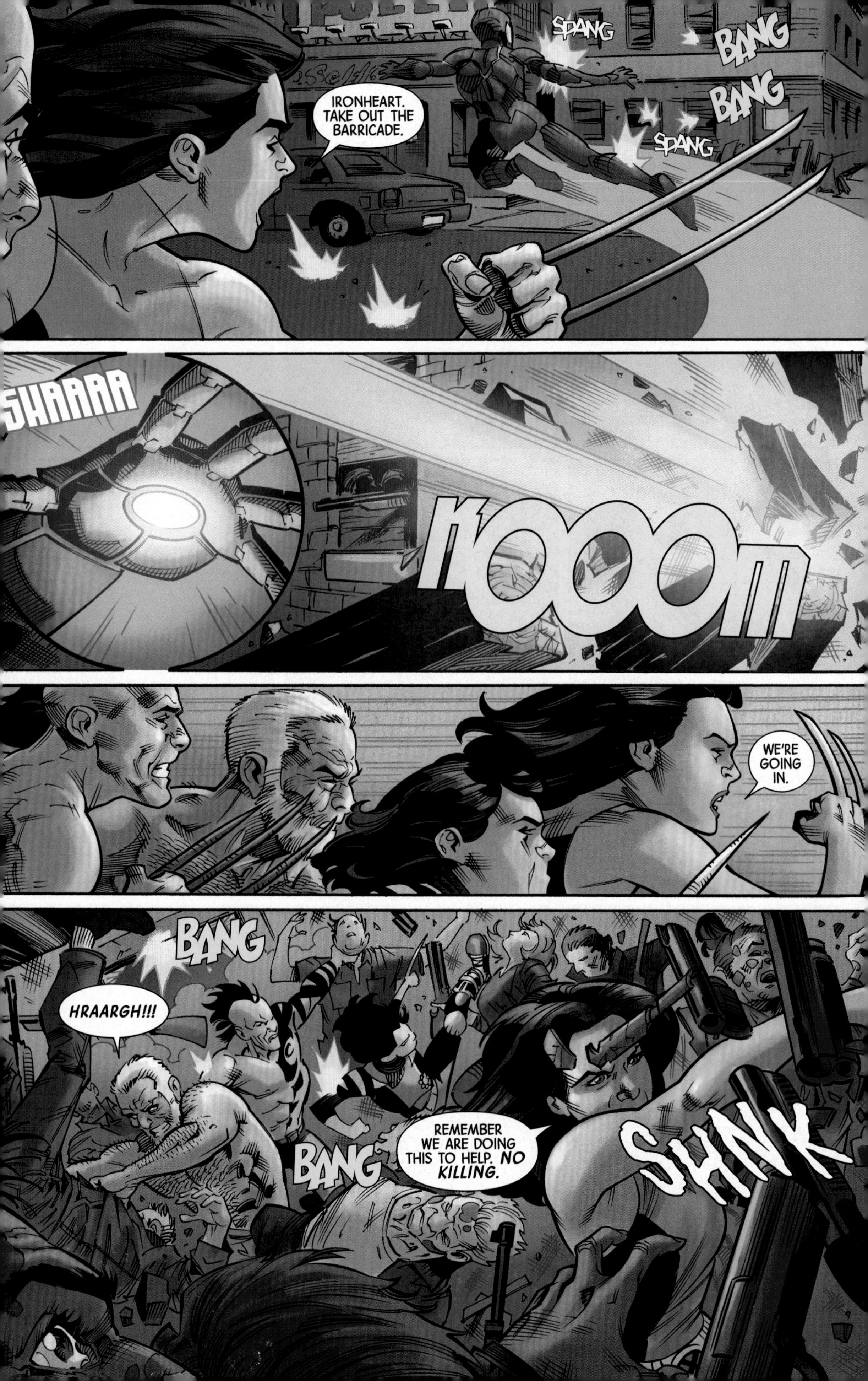
SPANG
BANG
IRONHEART. TAKE OUT THE BARRICADE.
BANG
SPANG
SHRRRR
KOOOM
WE'RE GOING IN.
BANG
HRAARGH!!!
REMEMBER WE ARE DOING THIS TO HELP. NO KILLING.
BANG
SHNK

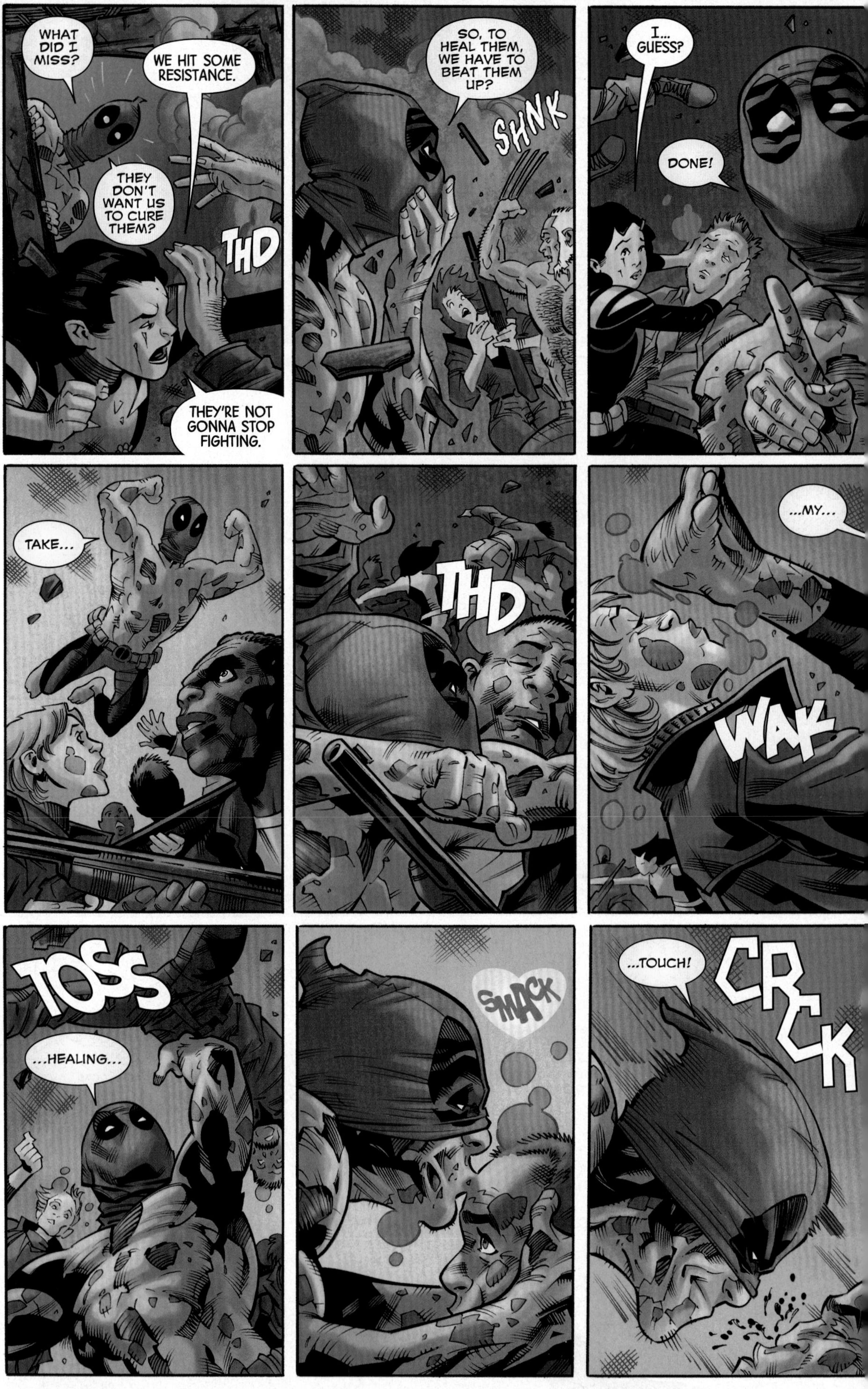
WHAT DID I MISS?
WE HIT SOME RESISTANCE.
THEY DON'T WANT US TO CURE THEM?
THD
THEY'RE NOT GONNA STOP FIGHTING.
SO, TO HEAL THEM, WE HAVE TO BEAT THEM UP?
SHNK
I... GUESS?
DONE!
TAKE...
THD
...MY...
WAK
TOSS
...HEALING...
SMACK
...TOUCH!
CRCK

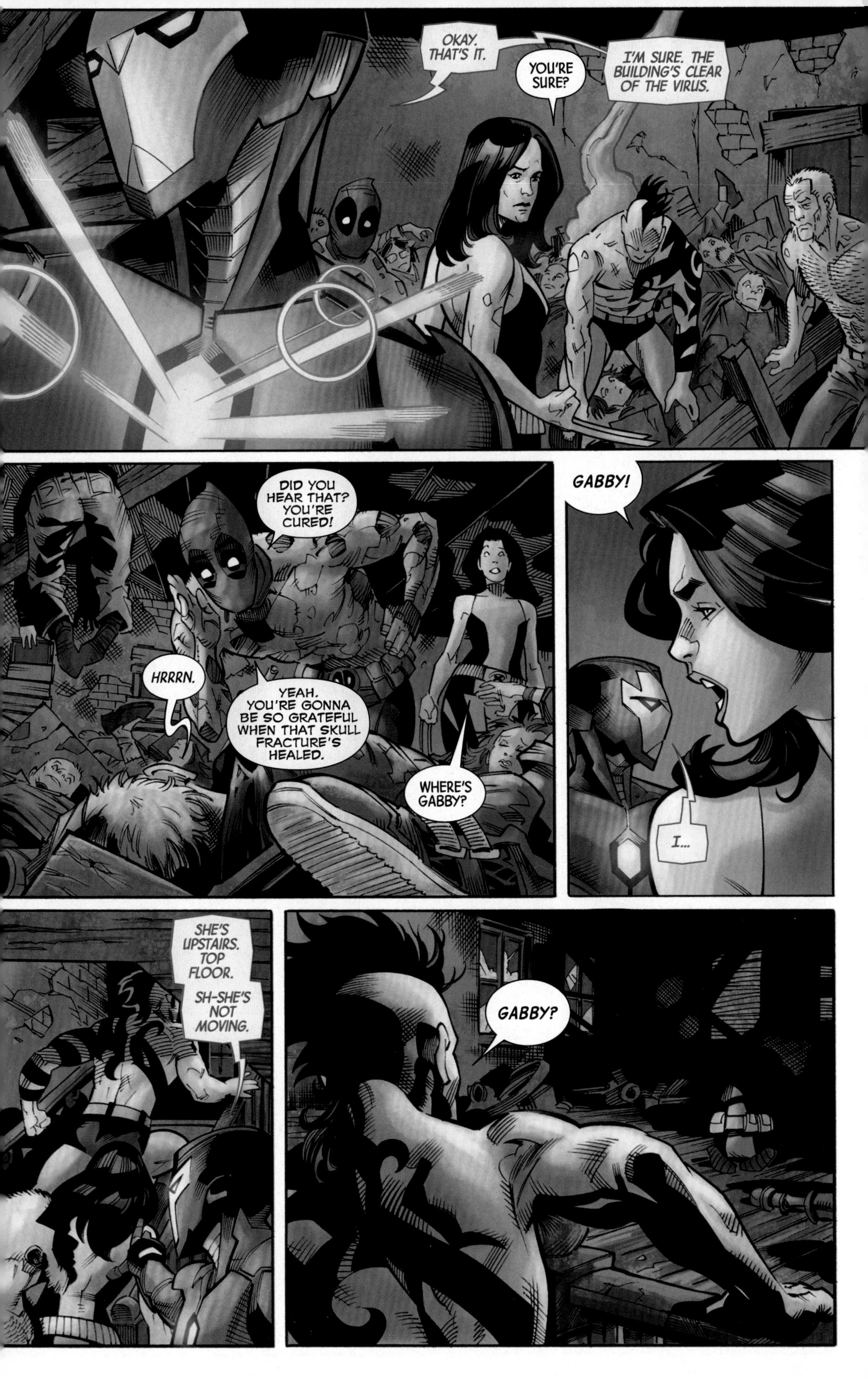
OKAY. THAT'S IT.
YOU'RE SURE?
I'M SURE. THE BUILDING'S CLEAR OF THE VIRUS.
DID YOU HEAR THAT? YOU'RE CURED!
HRRRN.
YEAH. YOU'RE GONNA BE SO GRATEFUL WHEN THAT SKULL FRACTURE'S HEALED.
WHERE'S GABBY?
GABBY!
I...
SHE'S UPSTAIRS. TOP FLOOR.
SH-SHE'S NOT MOVING.
GABBY?

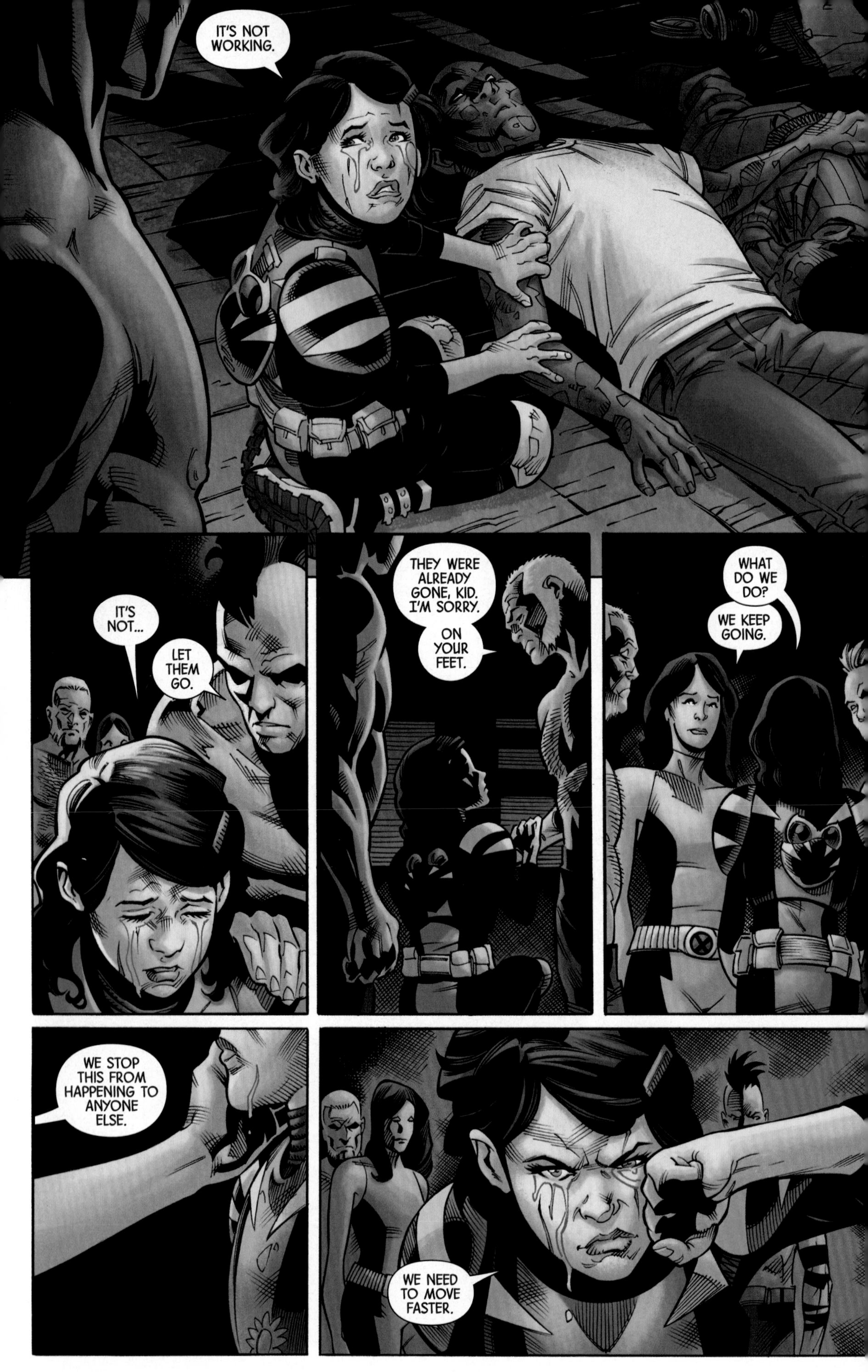
IT'S NOT WORKING.
IT'S NOT...
LET THEM GO.
THEY WERE ALREADY GONE, KID. I'M SORRY.
ON YOUR FEET.
WHAT DO WE DO?
WE KEEP GOING.
WE STOP THIS FROM HAPPENING TO ANYONE ELSE.
WE NEED TO MOVE FASTER.

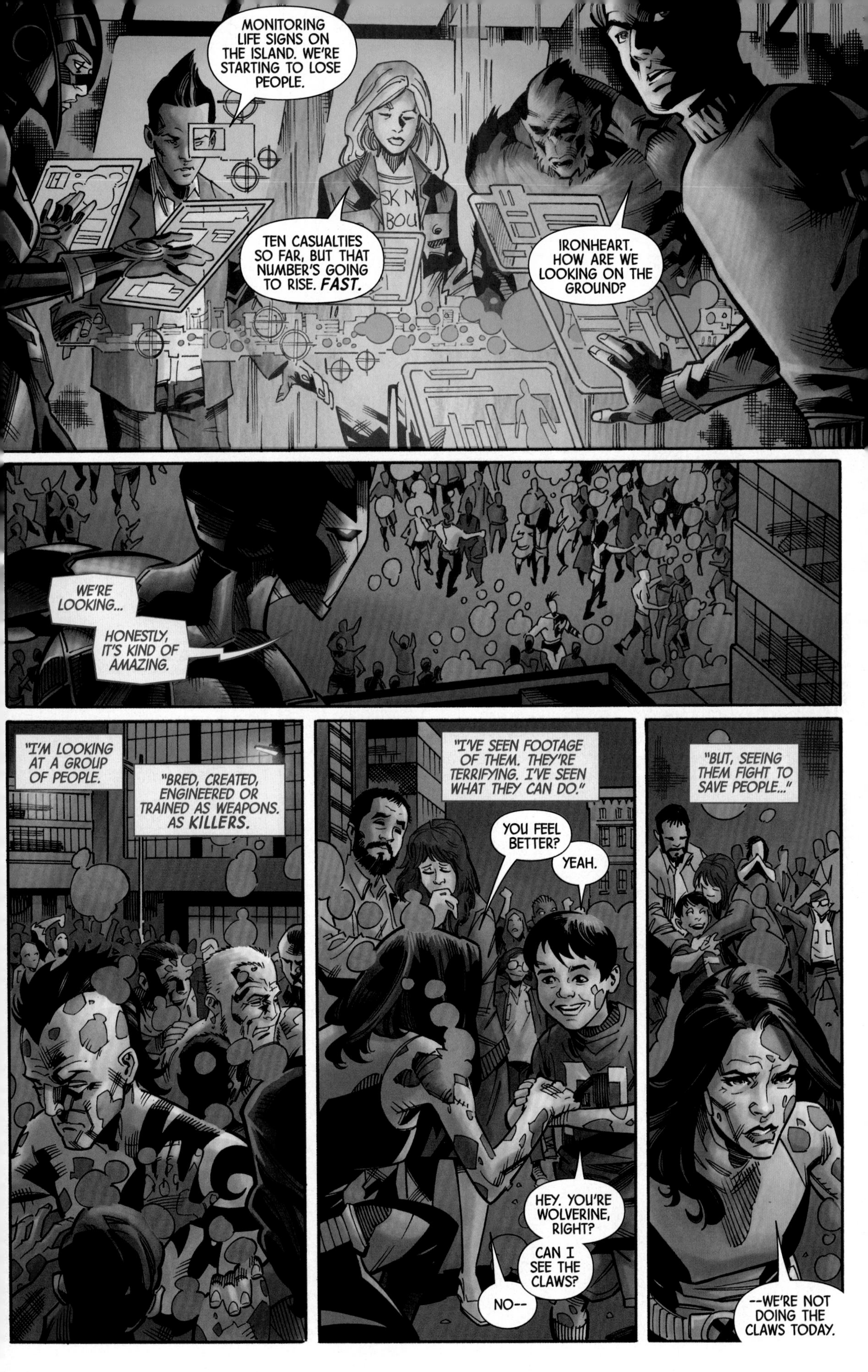
MONITORING LIFE SIGNS ON THE ISLAND. WE'RE STARTING TO LOSE PEOPLE.
TEN CASUALTIES SO FAR, BUT THAT NUMBER'S GOING TO RISE. **FAST.**
IRONHEART. HOW ARE WE LOOKING ON THE GROUND?
WE'RE LOOKING...
HONESTLY, IT'S KIND OF AMAZING.
"I'M LOOKING AT A GROUP OF PEOPLE.
"BRED, CREATED, ENGINEERED OR TRAINED AS WEAPONS. AS **KILLERS.**
"I'VE SEEN FOOTAGE OF THEM. THEY'RE TERRIFYING. I'VE SEEN WHAT THEY CAN DO."
YOU FEEL BETTER?
YEAH.
HEY. YOU'RE WOLVERINE, RIGHT?
CAN I SEE THE CLAWS?
NO--
"BUT, SEEING THEM FIGHT TO SAVE PEOPLE..."
--WE'RE NOT DOING THE CLAWS TODAY.

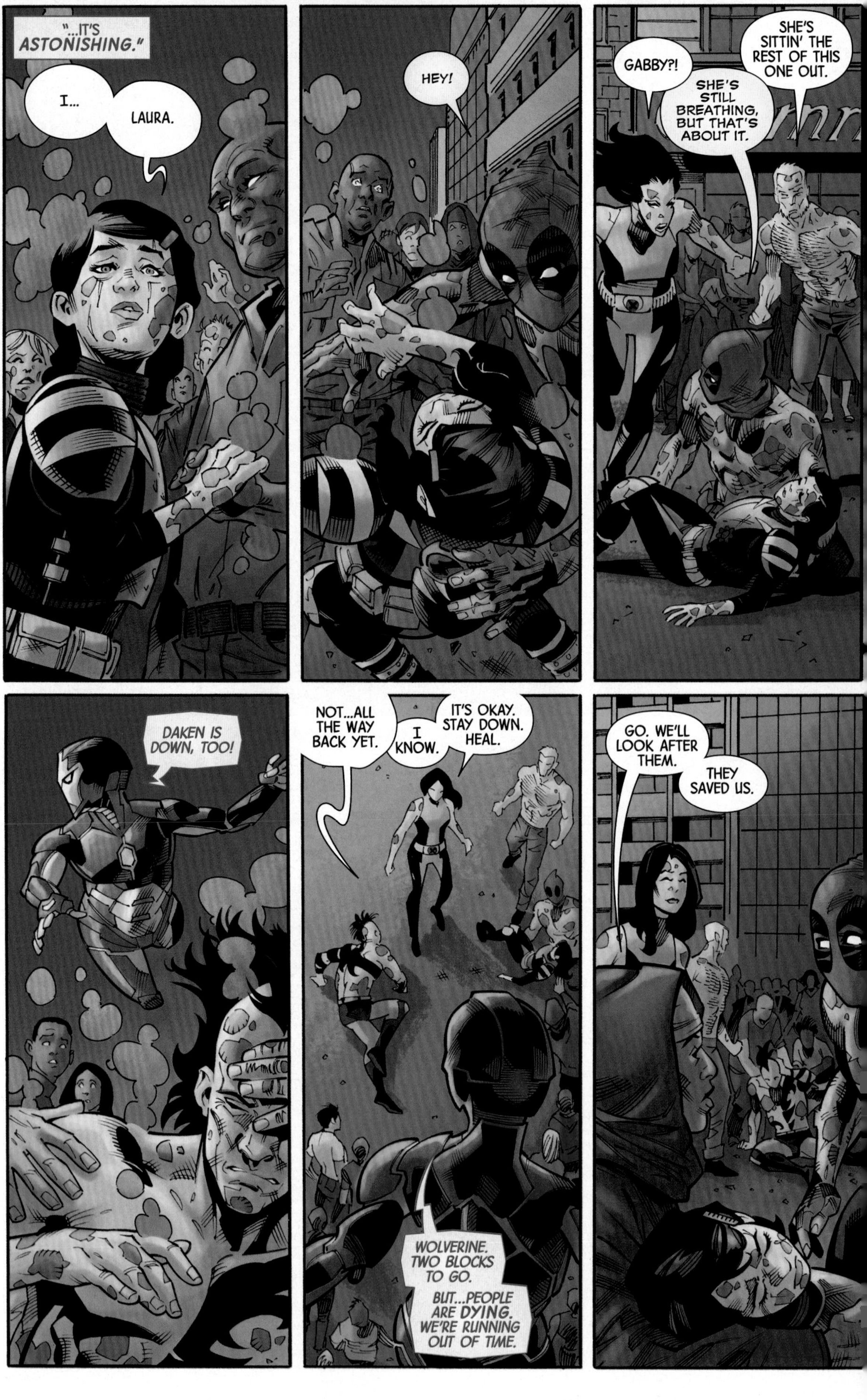
"...IT'S ASTONISHING."
I...
LAURA.
HEY!
GABBY?!
SHE'S STILL BREATHING, BUT THAT'S ABOUT IT.
SHE'S SITTIN' THE REST OF THIS ONE OUT.
DAKEN IS DOWN, TOO!
NOT...ALL THE WAY BACK YET.
I KNOW.
IT'S OKAY. STAY DOWN. HEAL.
WOLVERINE. TWO BLOCKS TO GO.
BUT...PEOPLE ARE DYING. WE'RE RUNNING OUT OF TIME.
GO. WE'LL LOOK AFTER THEM.
THEY SAVED US.

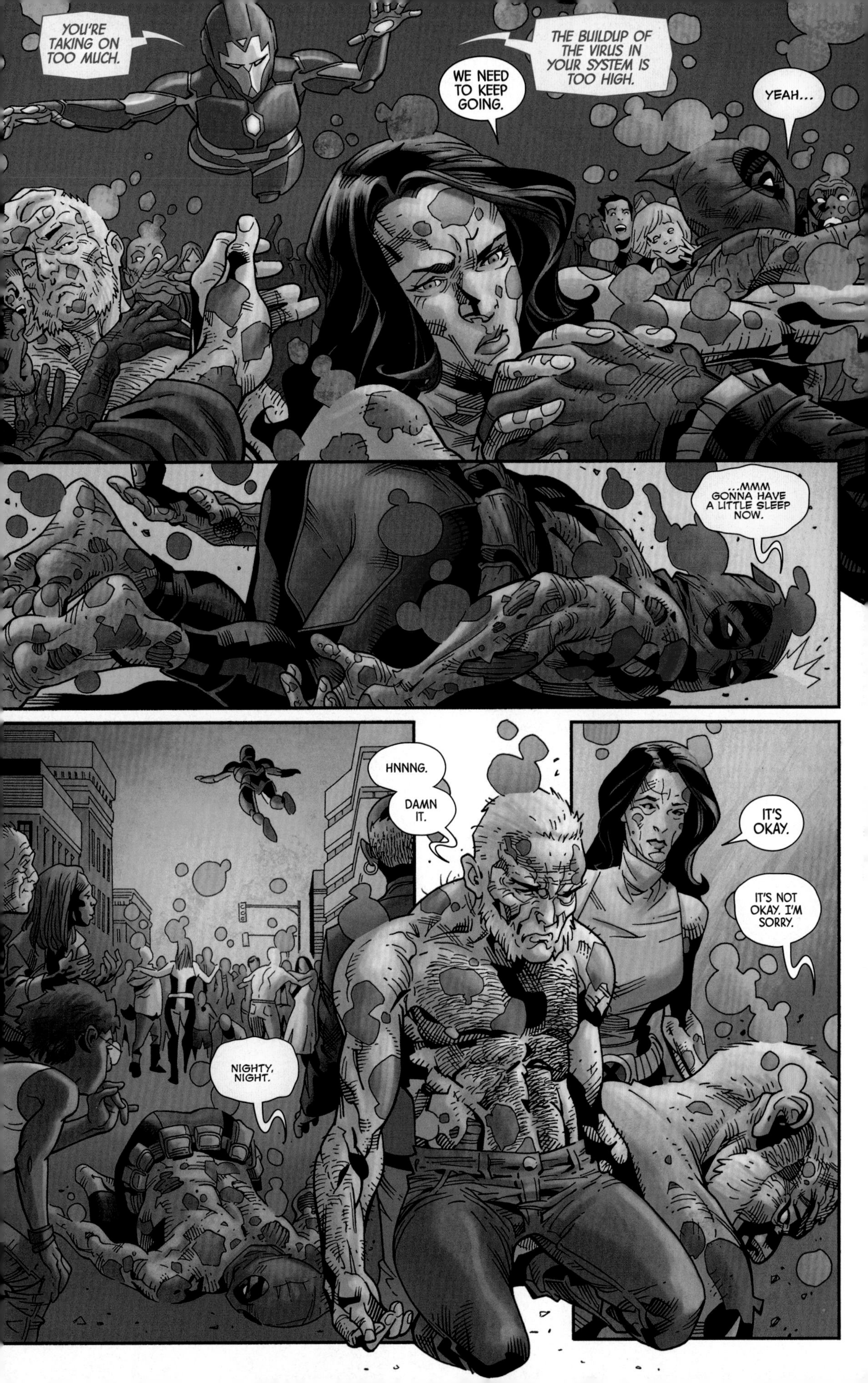
YOU'RE TAKING ON TOO MUCH.
THE BUILDUP OF THE VIRUS IN YOUR SYSTEM IS TOO HIGH.
WE NEED TO KEEP GOING.
YEAH...
...MMM GONNA HAVE A LITTLE SLEEP NOW.
HNNNG.
DAMN IT.
IT'S OKAY.
IT'S NOT OKAY. I'M SORRY.
NIGHTY, NIGHT.

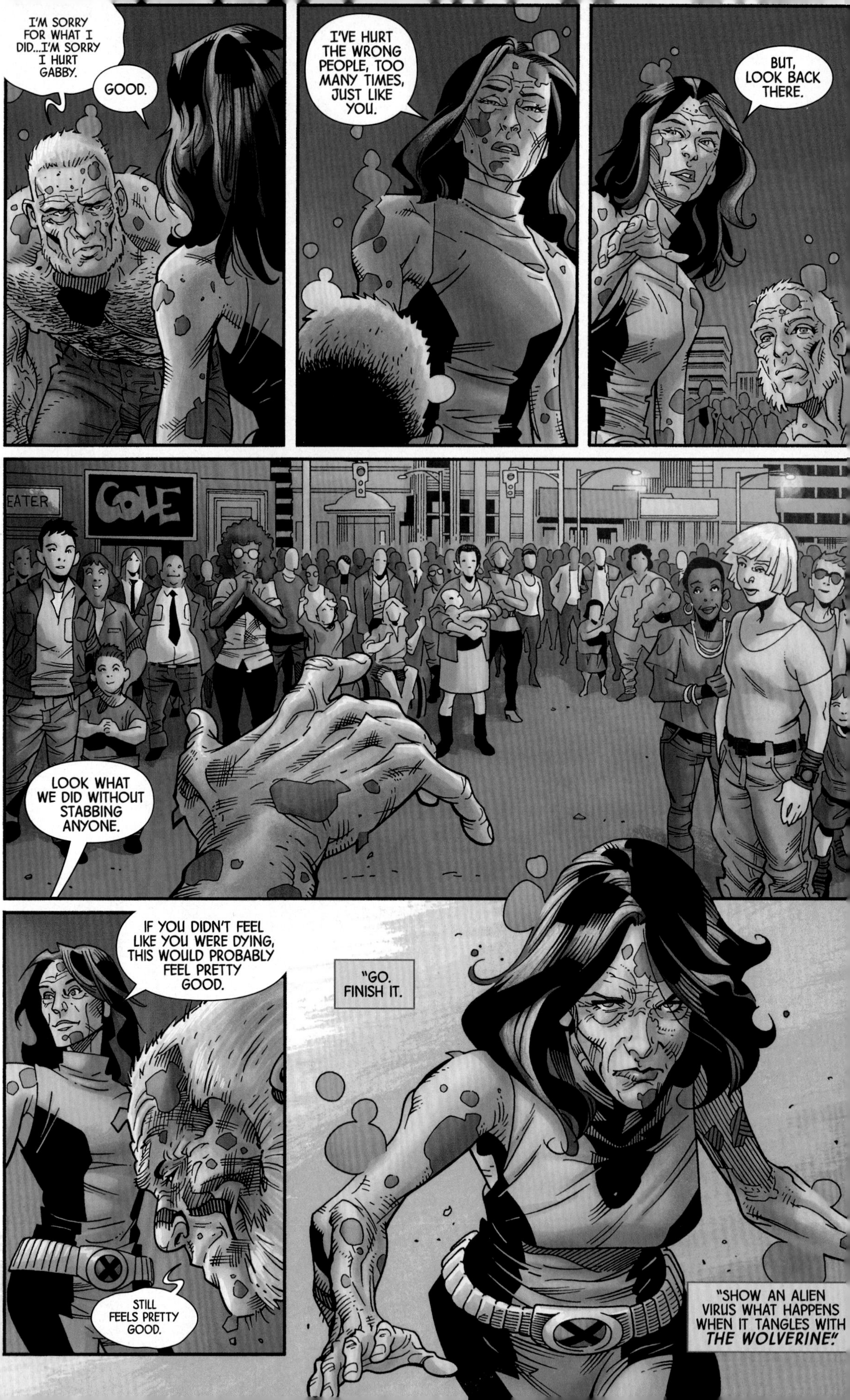
I'M SORRY FOR WHAT I DID...I'M SORRY I HURT GABBY.
GOOD.
I'VE HURT THE WRONG PEOPLE, TOO MANY TIMES, JUST LIKE YOU.
BUT, LOOK BACK THERE.
EATER
COLE
LOOK WHAT WE DID WITHOUT STABBING ANYONE.
IF YOU DIDN'T FEEL LIKE YOU WERE DYING, THIS WOULD PROBABLY FEEL PRETTY GOOD.
STILL FEELS PRETTY GOOD.
"GO. FINISH IT.
"SHOW AN ALIEN VIRUS WHAT HAPPENS WHEN IT TANGLES WITH *THE WOLVERINE!"*

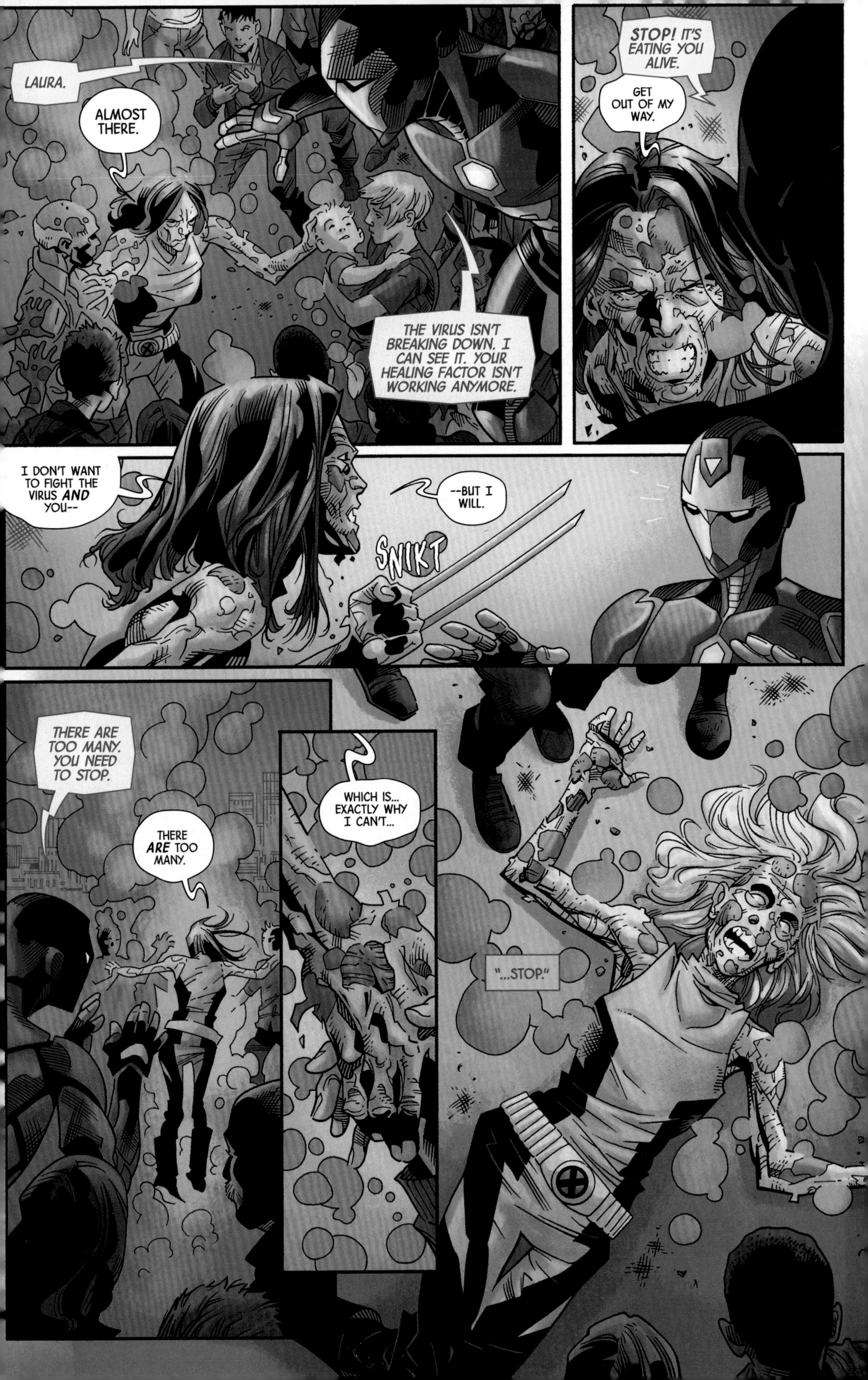

LAURA.
ALMOST THERE.
THE VIRUS ISN'T BREAKING DOWN. I CAN SEE IT. YOUR HEALING FACTOR ISN'T WORKING ANYMORE.
STOP! IT'S EATING YOU ALIVE.
GET OUT OF MY WAY.
I DON'T WANT TO FIGHT THE VIRUS AND YOU--
--BUT I WILL.
SNIKT
THERE ARE TOO MANY. YOU NEED TO STOP.
THERE ARE TOO MANY.
WHICH IS... EXACTLY WHY I CAN'T...
"...STOP."

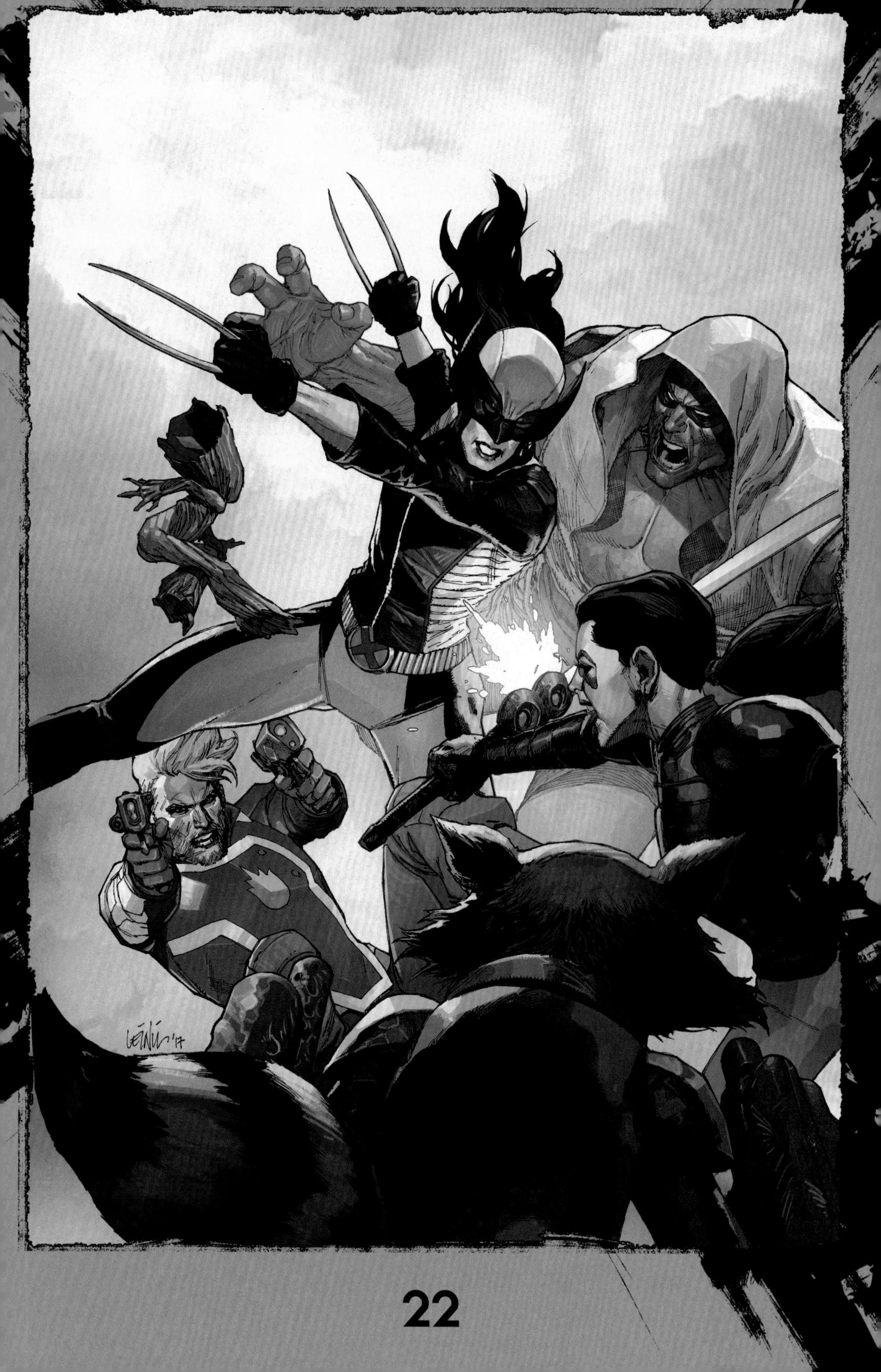

22

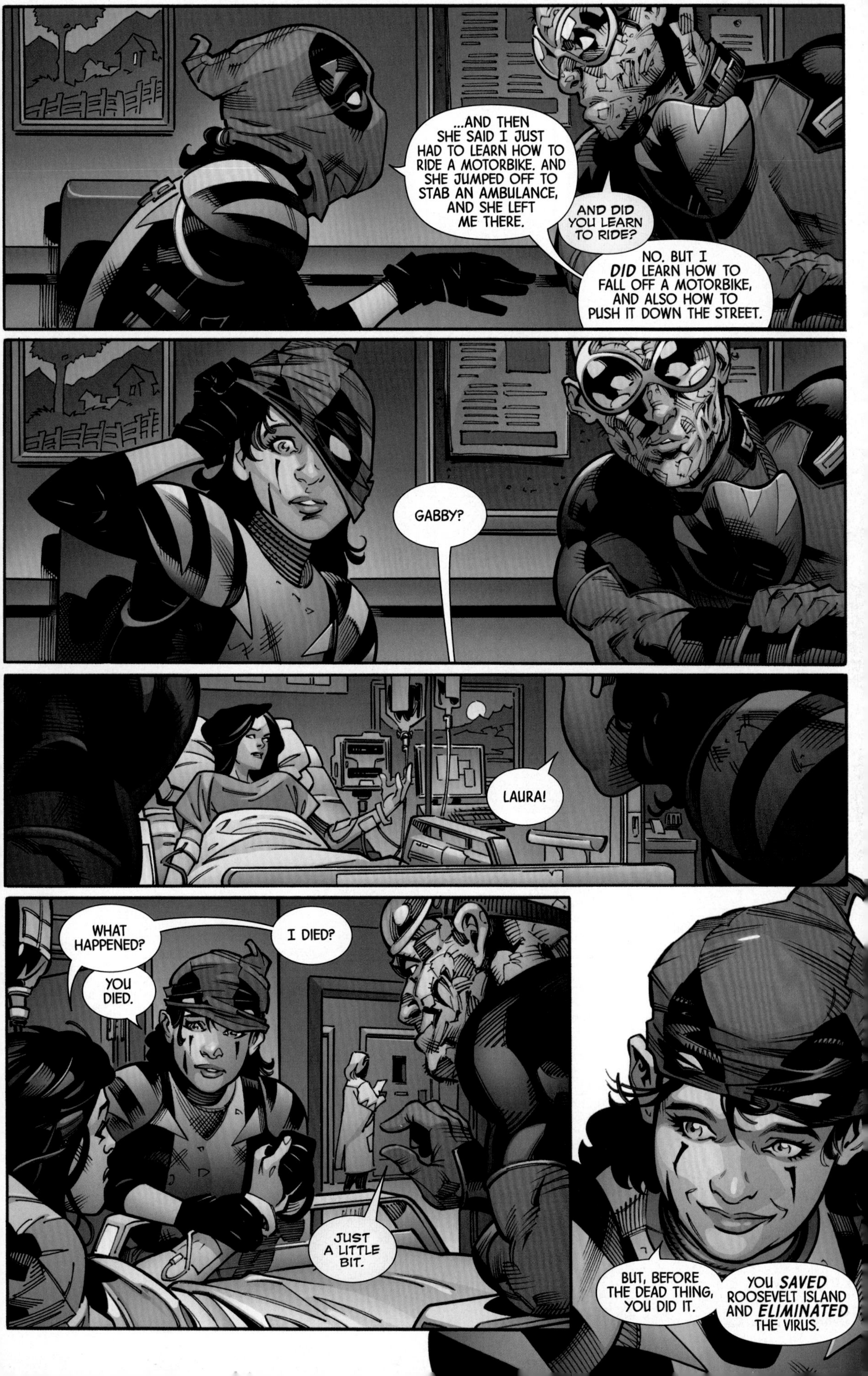
...AND THEN SHE SAID I JUST HAD TO LEARN HOW TO RIDE A MOTORBIKE. AND SHE JUMPED OFF TO STAB AN AMBULANCE, AND SHE LEFT ME THERE.
AND DID YOU LEARN TO RIDE?
NO. BUT I *DID* LEARN HOW TO FALL OFF A MOTORBIKE, AND ALSO HOW TO PUSH IT DOWN THE STREET.
GABBY?
LAURA!
WHAT HAPPENED?
YOU DIED.
I DIED?
JUST A LITTLE BIT.
BUT, BEFORE THE DEAD THING, YOU DID IT.
YOU *SAVED* ROOSEVELT ISLAND AND *ELIMINATED* THE VIRUS.

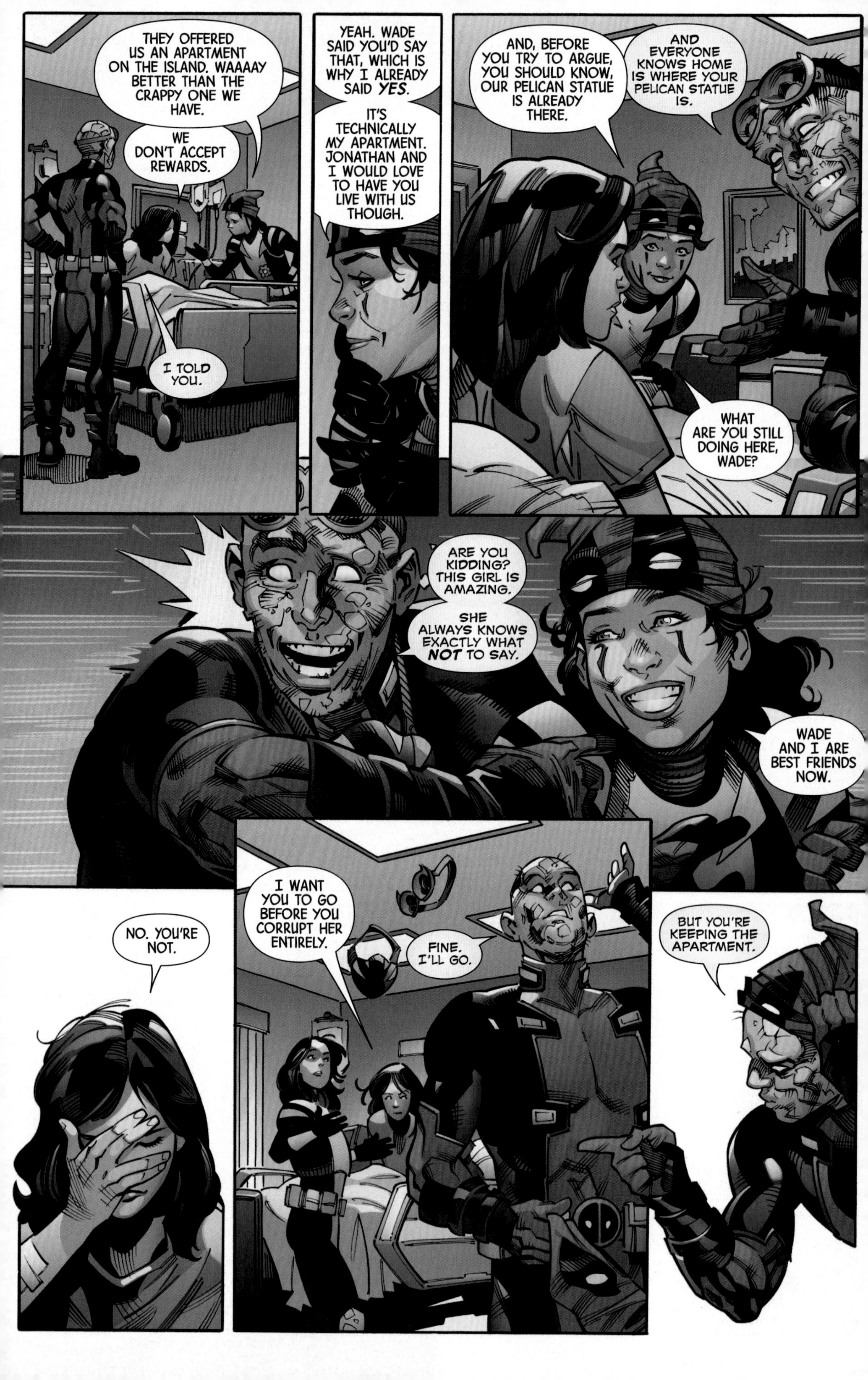
THEY OFFERED US AN APARTMENT ON THE ISLAND. WAAAAY BETTER THAN THE CRAPPY ONE WE HAVE.
WE DON'T ACCEPT REWARDS.
I TOLD YOU.
YEAH. WADE SAID YOU'D SAY THAT, WHICH IS WHY I ALREADY SAID **YES**.
IT'S TECHNICALLY MY APARTMENT. JONATHAN AND I WOULD LOVE TO HAVE YOU LIVE WITH US THOUGH.
AND, BEFORE YOU TRY TO ARGUE, YOU SHOULD KNOW, OUR PELICAN STATUE IS ALREADY THERE.
AND EVERYONE KNOWS HOME IS WHERE YOUR PELICAN STATUE IS.
WHAT ARE YOU STILL DOING HERE, WADE?
ARE YOU KIDDING? THIS GIRL IS AMAZING.
SHE ALWAYS KNOWS EXACTLY WHAT **NOT** TO SAY.
WADE AND I ARE BEST FRIENDS NOW.
NO. YOU'RE NOT.
I WANT YOU TO GO BEFORE YOU CORRUPT HER ENTIRELY.
FINE. I'LL GO.
BUT YOU'RE KEEPING THE APARTMENT.

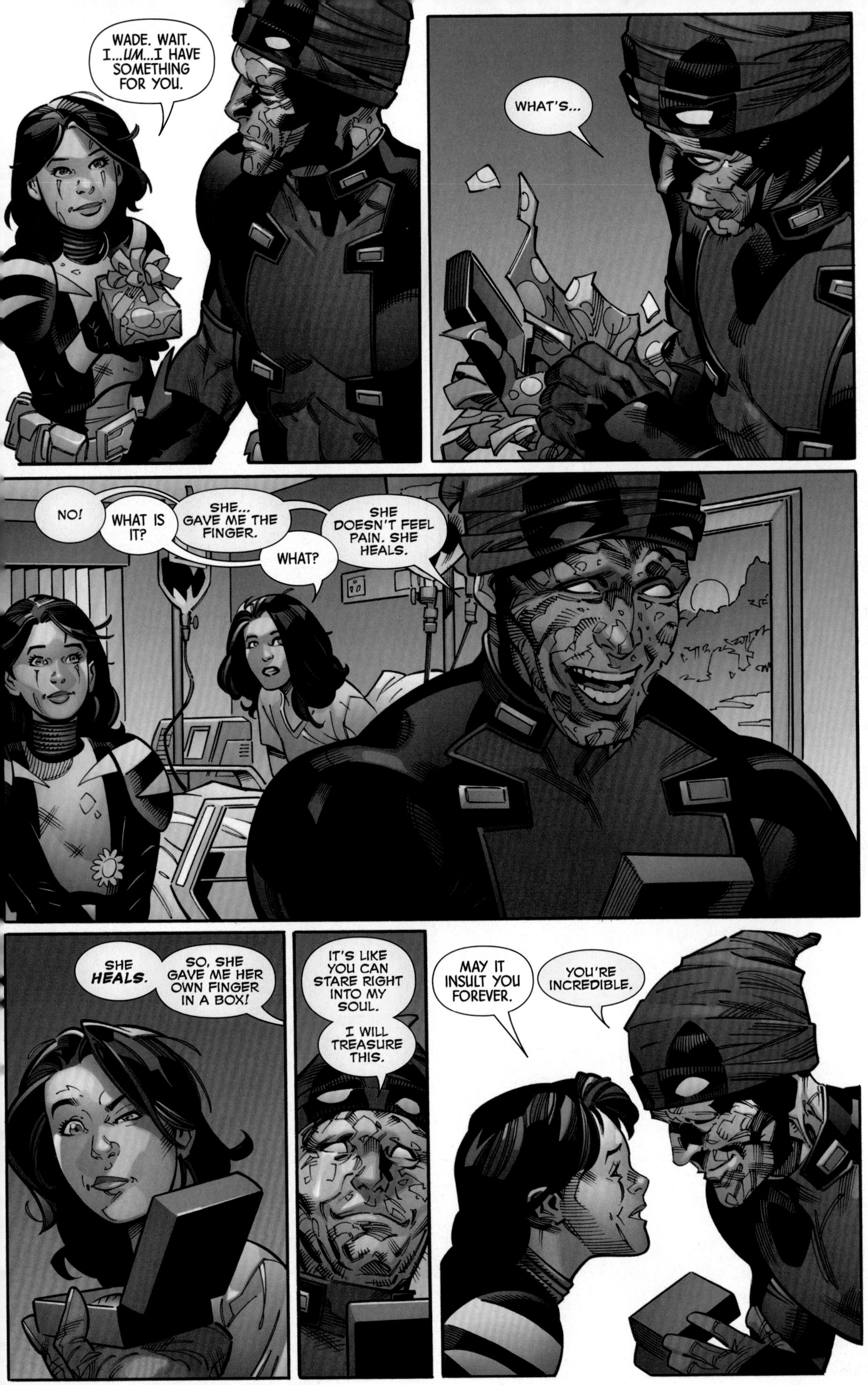
WADE. WAIT. I...*UM*...I HAVE SOMETHING FOR YOU.
WHAT'S...
NO!
WHAT IS IT?
SHE... GAVE ME THE FINGER.
WHAT?
SHE DOESN'T FEEL PAIN. SHE HEALS.
SHE *HEALS*.
SO, SHE GAVE ME HER OWN FINGER IN A BOX!
IT'S LIKE YOU CAN STARE RIGHT INTO MY SOUL.
I WILL TREASURE THIS.
MAY IT INSULT YOU FOREVER.
YOU'RE INCREDIBLE.

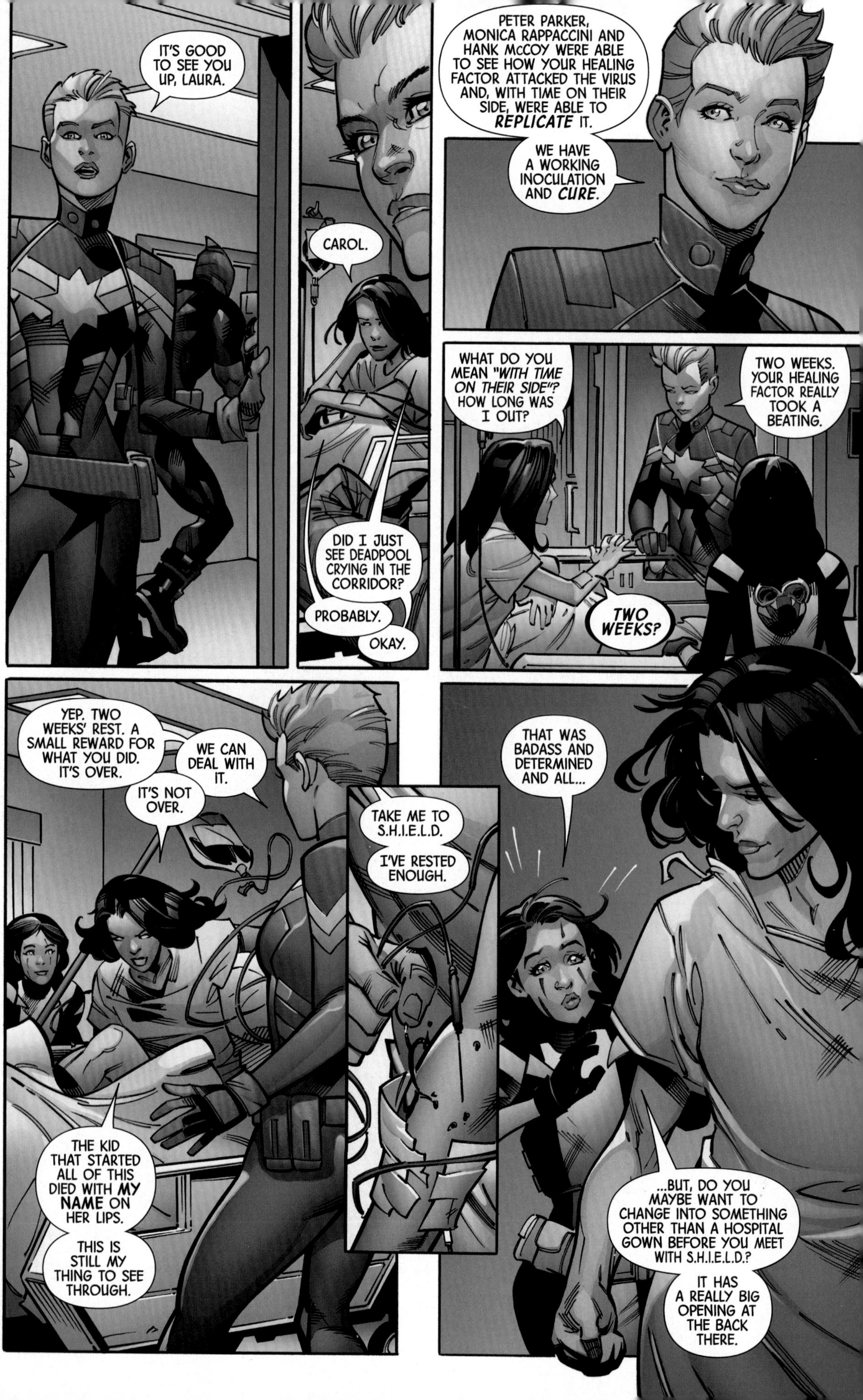
IT'S GOOD TO SEE YOU UP, LAURA.
CAROL.
DID I JUST SEE DEADPOOL CRYING IN THE CORRIDOR?
PROBABLY.
OKAY.
PETER PARKER, MONICA RAPPACCINI AND HANK McCOY WERE ABLE TO SEE HOW YOUR HEALING FACTOR ATTACKED THE VIRUS AND, WITH TIME ON THEIR SIDE, WERE ABLE TO REPLICATE IT.
WE HAVE A WORKING INOCULATION AND CURE.
WHAT DO YOU MEAN "WITH TIME ON THEIR SIDE"? HOW LONG WAS I OUT?
TWO WEEKS. YOUR HEALING FACTOR REALLY TOOK A BEATING.
TWO WEEKS?
YEP. TWO WEEKS' REST. A SMALL REWARD FOR WHAT YOU DID. IT'S OVER.
IT'S NOT OVER.
WE CAN DEAL WITH IT.
THE KID THAT STARTED ALL OF THIS DIED WITH MY NAME ON HER LIPS.
THIS IS STILL MY THING TO SEE THROUGH.
TAKE ME TO S.H.I.E.L.D.
I'VE RESTED ENOUGH.
THAT WAS BADASS AND DETERMINED AND ALL...
...BUT, DO YOU MAYBE WANT TO CHANGE INTO SOMETHING OTHER THAN A HOSPITAL GOWN BEFORE YOU MEET WITH S.H.I.E.L.D.?
IT HAS A REALLY BIG OPENING AT THE BACK THERE.

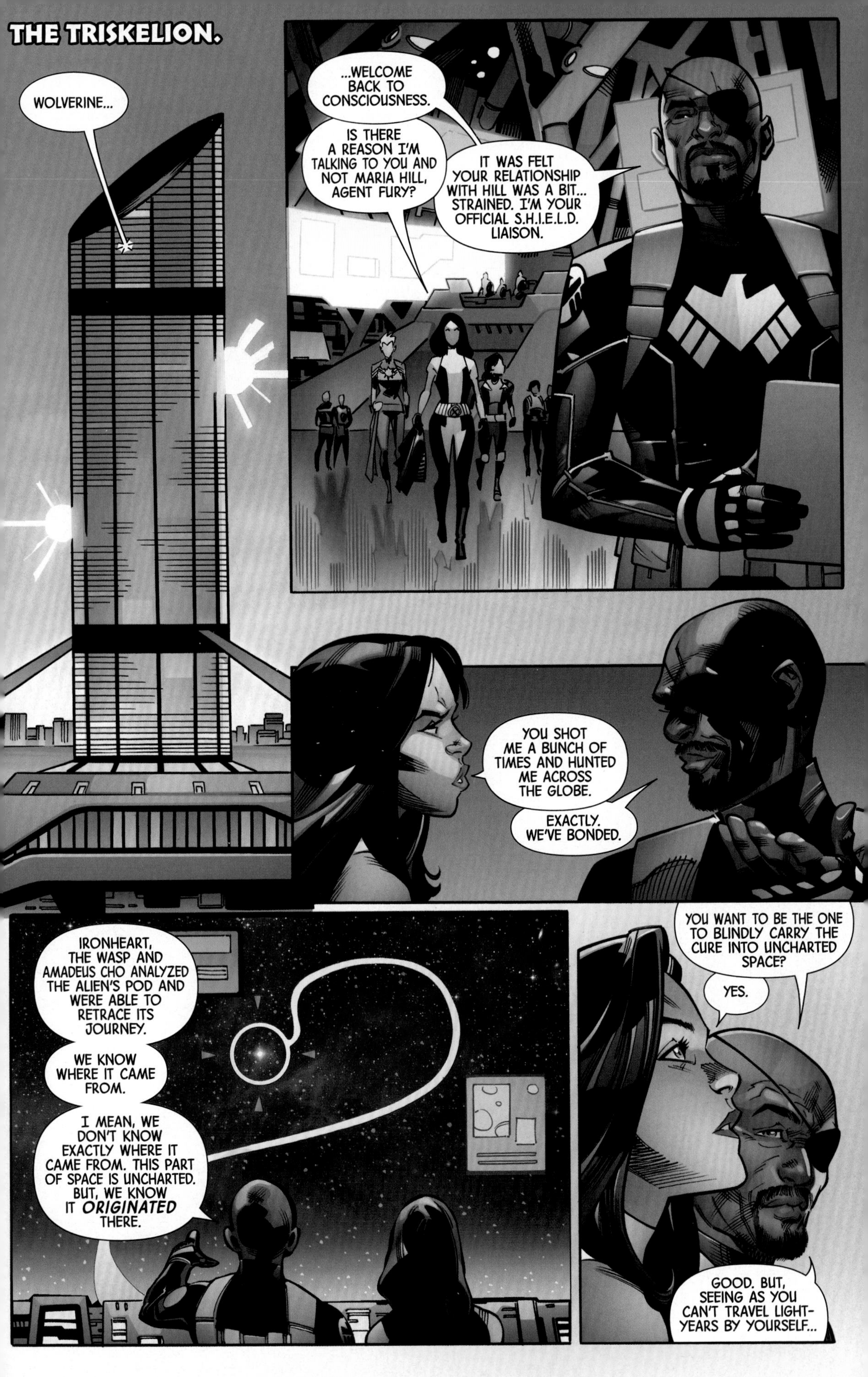
THE TRISKELION.
WOLVERINE...
...WELCOME BACK TO CONSCIOUSNESS.
IS THERE A REASON I'M TALKING TO YOU AND NOT MARIA HILL, AGENT FURY?
IT WAS FELT YOUR RELATIONSHIP WITH HILL WAS A BIT... STRAINED. I'M YOUR OFFICIAL S.H.I.E.L.D. LIAISON.
YOU SHOT ME A BUNCH OF TIMES AND HUNTED ME ACROSS THE GLOBE.
EXACTLY. WE'VE BONDED.
IRONHEART, THE WASP AND AMADEUS CHO ANALYZED THE ALIEN'S POD AND WERE ABLE TO RETRACE ITS JOURNEY.
WE KNOW WHERE IT CAME FROM.
I MEAN, WE DON'T KNOW EXACTLY WHERE IT CAME FROM. THIS PART OF SPACE IS UNCHARTED. BUT, WE KNOW IT *ORIGINATED* THERE.
YOU WANT TO BE THE ONE TO BLINDLY CARRY THE CURE INTO UNCHARTED SPACE?
YES.
GOOD. BUT, SEEING AS YOU CAN'T TRAVEL LIGHT-YEARS BY YOURSELF...

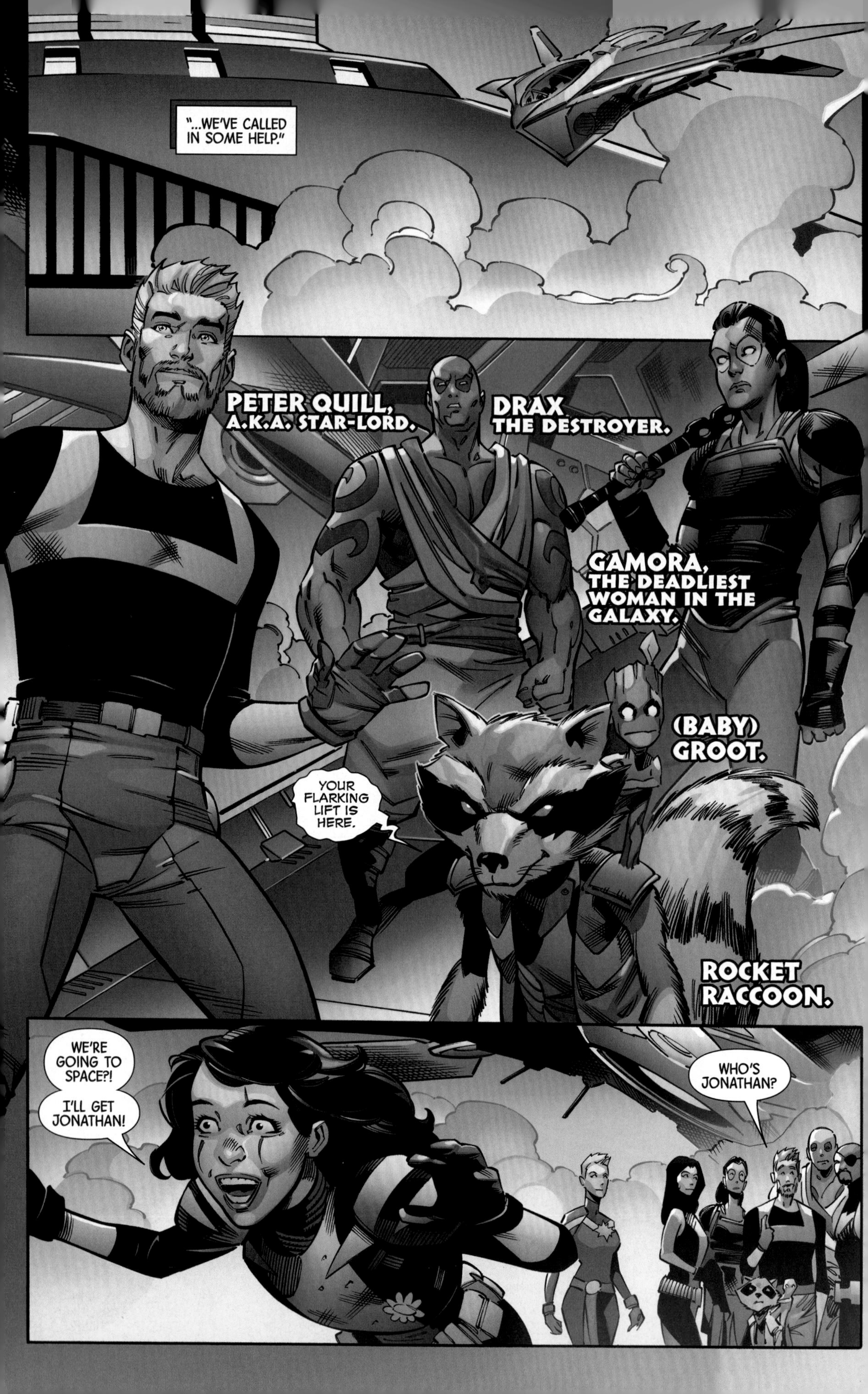
"...WE'VE CALLED IN SOME HELP."
PETER QUILL, A.K.A. STAR-LORD.
DRAX THE DESTROYER.
GAMORA, THE DEADLIEST WOMAN IN THE GALAXY.
(BABY) GROOT.
YOUR FLARKING LIFT IS HERE.
ROCKET RACCOON.
WE'RE GOING TO SPACE?!
I'LL GET JONATHAN!
WHO'S JONATHAN?

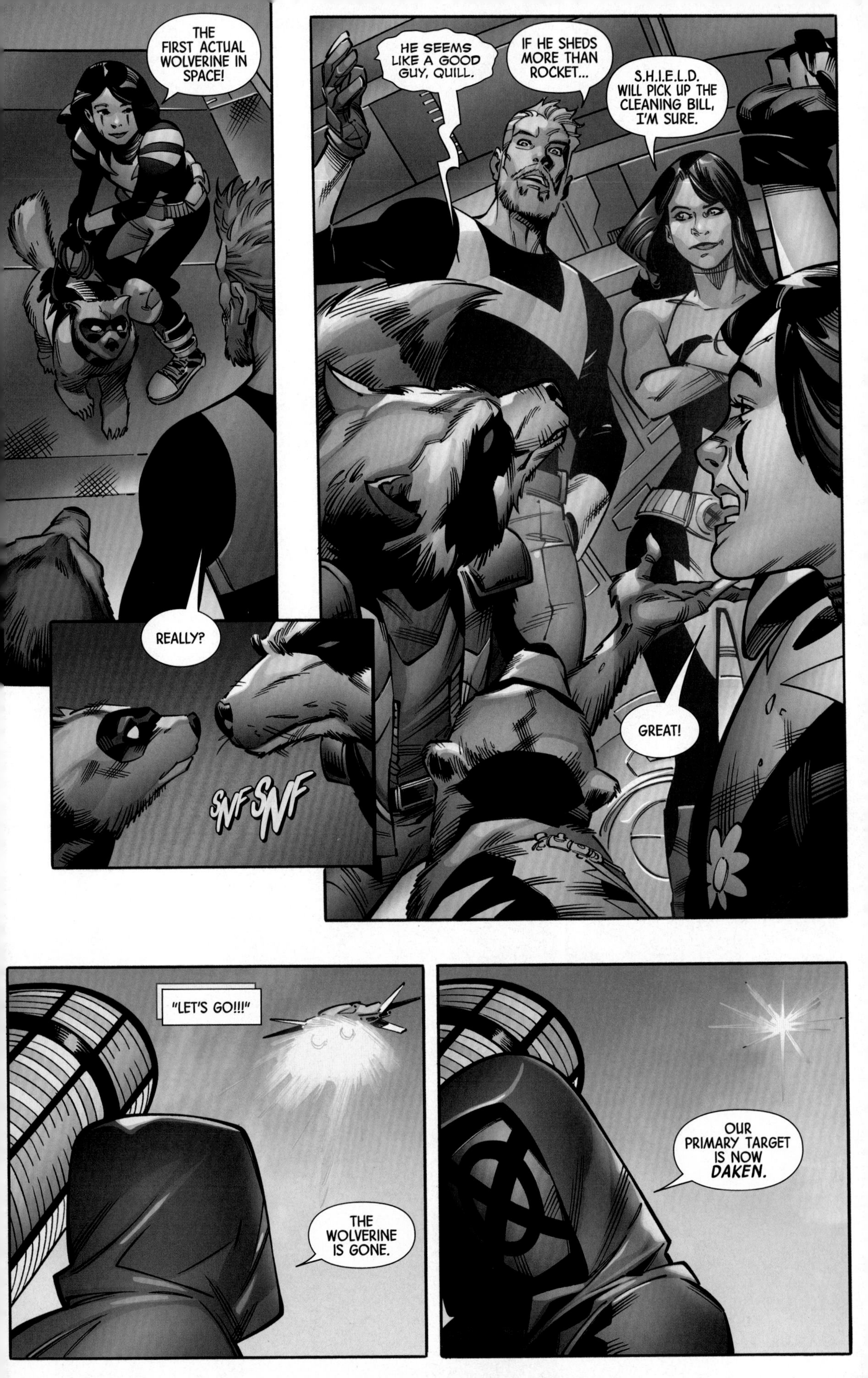
THE FIRST ACTUAL WOLVERINE IN SPACE!
REALLY?
SNF SNF
HE SEEMS LIKE A GOOD GUY, QUILL.
IF HE SHEDS MORE THAN ROCKET...
S.H.I.E.L.D. WILL PICK UP THE CLEANING BILL, I'M SURE.
GREAT!
"LET'S GO!!!"
THE WOLVERINE IS GONE.
OUR PRIMARY TARGET IS NOW DAKEN.

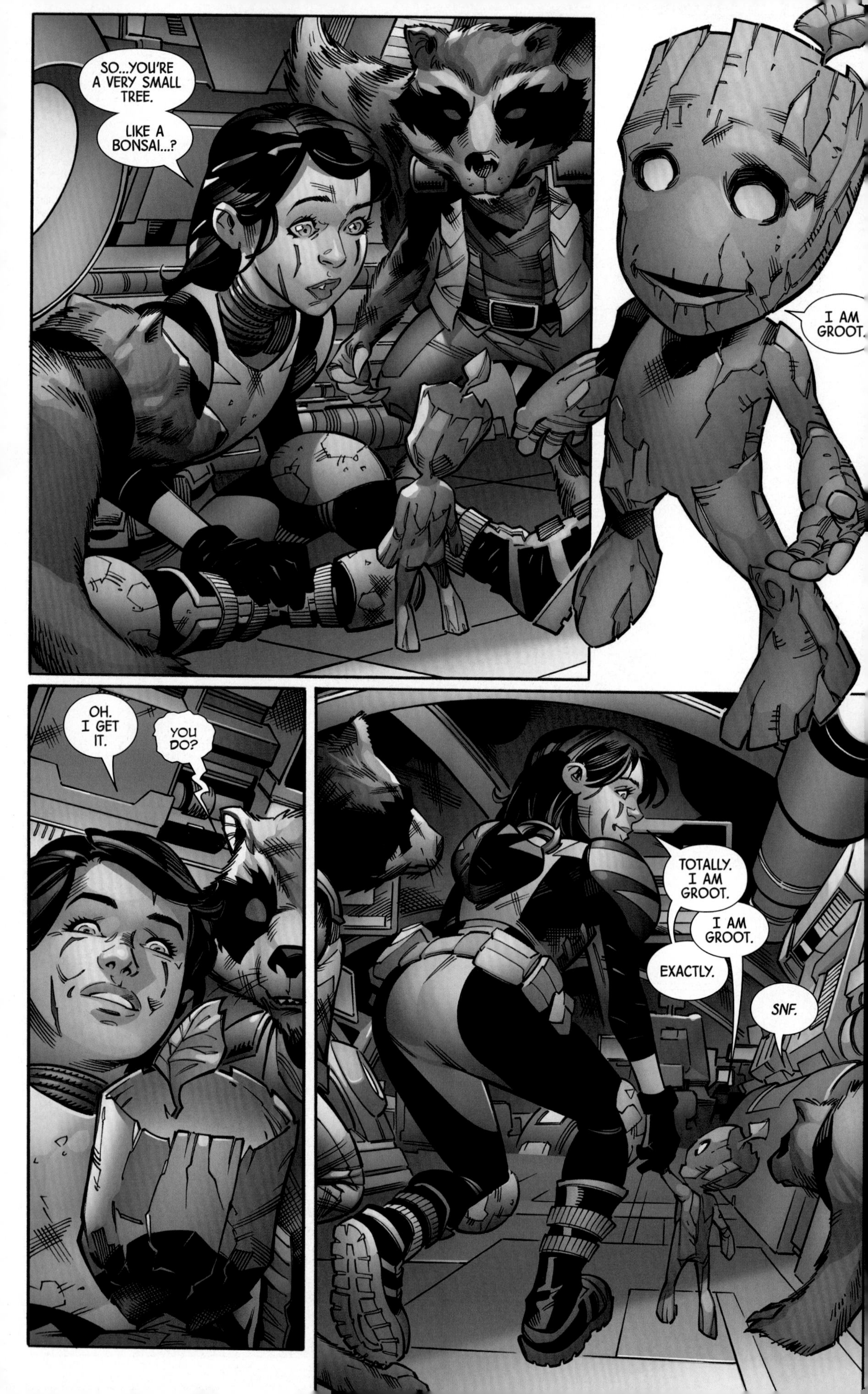
SO...YOU'RE A VERY SMALL TREE.
LIKE A BONSAI...?
I AM GROOT.
OH. I GET IT.
YOU DO?
TOTALLY. I AM GROOT.
I AM GROOT.
EXACTLY.
SNF.

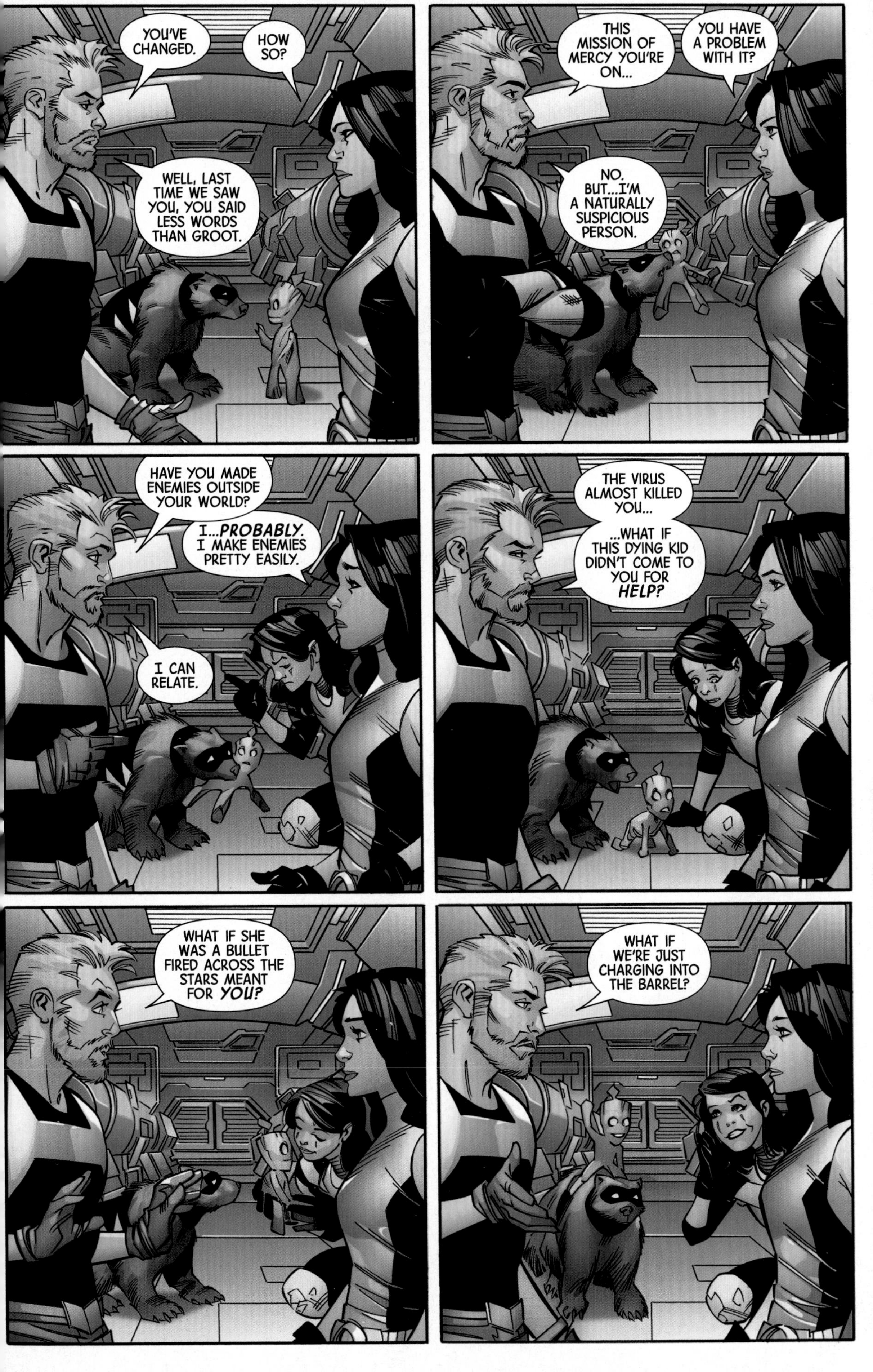
YOU'VE CHANGED.
HOW SO?
WELL, LAST TIME WE SAW YOU, YOU SAID LESS WORDS THAN GROOT.
THIS MISSION OF MERCY YOU'RE ON...
YOU HAVE A PROBLEM WITH IT?
NO. BUT...I'M A NATURALLY SUSPICIOUS PERSON.
HAVE YOU MADE ENEMIES OUTSIDE YOUR WORLD?
I...*PROBABLY*. I MAKE ENEMIES PRETTY EASILY.
I CAN RELATE.
THE VIRUS ALMOST KILLED YOU...
...WHAT IF THIS DYING KID DIDN'T COME TO YOU FOR *HELP?*
WHAT IF SHE WAS A BULLET FIRED ACROSS THE STARS MEANT FOR *YOU?*
WHAT IF WE'RE JUST CHARGING INTO THE BARREL?

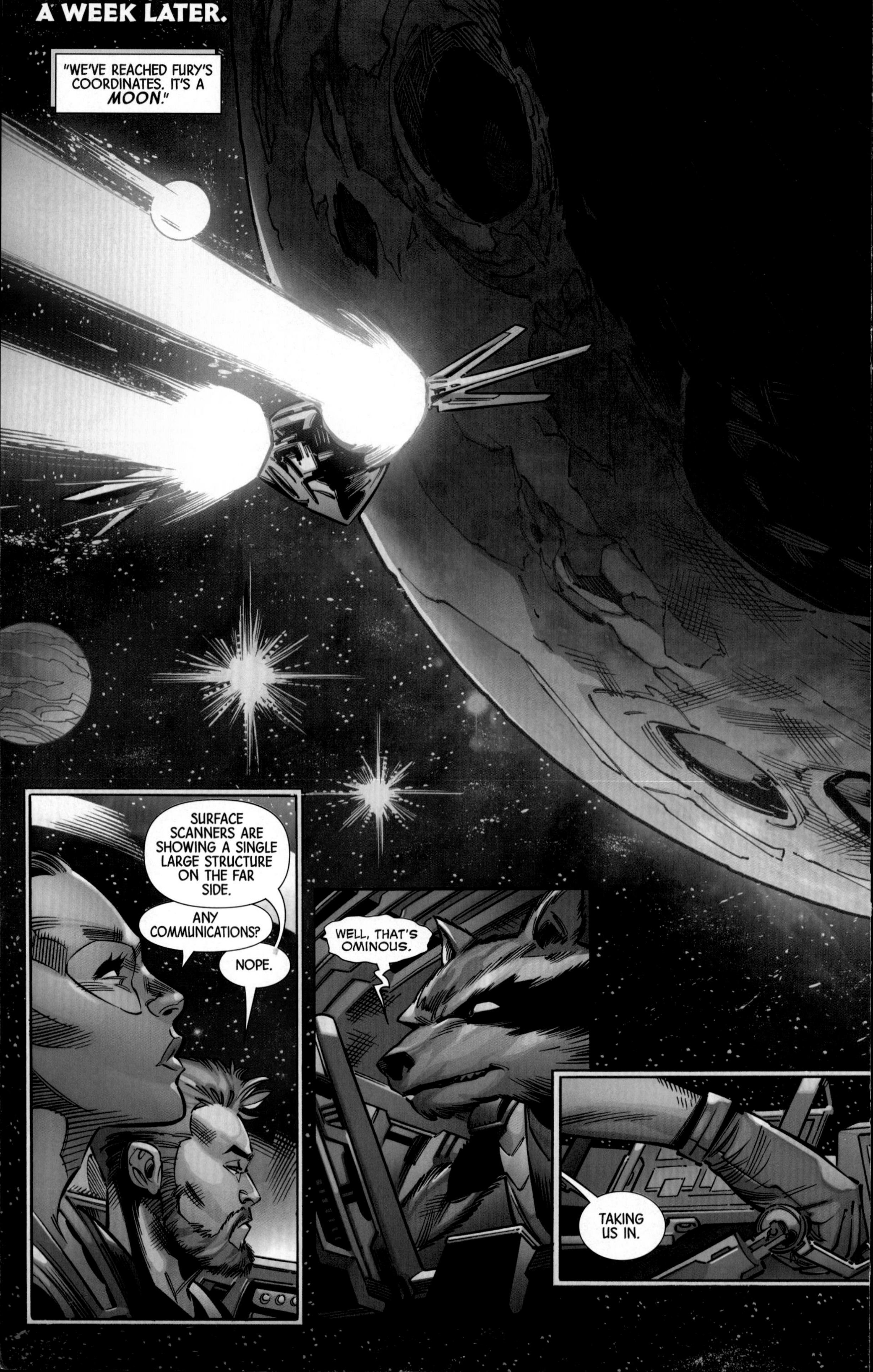
A WEEK LATER.
"WE'VE REACHED FURY'S COORDINATES. IT'S A MOON."
SURFACE SCANNERS ARE SHOWING A SINGLE LARGE STRUCTURE ON THE FAR SIDE.
ANY COMMUNICATIONS?
NOPE.
WELL, THAT'S OMINOUS.
TAKING US IN.

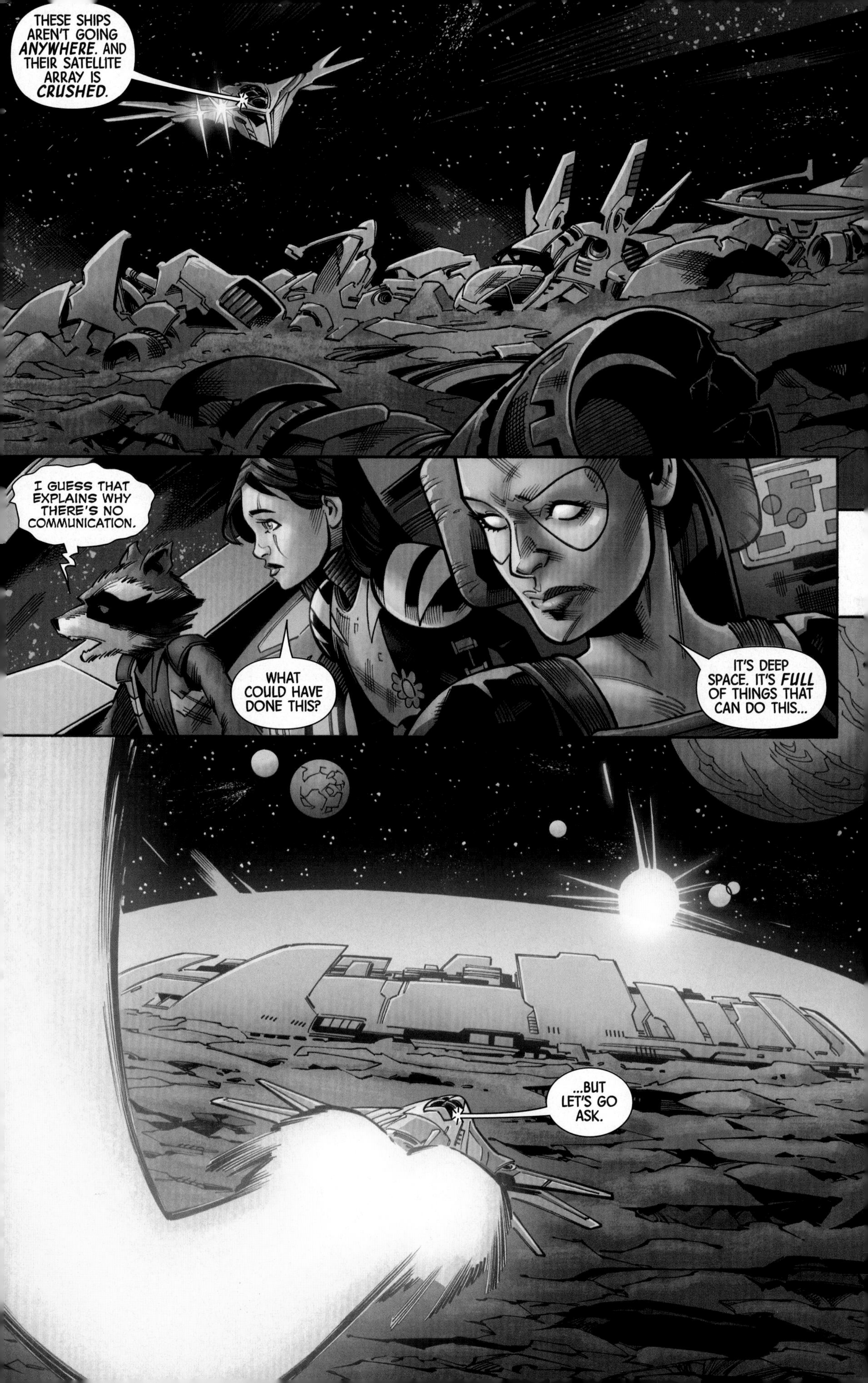

THESE SHIPS AREN'T GOING ANYWHERE. AND THEIR SATELLITE ARRAY IS CRUSHED.
I GUESS THAT EXPLAINS WHY THERE'S NO COMMUNICATION.
WHAT COULD HAVE DONE THIS?
IT'S DEEP SPACE. IT'S FULL OF THINGS THAT CAN DO THIS...
...BUT LET'S GO ASK.

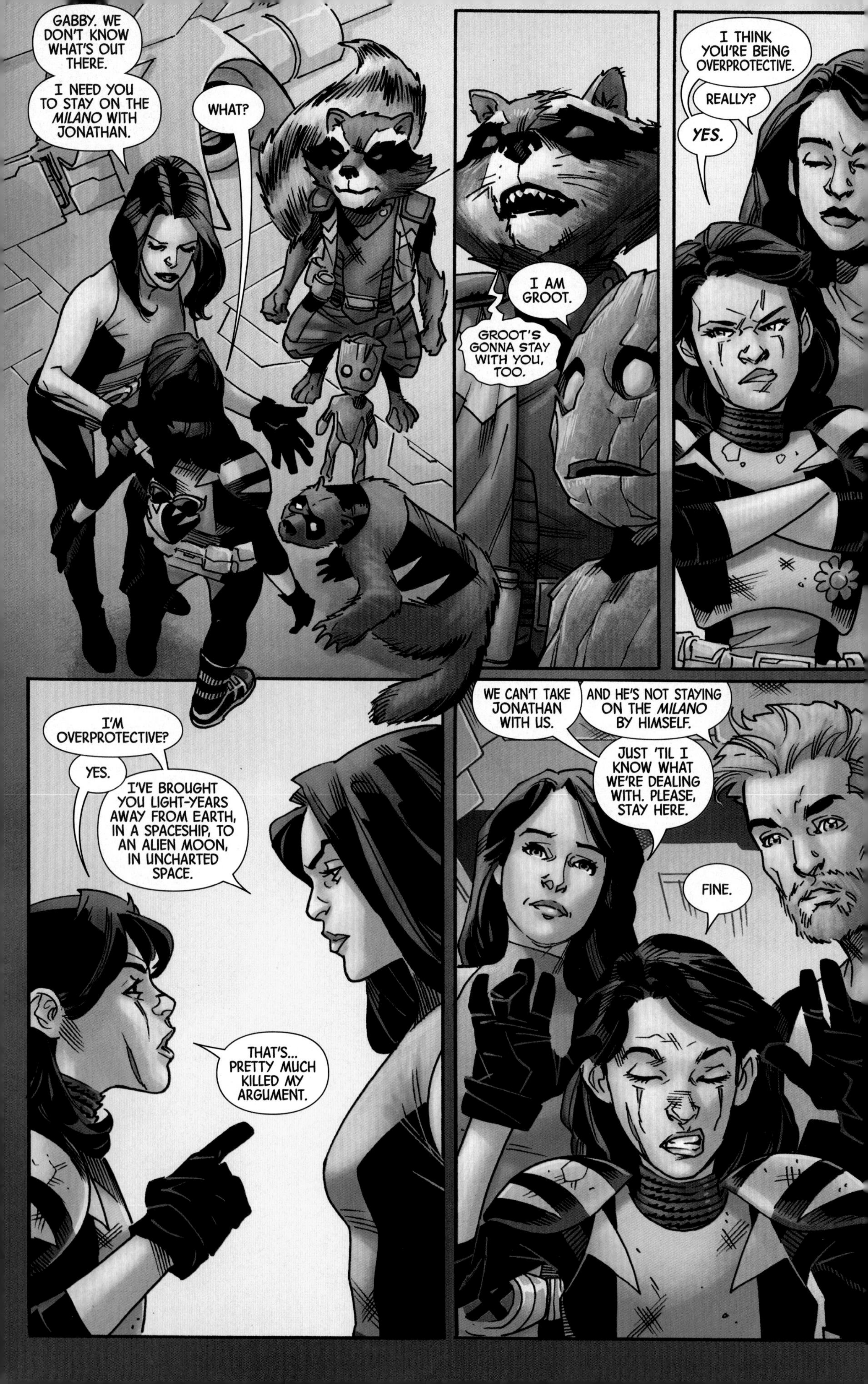
GABBY. WE DON'T KNOW WHAT'S OUT THERE.
I NEED YOU TO STAY ON THE *MILANO* WITH JONATHAN.
WHAT?
I AM GROOT.
GROOT'S GONNA STAY WITH YOU, TOO.
I THINK YOU'RE BEING OVERPROTECTIVE.
REALLY?
YES.
I'M OVERPROTECTIVE?
YES.
I'VE BROUGHT YOU LIGHT-YEARS AWAY FROM EARTH, IN A SPACESHIP, TO AN ALIEN MOON, IN UNCHARTED SPACE.
THAT'S... PRETTY MUCH KILLED MY ARGUMENT.
WE CAN'T TAKE JONATHAN WITH US.
AND HE'S NOT STAYING ON THE *MILANO* BY HIMSELF.
JUST 'TIL I KNOW WHAT WE'RE DEALING WITH. PLEASE, STAY HERE.
FINE.

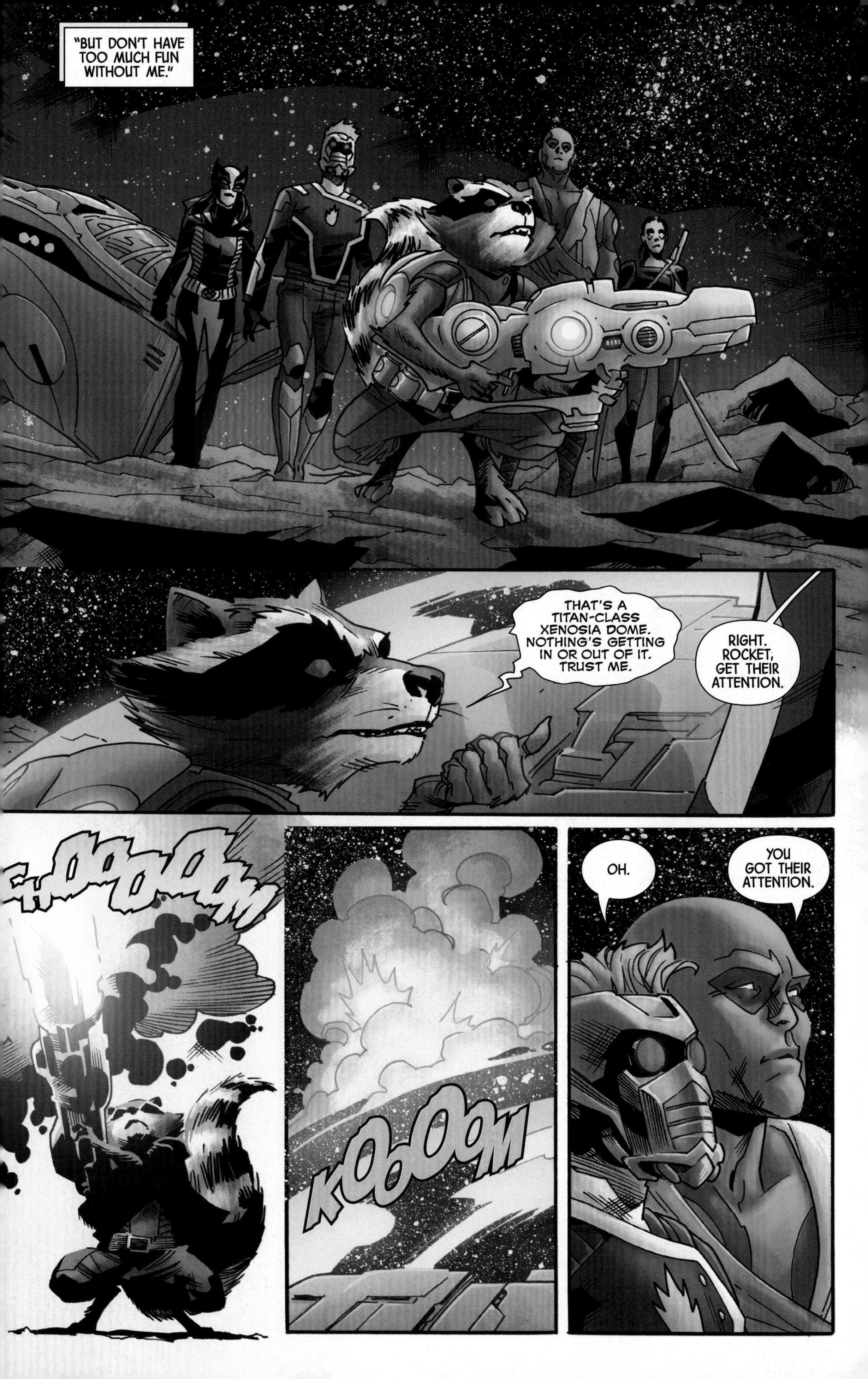
"BUT DON'T HAVE TOO MUCH FUN WITHOUT ME."
THAT'S A TITAN-CLASS XENOSIA DOME. NOTHING'S GETTING IN OR OUT OF IT. TRUST ME.
RIGHT. ROCKET, GET THEIR ATTENTION.
CHOOOOOM
KOOOOM
OH.
YOU GOT THEIR ATTENTION.

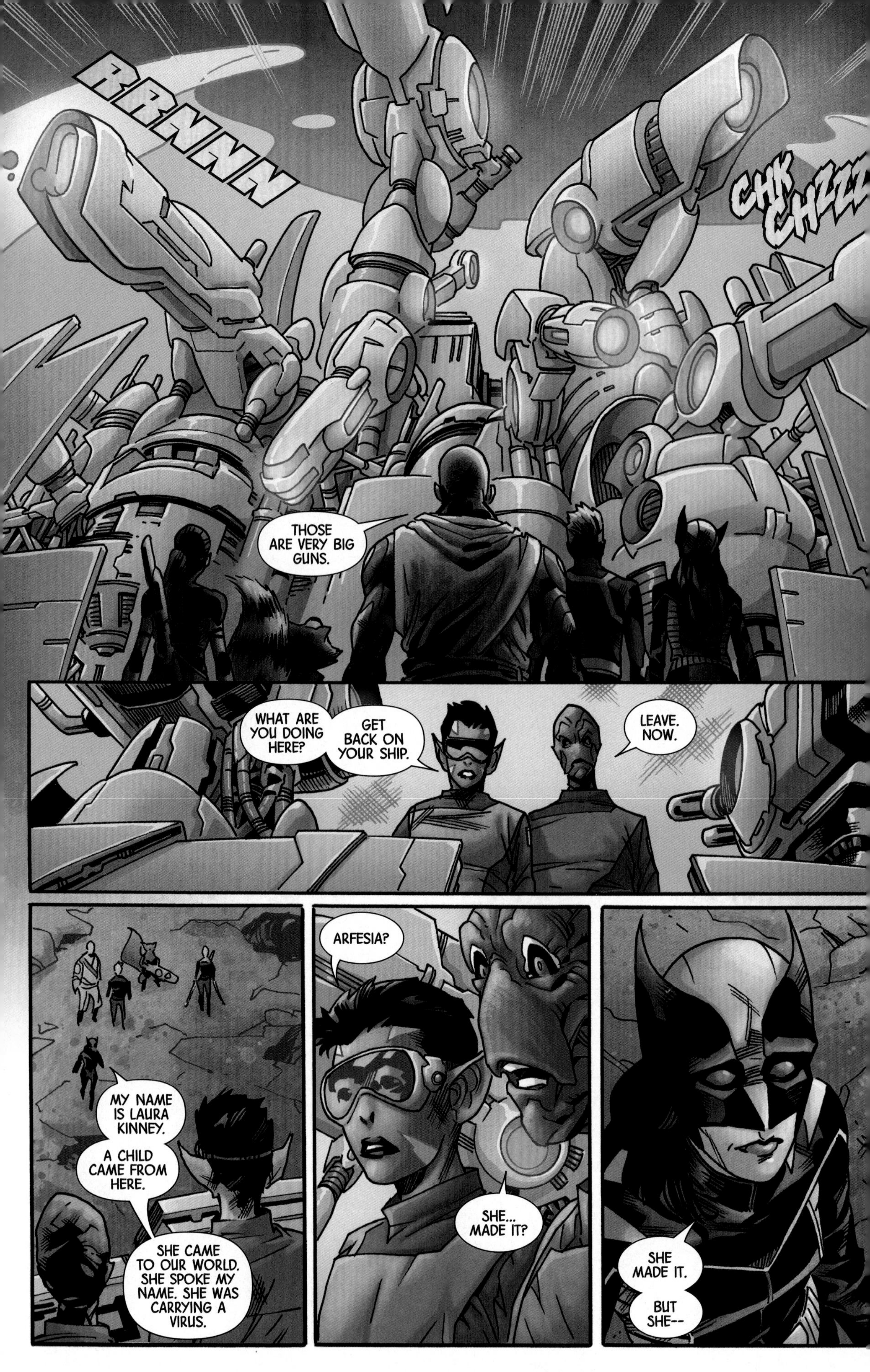
RRNNNN
CHK CHZZZ
THOSE ARE VERY BIG GUNS.
WHAT ARE YOU DOING HERE?
GET BACK ON YOUR SHIP.
LEAVE. NOW.
MY NAME IS LAURA KINNEY.
A CHILD CAME FROM HERE.
SHE CAME TO OUR WORLD. SHE SPOKE MY NAME. SHE WAS CARRYING A VIRUS.
ARFESIA?
SHE... MADE IT?
SHE MADE IT.
BUT SHE--

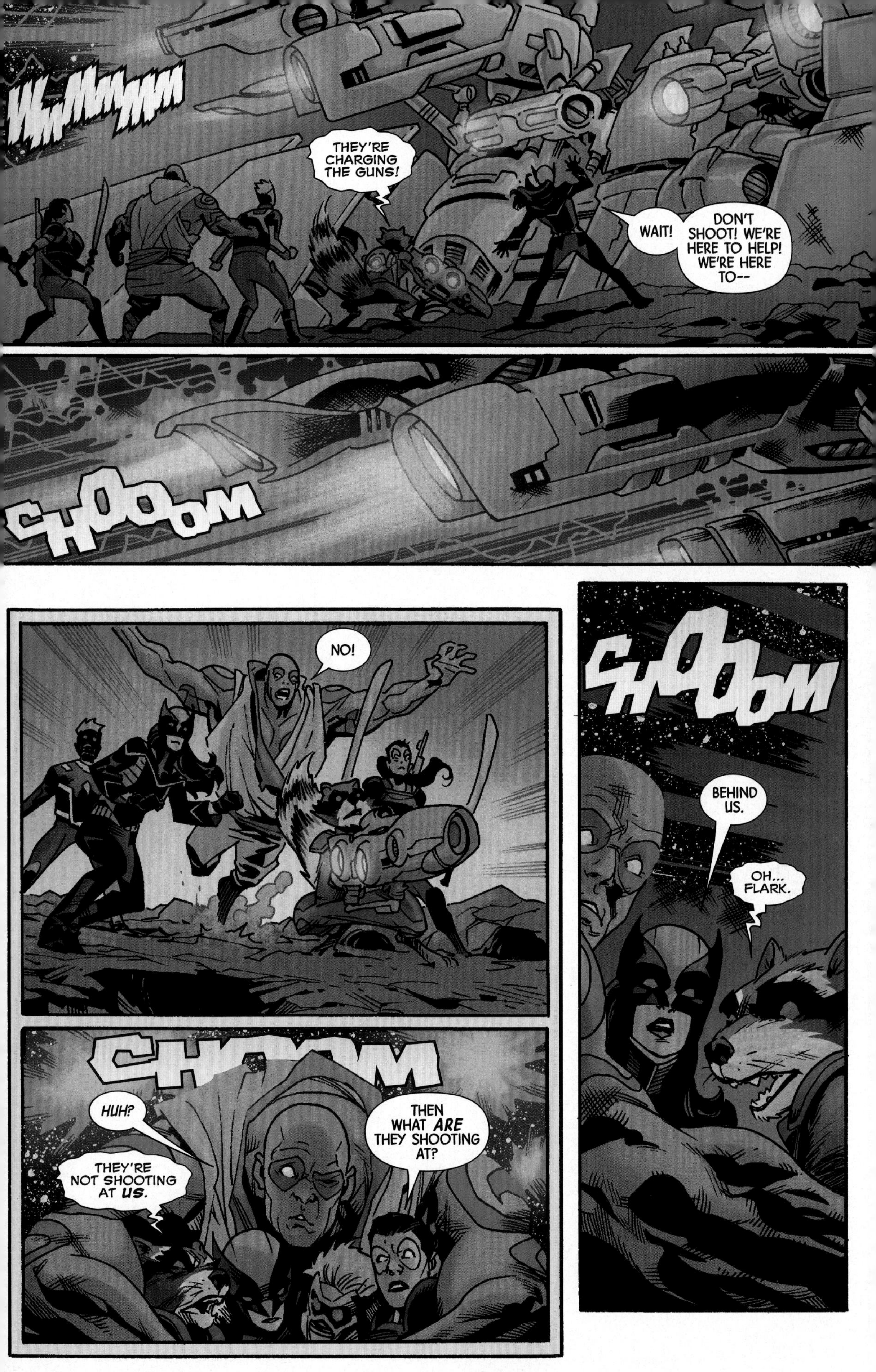
WHMMMMM
THEY'RE CHARGING THE GUNS!
WAIT!
DON'T SHOOT! WE'RE HERE TO HELP! WE'RE HERE TO--
CHOOOOM
NO!
CHOOOOM
HUH?
THEY'RE NOT SHOOTING AT US.
THEN WHAT ARE THEY SHOOTING AT?
CHOOOOM
BEHIND US.
OH... FLARK.

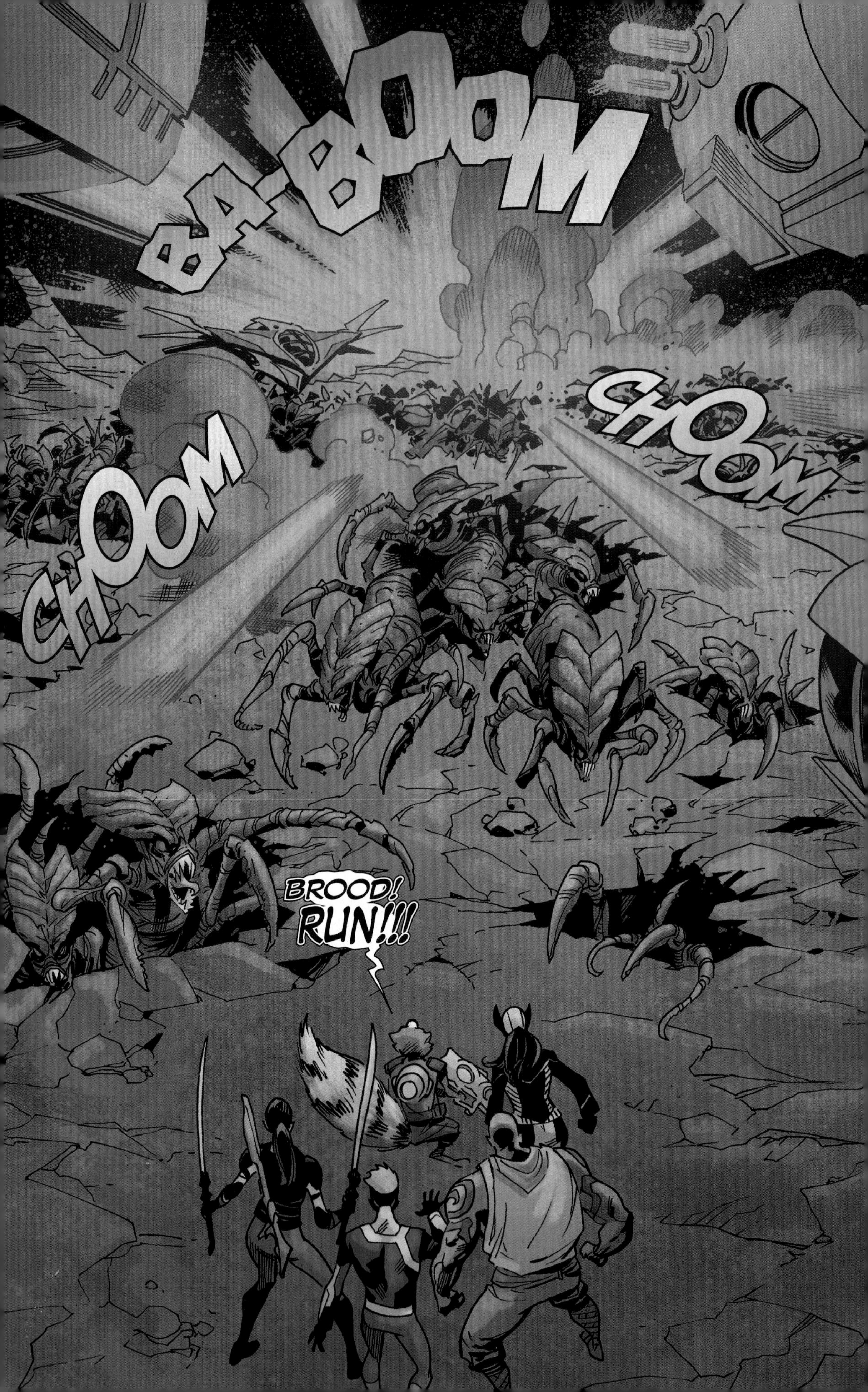
BA-BOOM
CHOOM
CHOOM
BROOD! RUN!!!

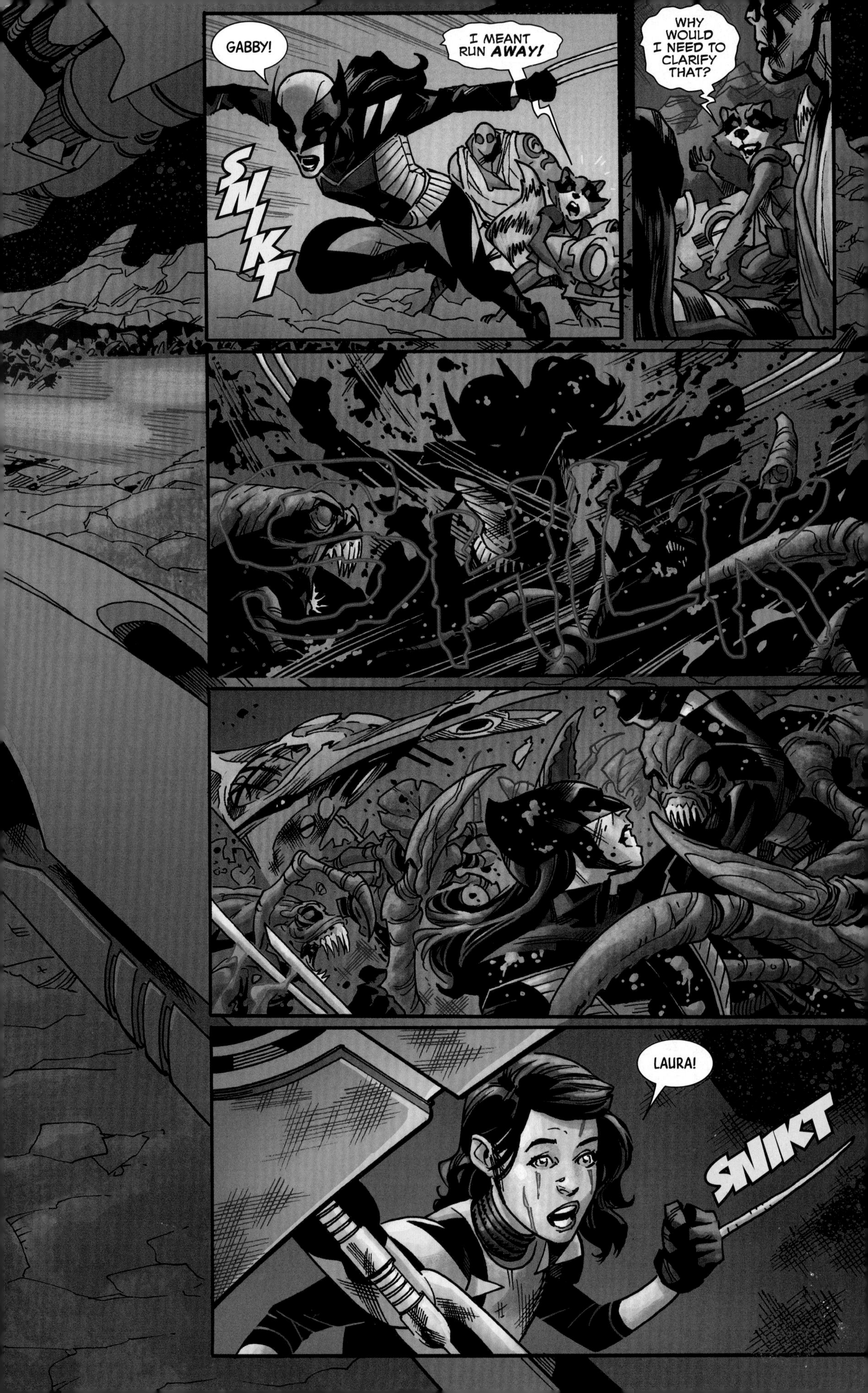
GABBY!
I MEANT RUN AWAY!
SNIKT
WHY WOULD I NEED TO CLARIFY THAT?
SHUNK
LAURA!
SNIKT

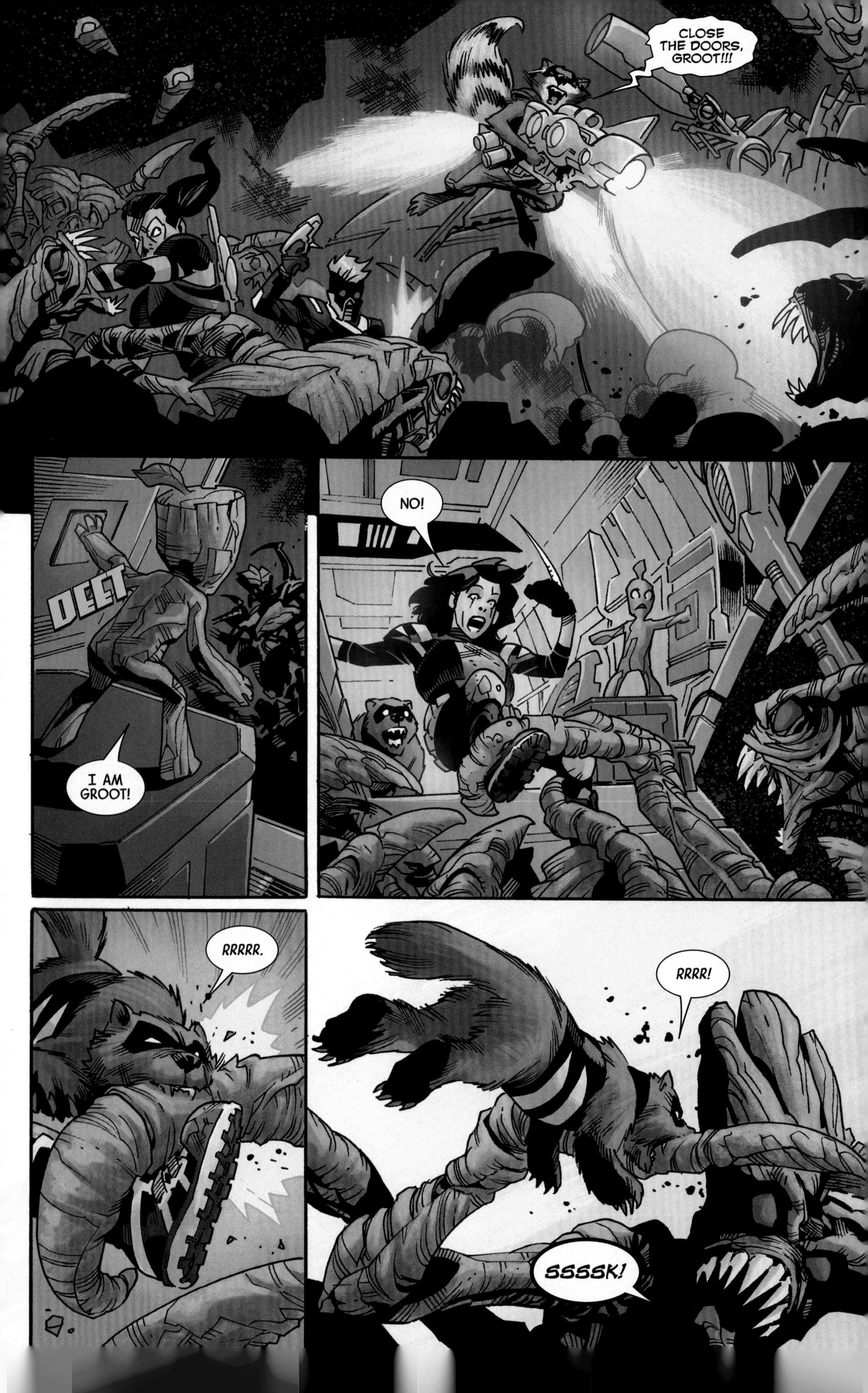
CLOSE THE DOORS, GROOT!!!
DEET
I AM GROOT!
NO!
RRRRR.
RRRR!
SSSSK!

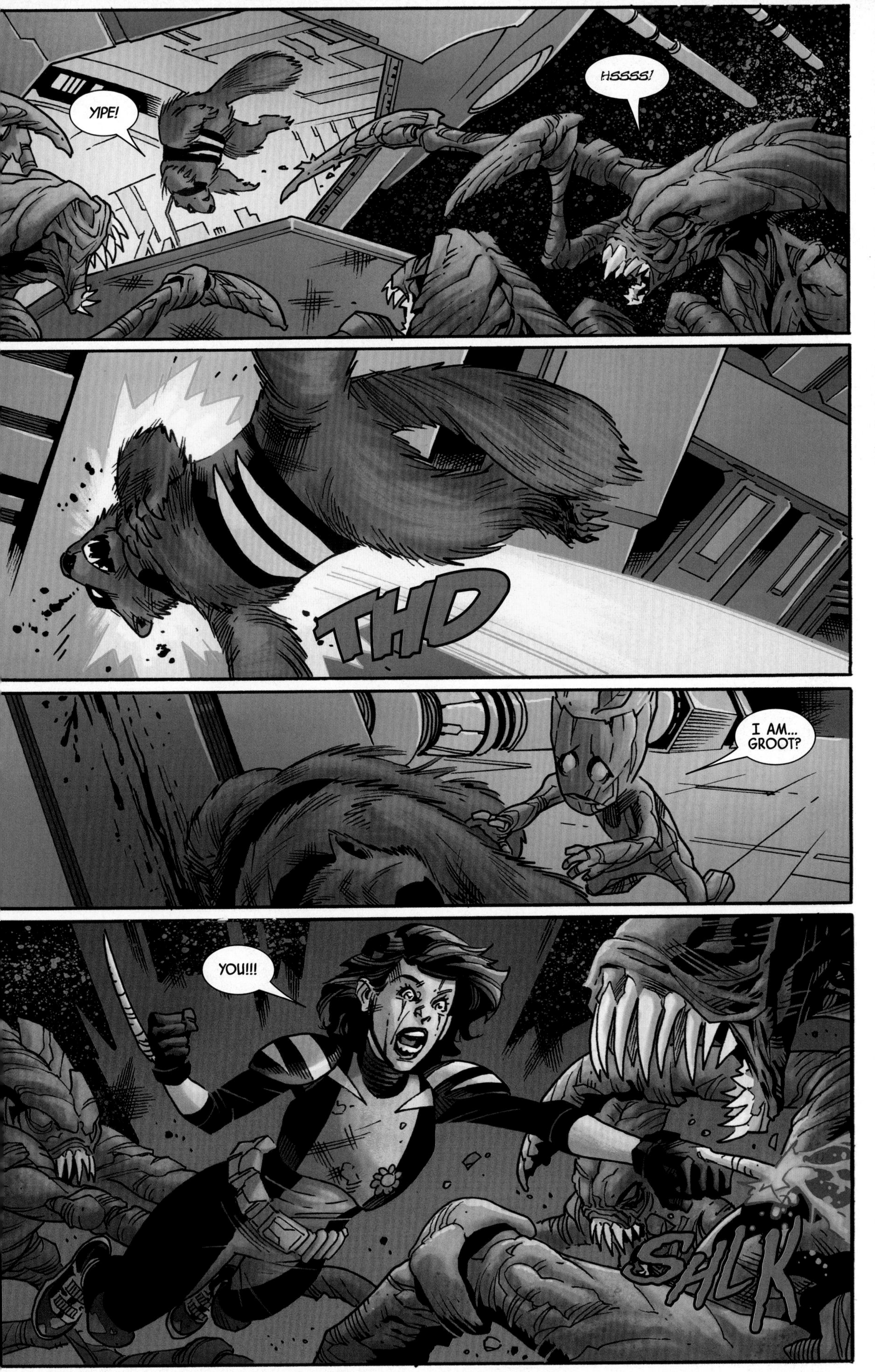
YIPE!
HSSSS!
THD
I AM... GROOT?
YOU!!!
SHLK

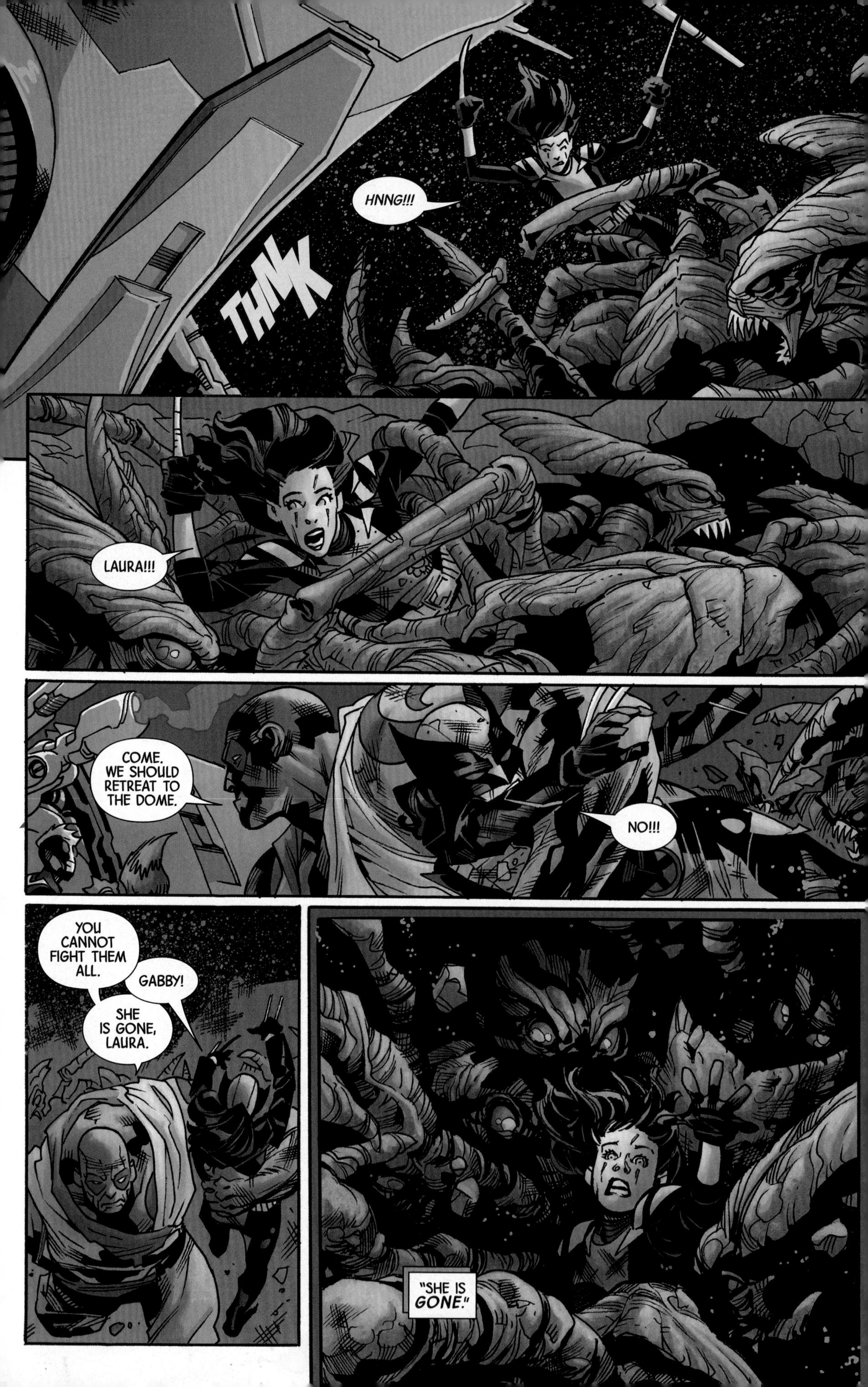
HNNG!!!
THNK
LAURA!!!
COME. WE SHOULD RETREAT TO THE DOME.
NO!!!
YOU CANNOT FIGHT THEM ALL.
GABBY!
SHE IS GONE, LAURA.
"SHE IS GONE."

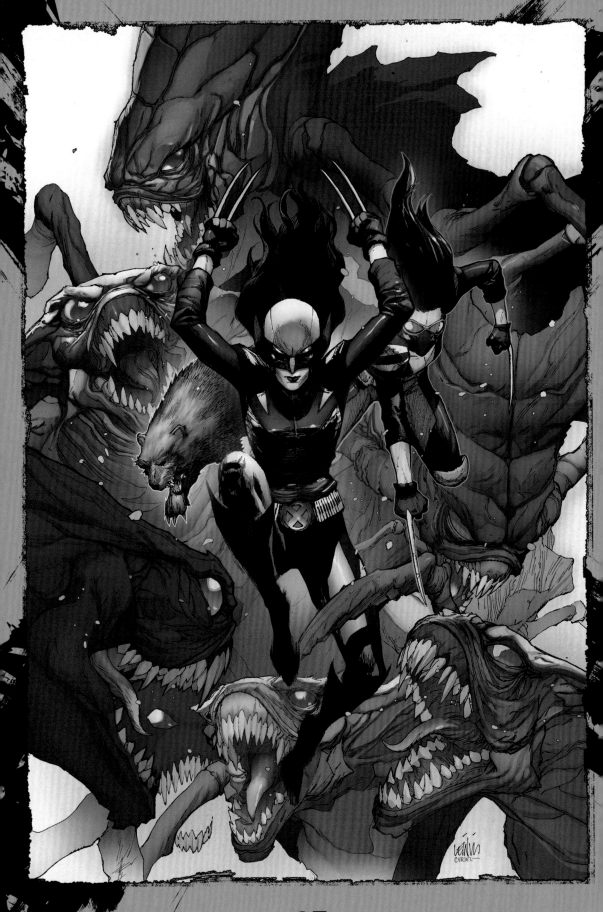

23

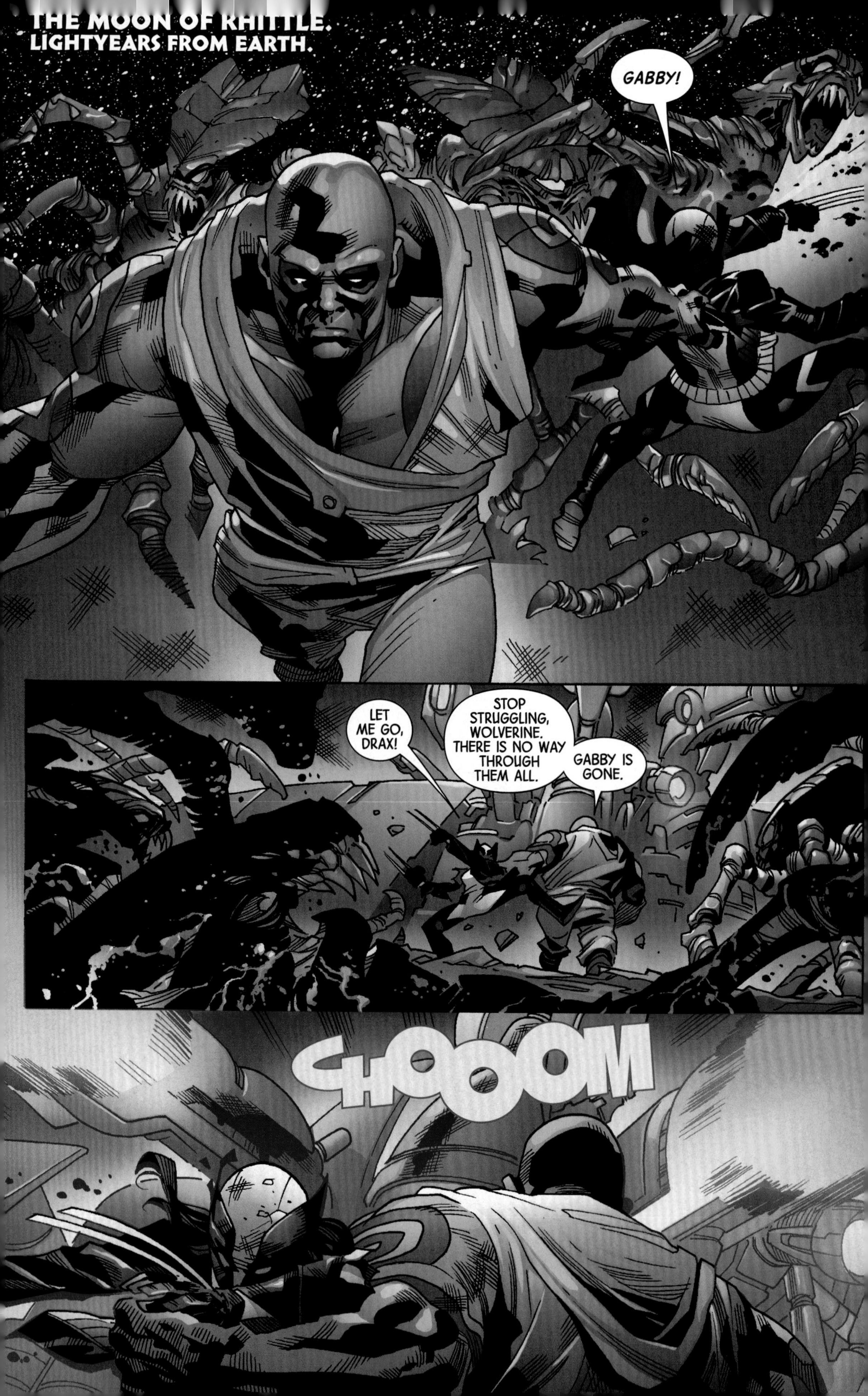
THE MOON OF KHITTLE.
LIGHTYEARS FROM EARTH.
GABBY!
LET ME GO, DRAX!
STOP STRUGGLING, WOLVERINE. THERE IS NO WAY THROUGH THEM ALL.
GABBY IS GONE.
CHOOOOM

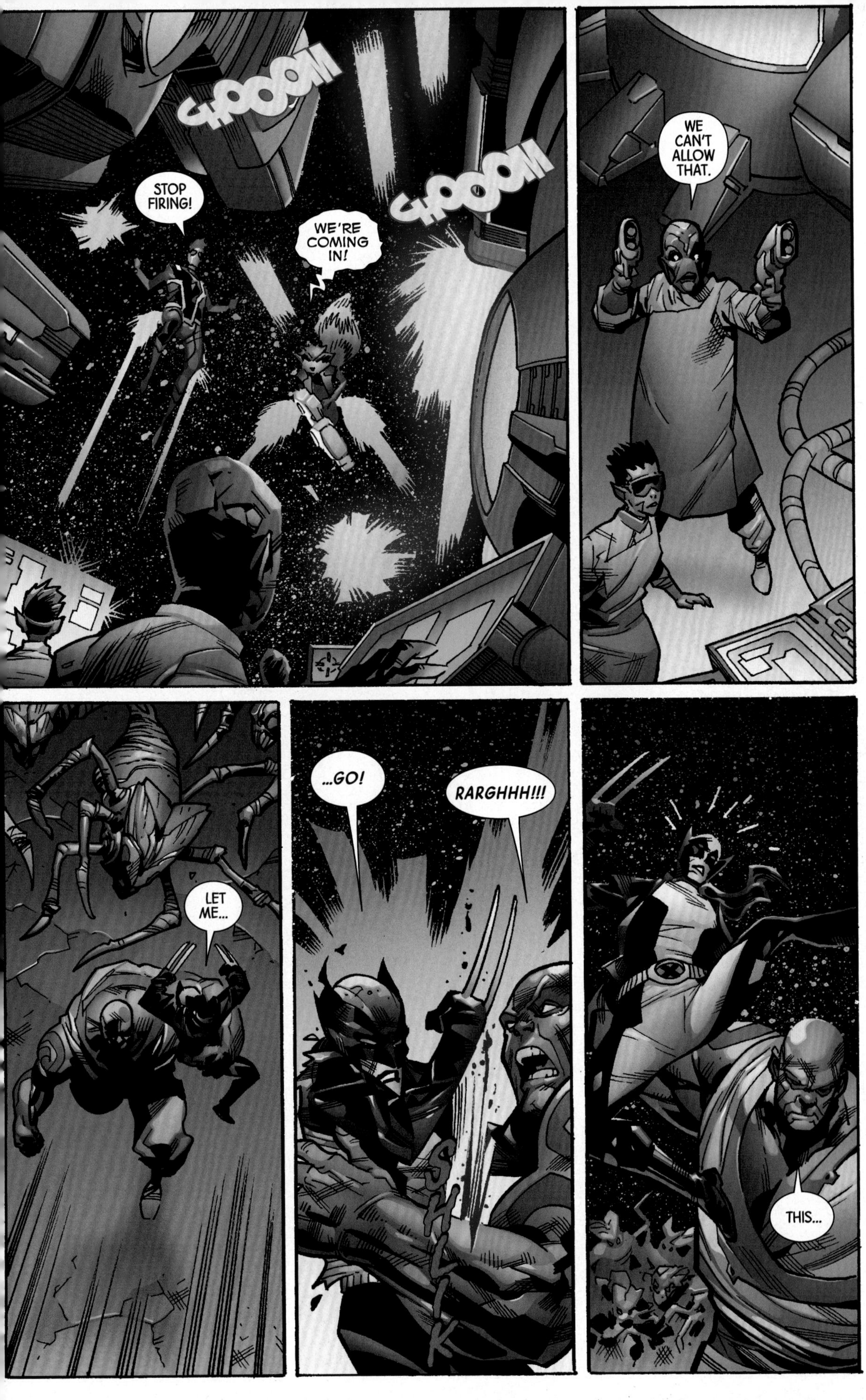
STOP FIRING!
WE'RE COMING IN!
WE CAN'T ALLOW THAT.
LET ME...
...GO!
RARGHHH!!!
THIS...

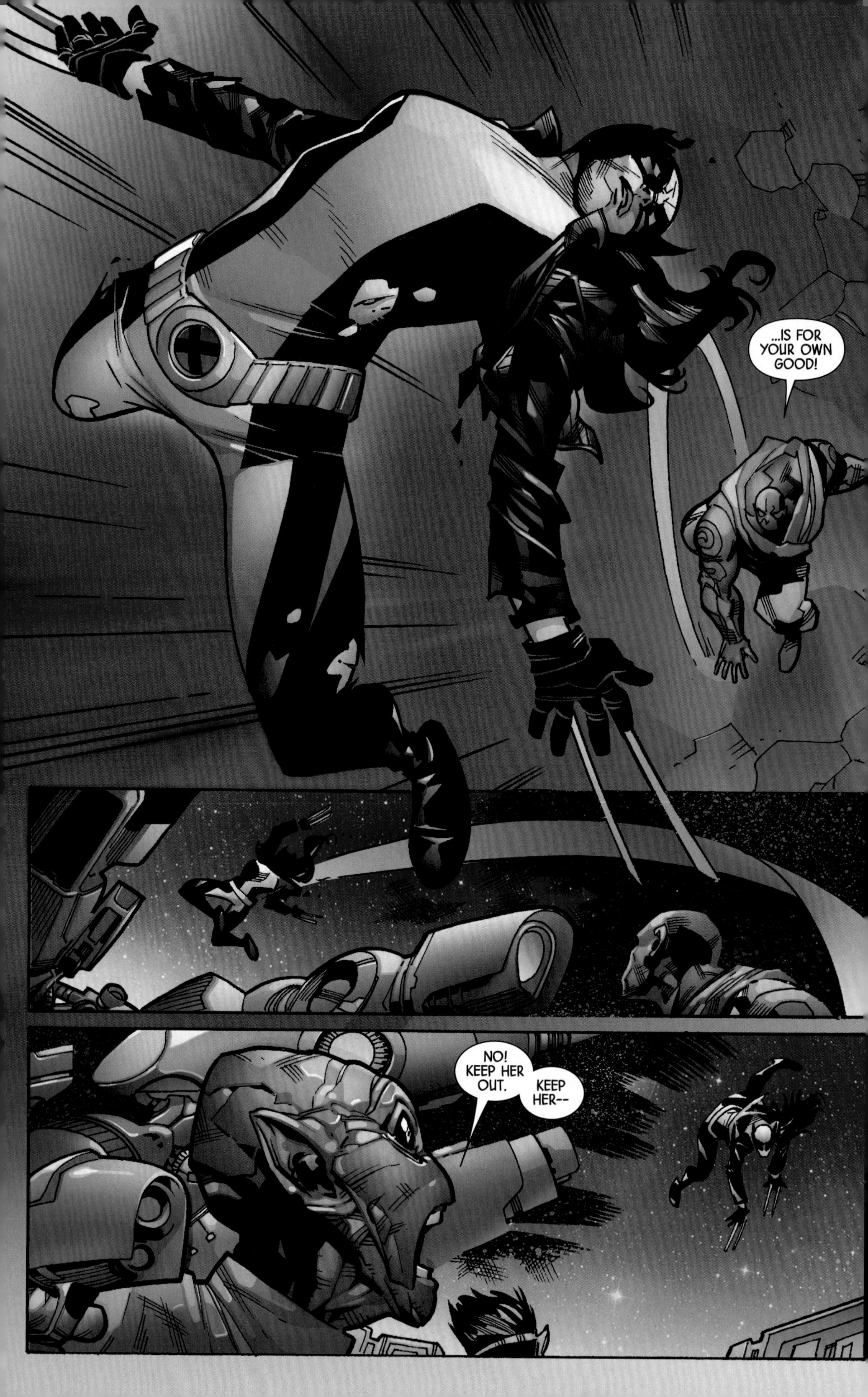
...IS FOR YOUR OWN GOOD!
NO! KEEP HER OUT.
KEEP HER--

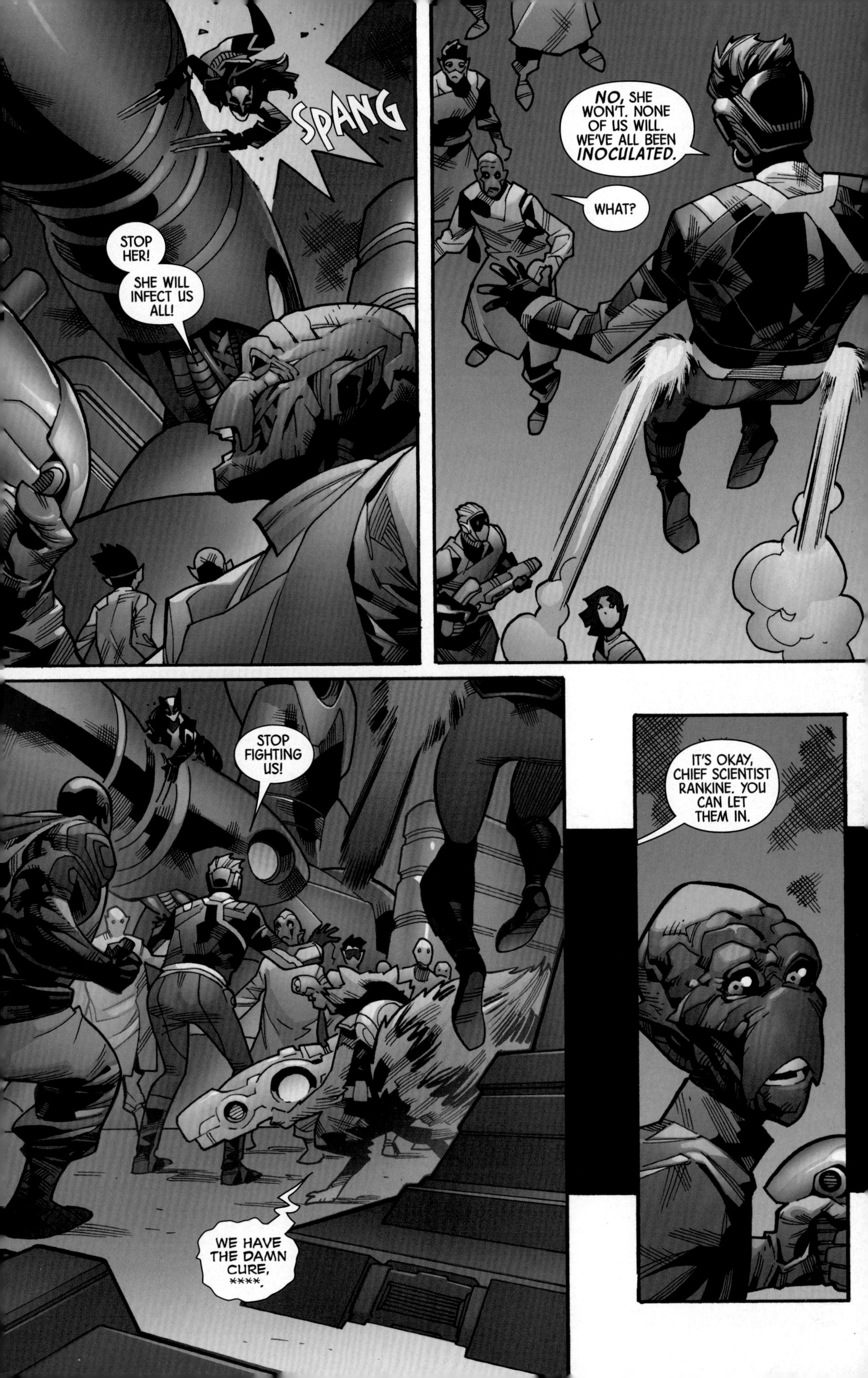
SPANG
STOP HER!
SHE WILL INFECT US ALL!
NO, SHE WON'T. NONE OF US WILL. WE'VE ALL BEEN INOCULATED.
WHAT?
STOP FIGHTING US!
WE HAVE THE DAMN CURE, ****.
IT'S OKAY, CHIEF SCIENTIST RANKINE. YOU CAN LET THEM IN.

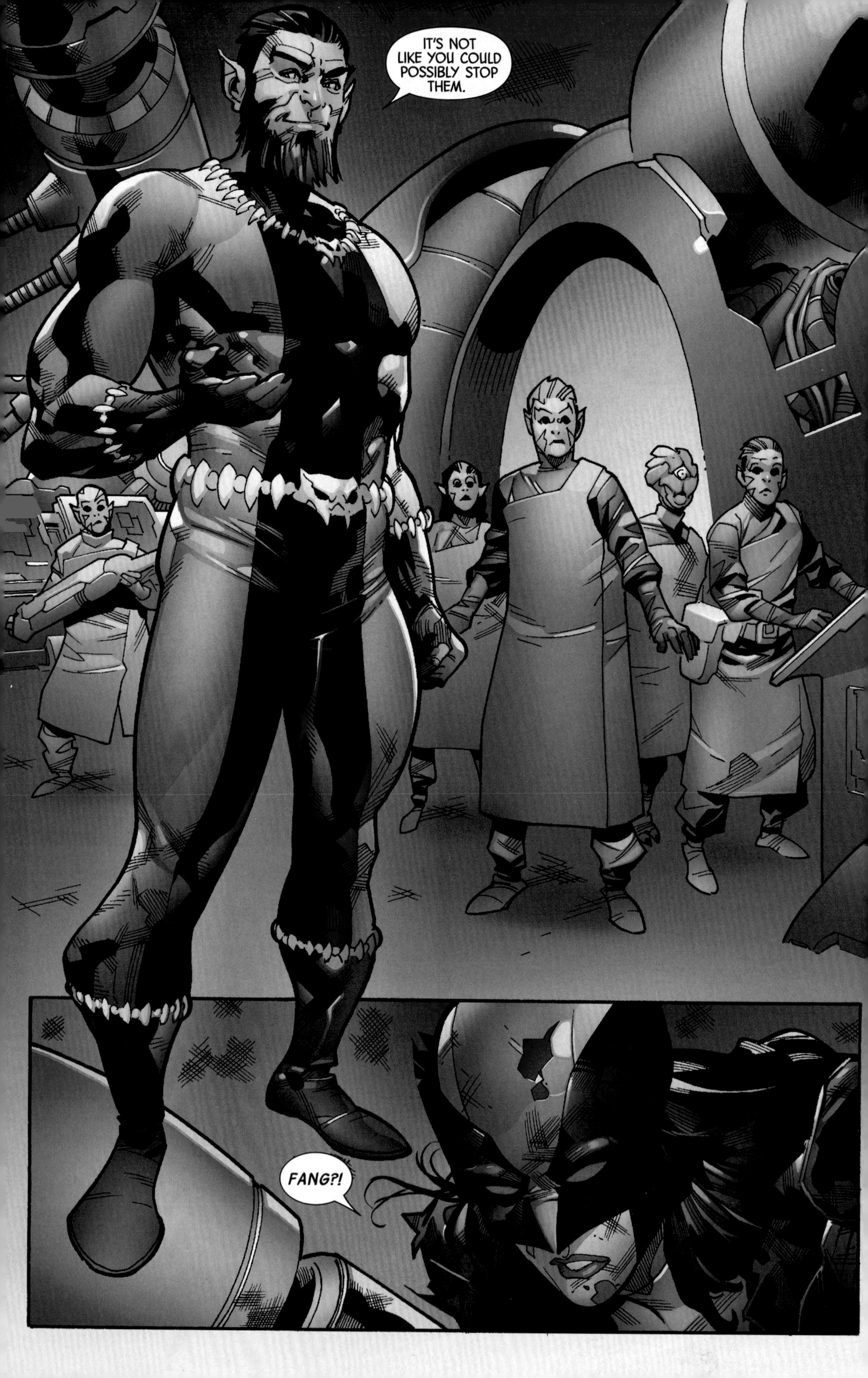
IT'S NOT LIKE YOU COULD POSSIBLY STOP THEM.
FANG?!

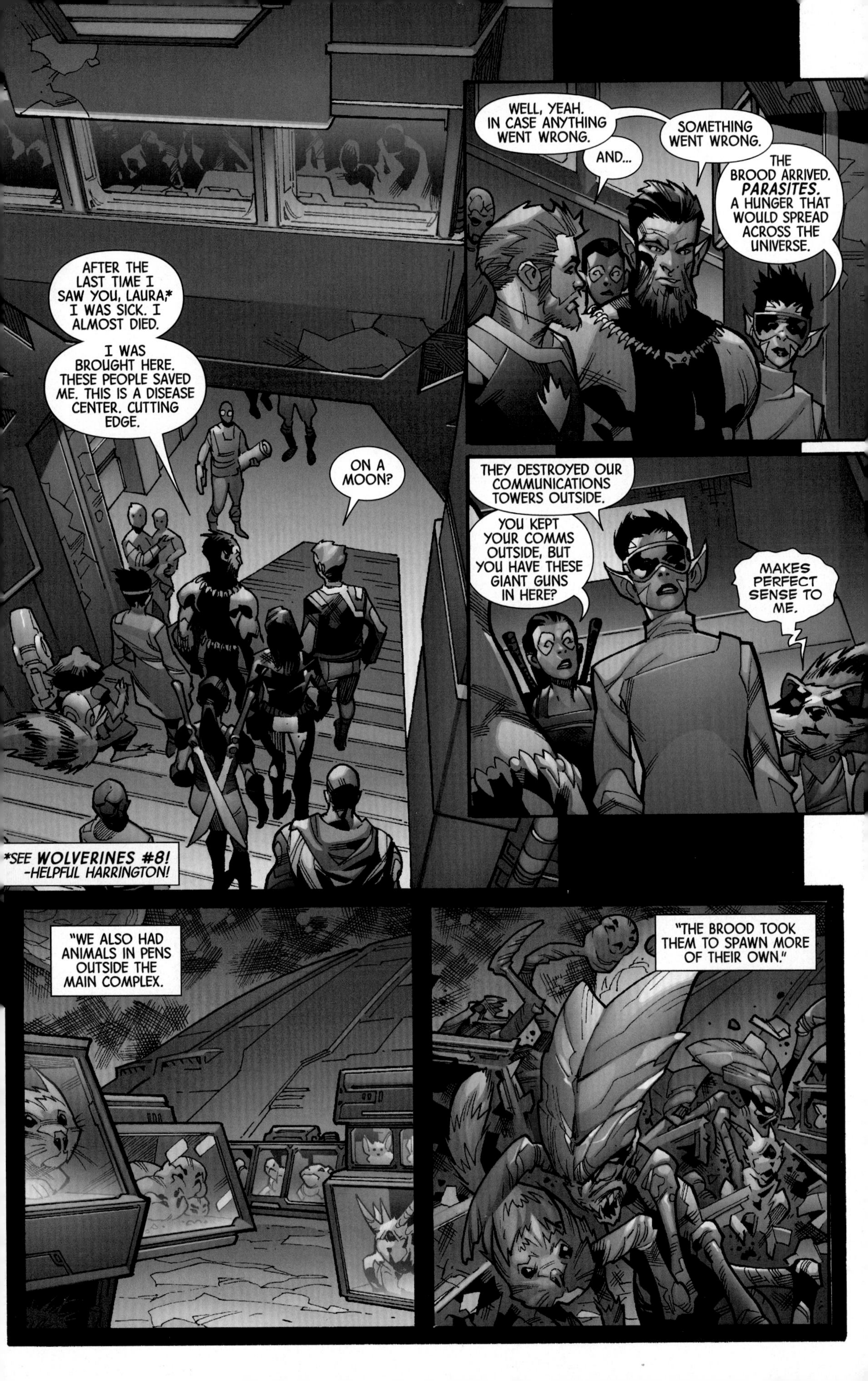
AFTER THE LAST TIME I SAW YOU, LAURA,* I WAS SICK. I ALMOST DIED.
I WAS BROUGHT HERE. THESE PEOPLE SAVED ME. THIS IS A DISEASE CENTER. CUTTING EDGE.
ON A MOON?
*SEE WOLVERINES #8! -HELPFUL HARRINGTON!
WELL, YEAH. IN CASE ANYTHING WENT WRONG.
AND...
SOMETHING WENT WRONG.
THE BROOD ARRIVED. PARASITES. A HUNGER THAT WOULD SPREAD ACROSS THE UNIVERSE.
THEY DESTROYED OUR COMMUNICATIONS TOWERS OUTSIDE.
YOU KEPT YOUR COMMS OUTSIDE, BUT YOU HAVE THESE GIANT GUNS IN HERE?
MAKES PERFECT SENSE TO ME.
"WE ALSO HAD ANIMALS IN PENS OUTSIDE THE MAIN COMPLEX.
"THE BROOD TOOK THEM TO SPAWN MORE OF THEIR OWN."

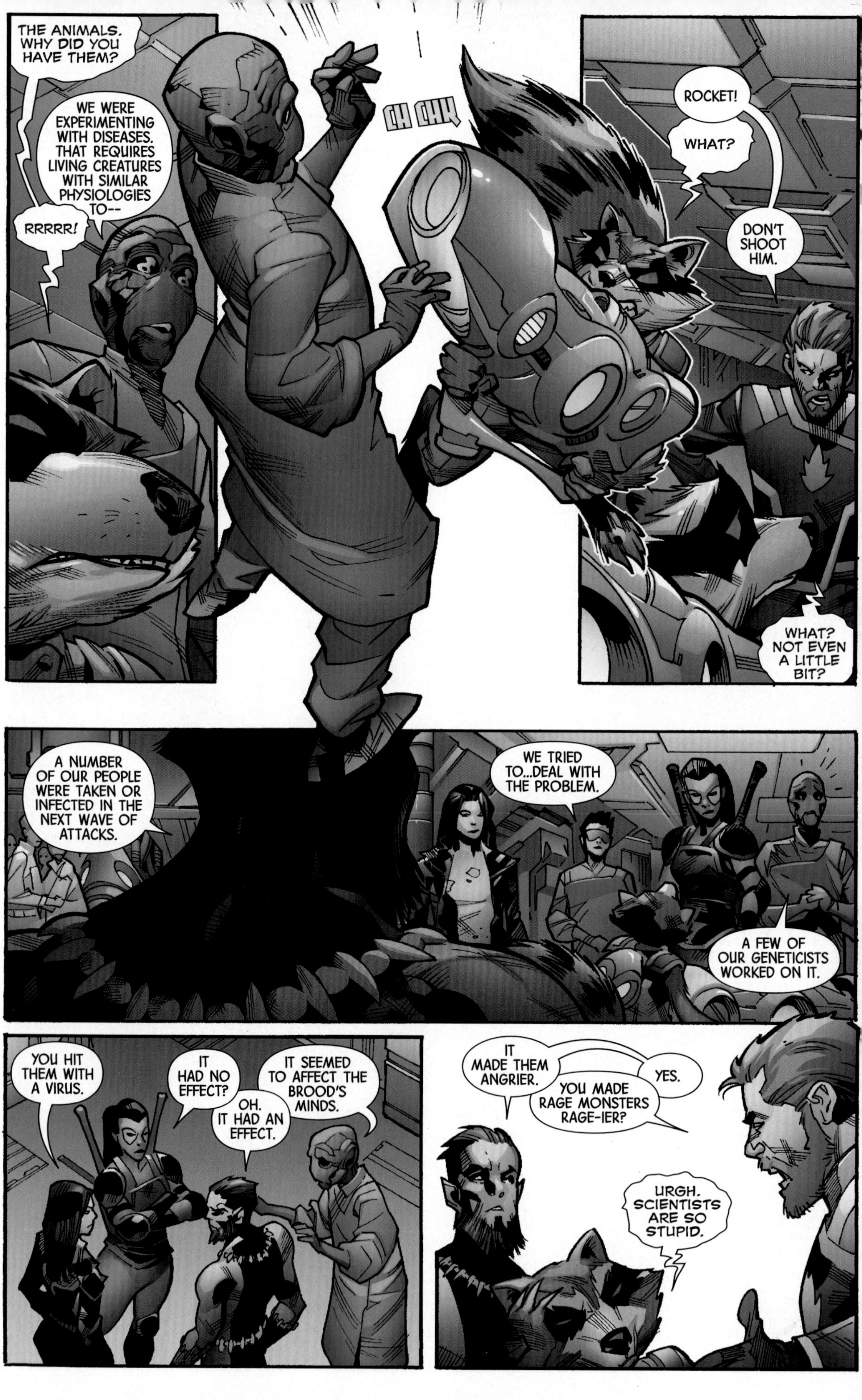
THE ANIMALS. WHY DID YOU HAVE THEM?
WE WERE EXPERIMENTING WITH DISEASES. THAT REQUIRES LIVING CREATURES WITH SIMILAR PHYSIOLOGIES TO--
RRRRR!
CH CHK
ROCKET!
WHAT?
DON'T SHOOT HIM.
WHAT? NOT EVEN A LITTLE BIT?
A NUMBER OF OUR PEOPLE WERE TAKEN OR INFECTED IN THE NEXT WAVE OF ATTACKS.
WE TRIED TO...DEAL WITH THE PROBLEM.
A FEW OF OUR GENETICISTS WORKED ON IT.
YOU HIT THEM WITH A VIRUS.
IT HAD NO EFFECT?
IT SEEMED TO AFFECT THE BROOD'S MINDS.
OH. IT HAD AN EFFECT.
IT MADE THEM ANGRIER.
YES.
YOU MADE RAGE MONSTERS RAGE-IER?
URGH. SCIENTISTS ARE SO STUPID.

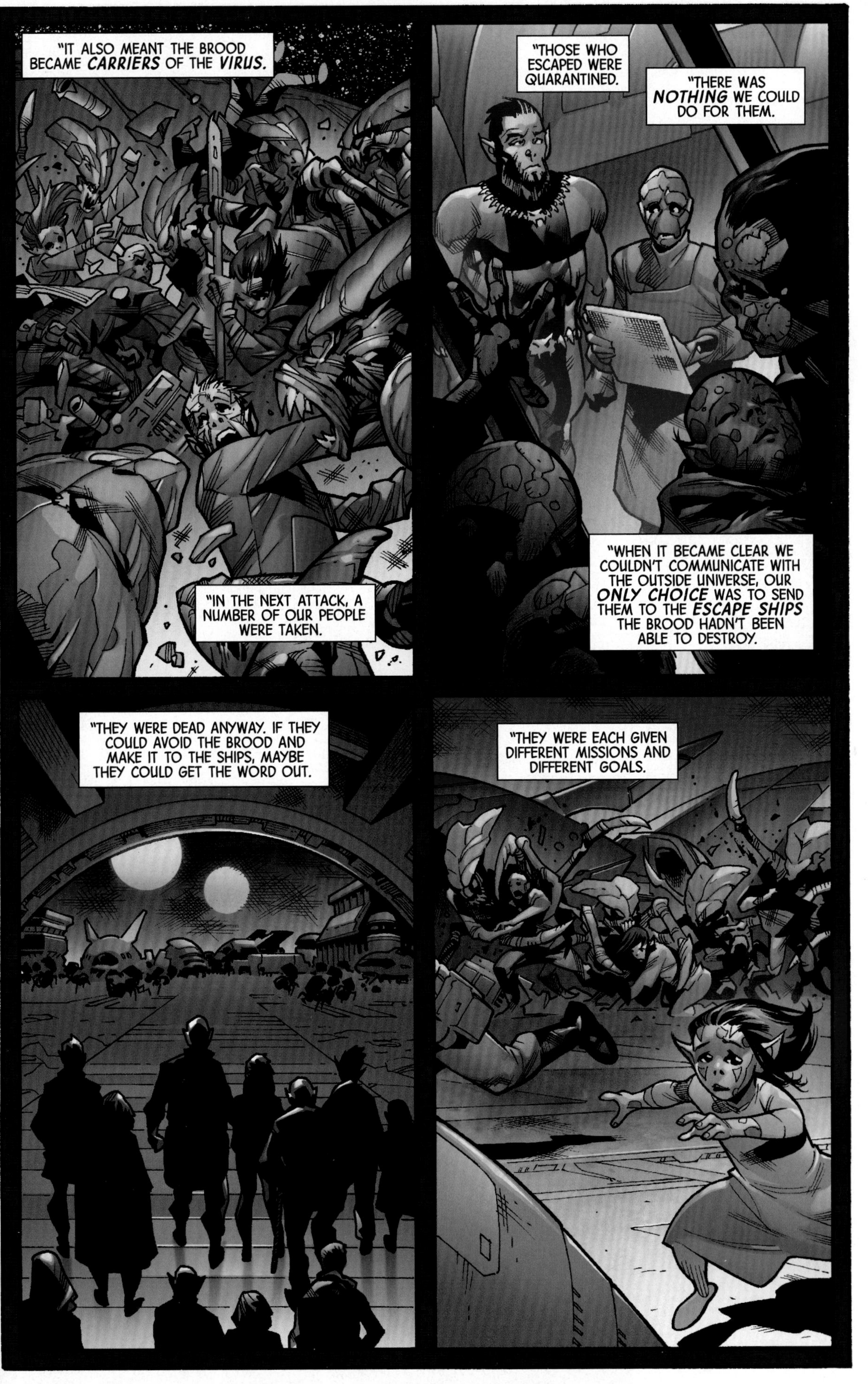
"IT ALSO MEANT THE BROOD BECAME CARRIERS OF THE VIRUS.
"IN THE NEXT ATTACK, A NUMBER OF OUR PEOPLE WERE TAKEN.
"THOSE WHO ESCAPED WERE QUARANTINED.
"THERE WAS NOTHING WE COULD DO FOR THEM.
"WHEN IT BECAME CLEAR WE COULDN'T COMMUNICATE WITH THE OUTSIDE UNIVERSE, OUR ONLY CHOICE WAS TO SEND THEM TO THE ESCAPE SHIPS THE BROOD HADN'T BEEN ABLE TO DESTROY.
"THEY WERE DEAD ANYWAY. IF THEY COULD AVOID THE BROOD AND MAKE IT TO THE SHIPS, MAYBE THEY COULD GET THE WORD OUT.
"THEY WERE EACH GIVEN DIFFERENT MISSIONS AND DIFFERENT GOALS.

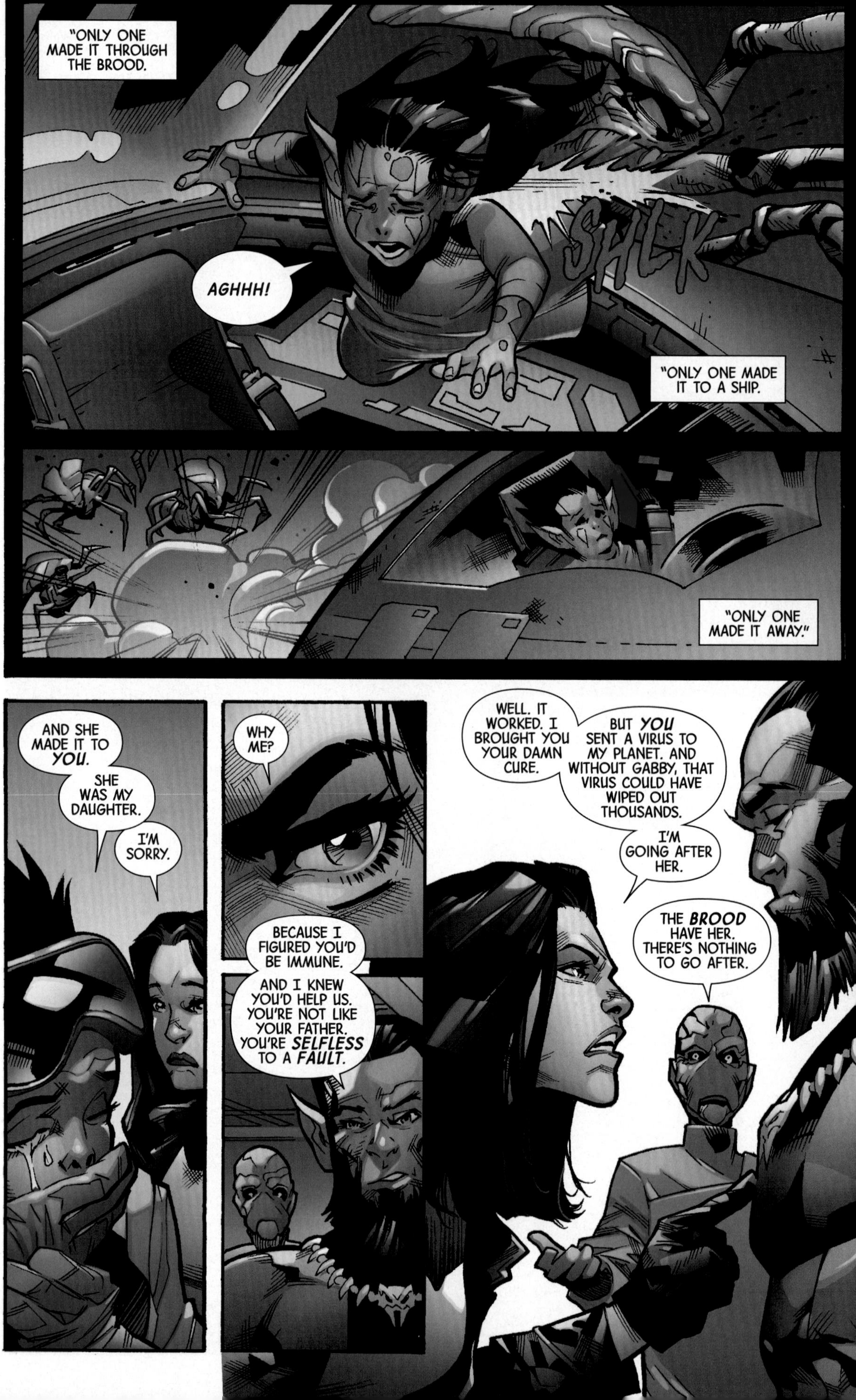
"ONLY ONE MADE IT THROUGH THE BROOD.
AGHHH!
SHLK
"ONLY ONE MADE IT TO A SHIP.
"ONLY ONE MADE IT AWAY."
AND SHE MADE IT TO YOU.
SHE WAS MY DAUGHTER.
I'M SORRY.
WHY ME?
BECAUSE I FIGURED YOU'D BE IMMUNE.
AND I KNEW YOU'D HELP US. YOU'RE NOT LIKE YOUR FATHER. YOU'RE SELFLESS TO A FAULT.
WELL. IT WORKED. I BROUGHT YOU YOUR DAMN CURE.
BUT YOU SENT A VIRUS TO MY PLANET. AND WITHOUT GABBY, THAT VIRUS COULD HAVE WIPED OUT THOUSANDS.
I'M GOING AFTER HER.
THE BROOD HAVE HER. THERE'S NOTHING TO GO AFTER.

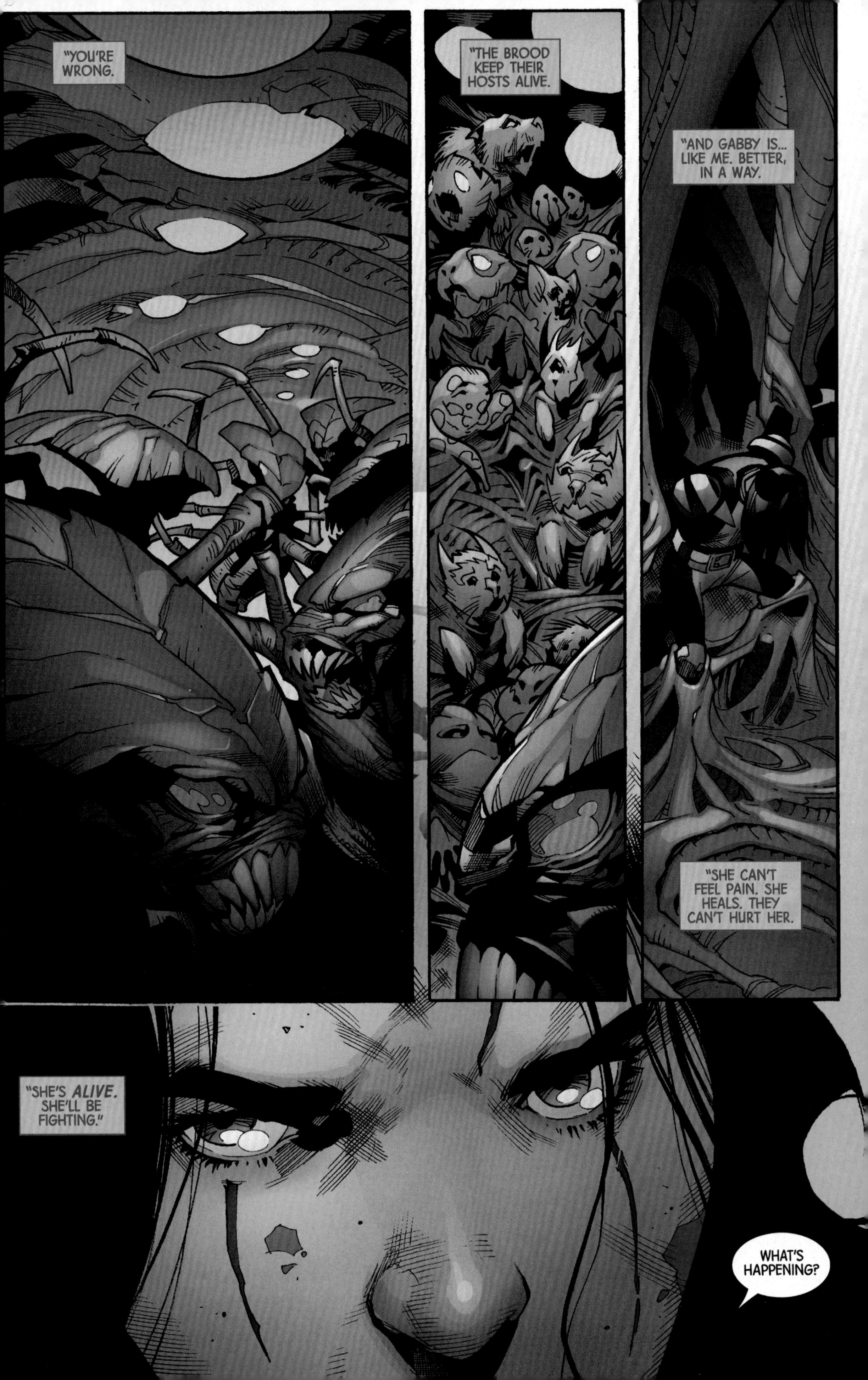
"YOU'RE WRONG.
"THE BROOD KEEP THEIR HOSTS ALIVE.
"AND GABBY IS... LIKE ME. BETTER, IN A WAY.
"SHE CAN'T FEEL PAIN. SHE HEALS. THEY CAN'T HURT HER.
"SHE'S *ALIVE.* SHE'LL BE FIGHTING."
WHAT'S HAPPENING?

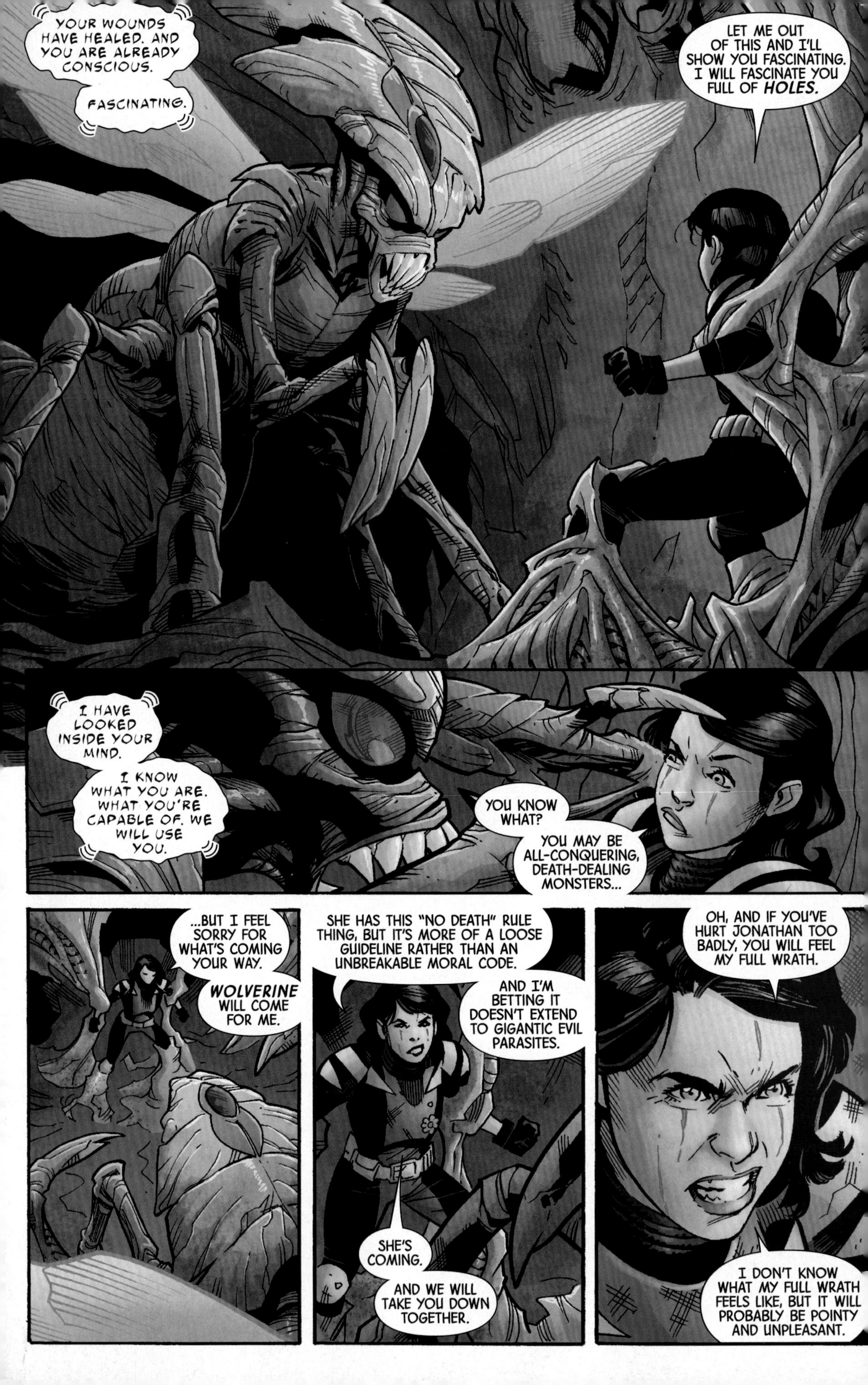
YOUR WOUNDS HAVE HEALED. AND YOU ARE ALREADY CONSCIOUS.
FASCINATING.
LET ME OUT OF THIS AND I'LL SHOW YOU FASCINATING. I WILL FASCINATE YOU FULL OF HOLES.
I HAVE LOOKED INSIDE YOUR MIND.
I KNOW WHAT YOU ARE. WHAT YOU'RE CAPABLE OF. WE WILL USE YOU.
YOU KNOW WHAT?
YOU MAY BE ALL-CONQUERING, DEATH-DEALING MONSTERS...
...BUT I FEEL SORRY FOR WHAT'S COMING YOUR WAY.
WOLVERINE WILL COME FOR ME.
SHE HAS THIS "NO DEATH" RULE THING, BUT IT'S MORE OF A LOOSE GUIDELINE RATHER THAN AN UNBREAKABLE MORAL CODE.
AND I'M BETTING IT DOESN'T EXTEND TO GIGANTIC EVIL PARASITES.
SHE'S COMING.
AND WE WILL TAKE YOU DOWN TOGETHER.
OH, AND IF YOU'VE HURT JONATHAN TOO BADLY, YOU WILL FEEL MY FULL WRATH.
I DON'T KNOW WHAT MY FULL WRATH FEELS LIKE, BUT IT WILL PROBABLY BE POINTY AND UNPLEASANT.

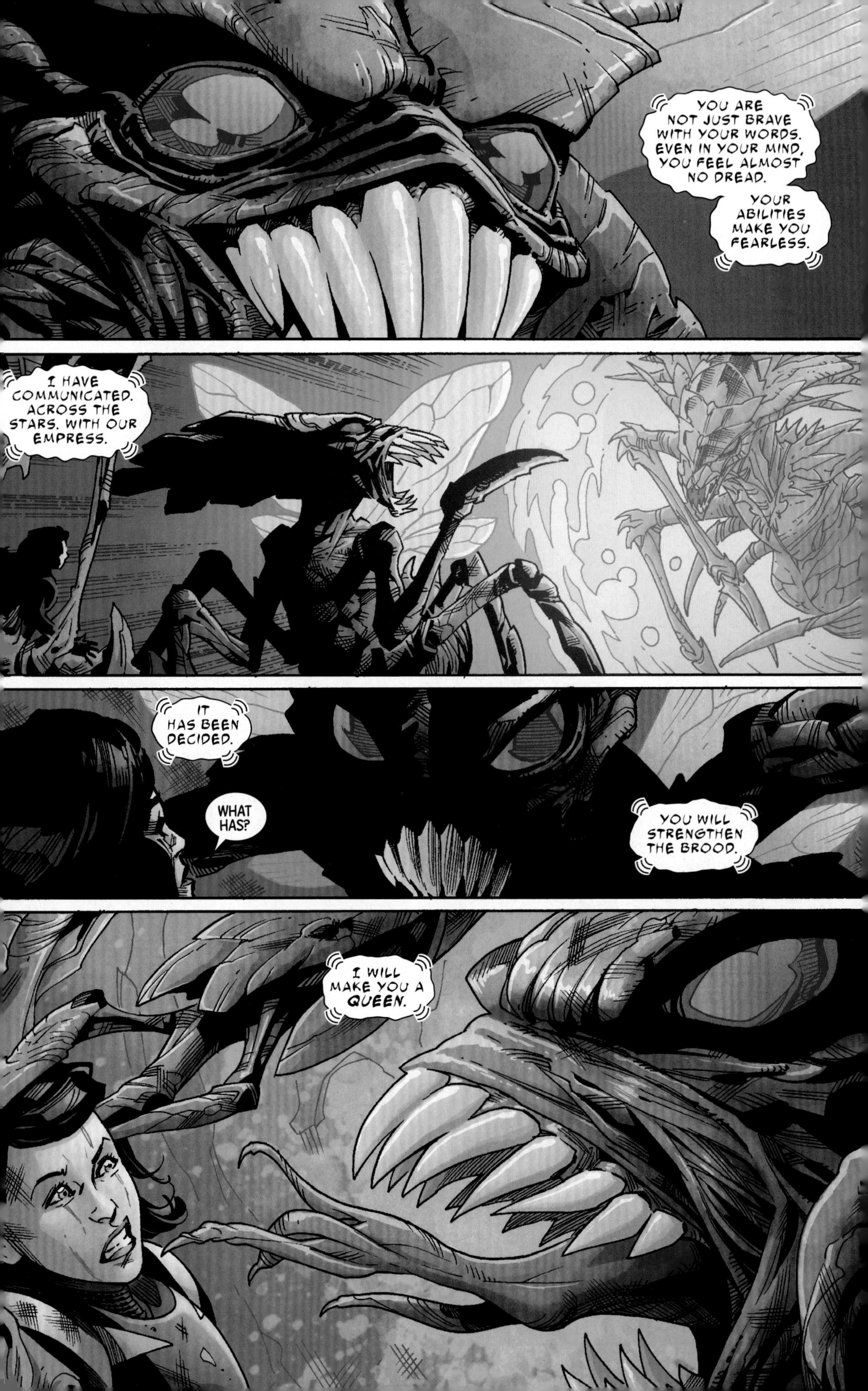
YOU ARE NOT JUST BRAVE WITH YOUR WORDS. EVEN IN YOUR MIND, YOU FEEL ALMOST NO DREAD.
YOUR ABILITIES MAKE YOU FEARLESS.
I HAVE COMMUNICATED. ACROSS THE STARS. WITH OUR EMPRESS.
IT HAS BEEN DECIDED.
WHAT HAS?
YOU WILL STRENGTHEN THE BROOD.
I WILL MAKE YOU A QUEEN.

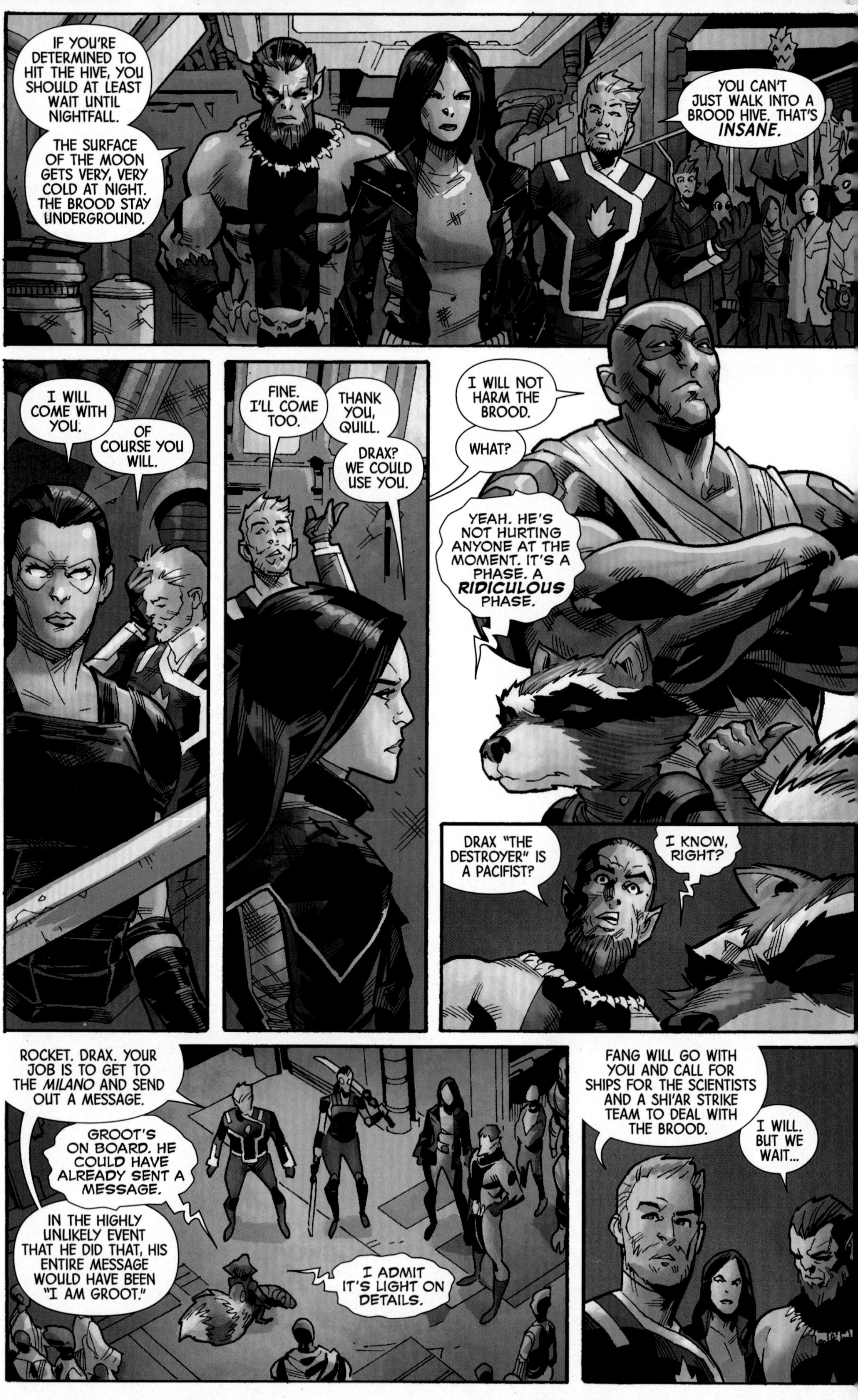
IF YOU'RE DETERMINED TO HIT THE HIVE, YOU SHOULD AT LEAST WAIT UNTIL NIGHTFALL.
THE SURFACE OF THE MOON GETS VERY, VERY COLD AT NIGHT. THE BROOD STAY UNDERGROUND.
YOU CAN'T JUST WALK INTO A BROOD HIVE. THAT'S *INSANE.*
I WILL COME WITH YOU.
OF COURSE YOU WILL.
FINE. I'LL COME TOO.
THANK YOU, QUILL.
DRAX? WE COULD USE YOU.
I WILL NOT HARM THE BROOD.
WHAT?
YEAH. HE'S NOT HURTING ANYONE AT THE MOMENT. IT'S A PHASE. A ***RIDICULOUS*** PHASE.
DRAX "THE DESTROYER" IS A PACIFIST?
I KNOW, RIGHT?
ROCKET. DRAX. YOUR JOB IS TO GET TO THE *MILANO* AND SEND OUT A MESSAGE.
GROOT'S ON BOARD. HE COULD HAVE ALREADY SENT A MESSAGE.
IN THE HIGHLY UNLIKELY EVENT THAT HE DID THAT, HIS ENTIRE MESSAGE WOULD HAVE BEEN "I AM GROOT."
I ADMIT IT'S LIGHT ON DETAILS.
FANG WILL GO WITH YOU AND CALL FOR SHIPS FOR THE SCIENTISTS AND A SHI'AR STRIKE TEAM TO DEAL WITH THE BROOD.
I WILL. BUT WE WAIT...

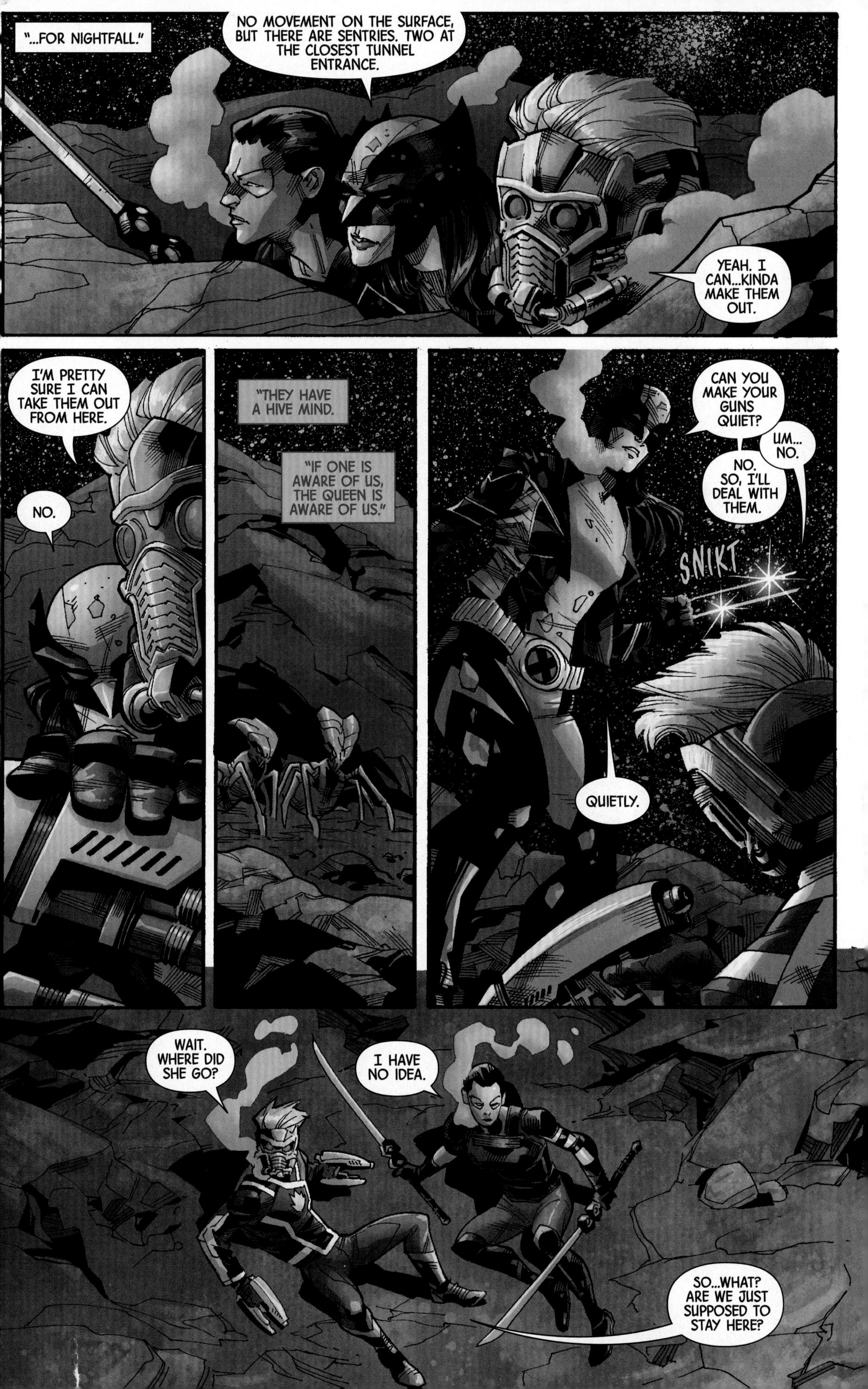
"...FOR NIGHTFALL."
NO MOVEMENT ON THE SURFACE, BUT THERE ARE SENTRIES. TWO AT THE CLOSEST TUNNEL ENTRANCE.
YEAH. I CAN...KINDA MAKE THEM OUT.
I'M PRETTY SURE I CAN TAKE THEM OUT FROM HERE.
NO.
"THEY HAVE A HIVE MIND.
"IF ONE IS AWARE OF US, THE QUEEN IS AWARE OF US."
CAN YOU MAKE YOUR GUNS QUIET?
UM... NO.
NO. SO, I'LL DEAL WITH THEM.
SNIKT
QUIETLY.
WAIT. WHERE DID SHE GO?
I HAVE NO IDEA.
SO...WHAT? ARE WE JUST SUPPOSED TO STAY HERE?

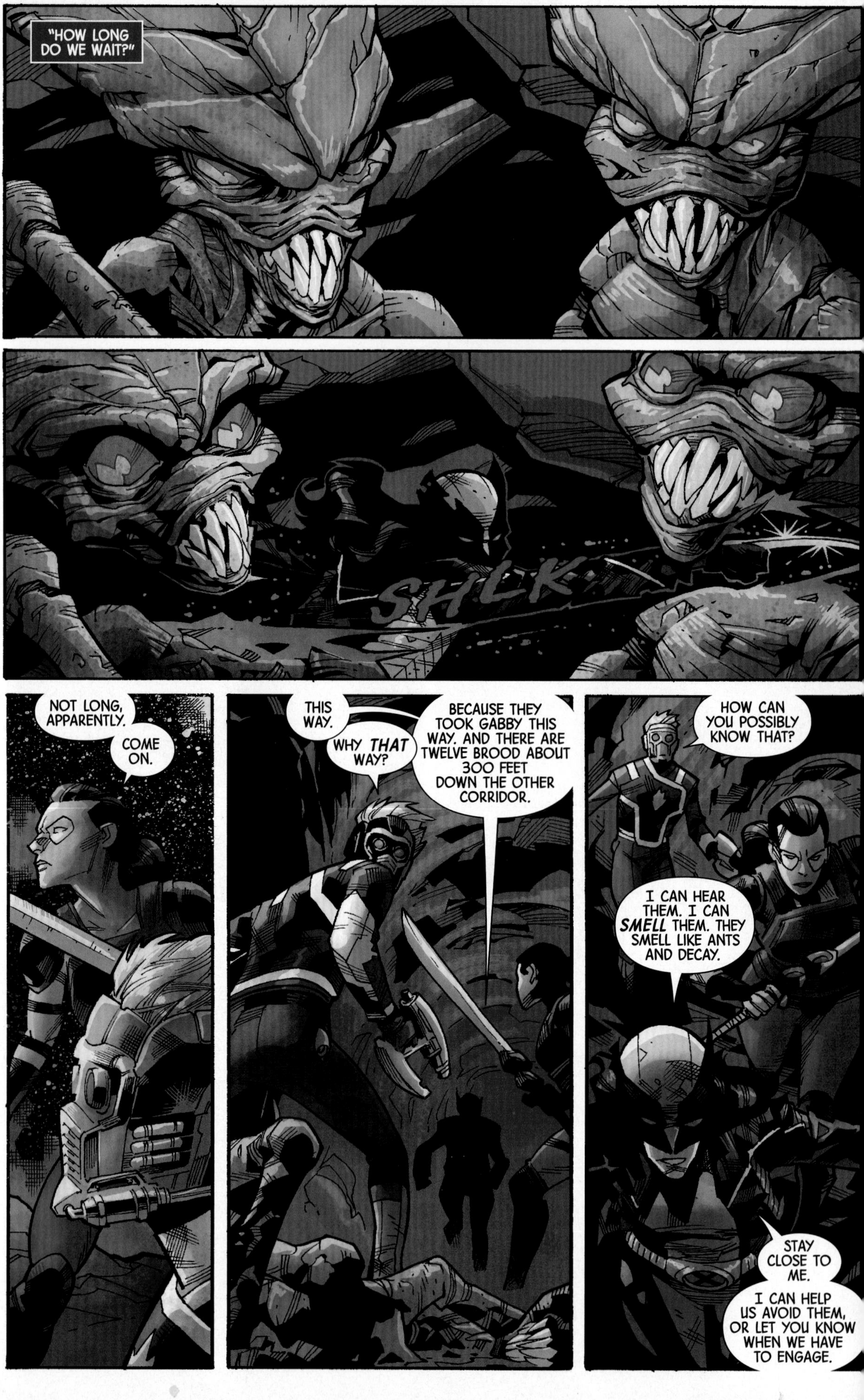
"HOW LONG DO WE WAIT?"
SHLK
NOT LONG, APPARENTLY.
COME ON.
THIS WAY.
WHY *THAT* WAY?
BECAUSE THEY TOOK GABBY THIS WAY. AND THERE ARE TWELVE BROOD ABOUT 300 FEET DOWN THE OTHER CORRIDOR.
HOW CAN YOU POSSIBLY KNOW THAT?
I CAN HEAR THEM. I CAN ***SMELL*** THEM. THEY SMELL LIKE ANTS AND DECAY.
STAY CLOSE TO ME.
I CAN HELP US AVOID THEM, OR LET YOU KNOW WHEN WE HAVE TO ENGAGE.

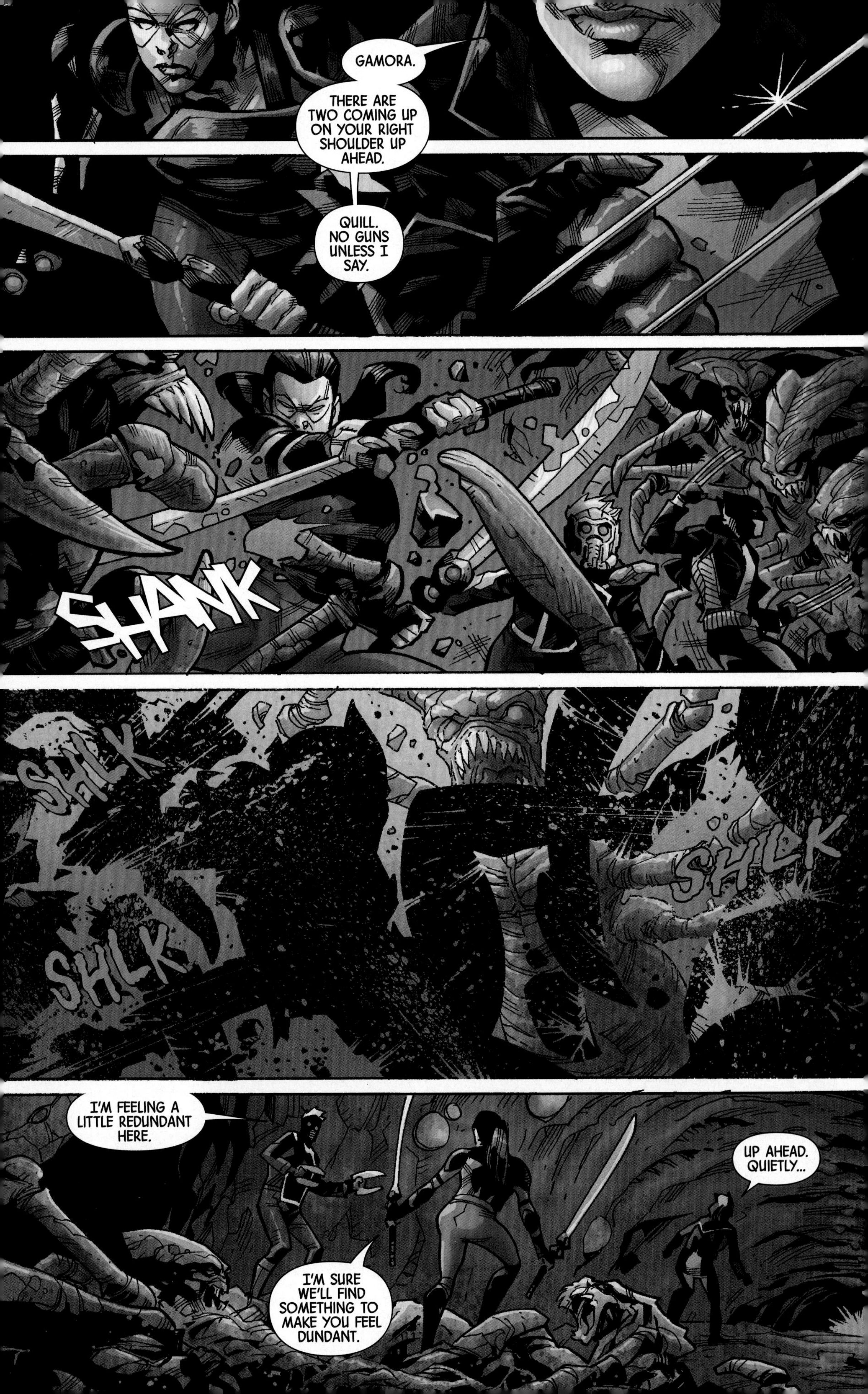
GAMORA.
THERE ARE TWO COMING UP ON YOUR RIGHT SHOULDER UP AHEAD.
QUILL. NO GUNS UNLESS I SAY.
SHANK
SHLK
SHLK
SHLK
I'M FEELING A LITTLE REDUNDANT HERE.
I'M SURE WE'LL FIND SOMETHING TO MAKE YOU FEEL DUNDANT.
UP AHEAD. QUIETLY...

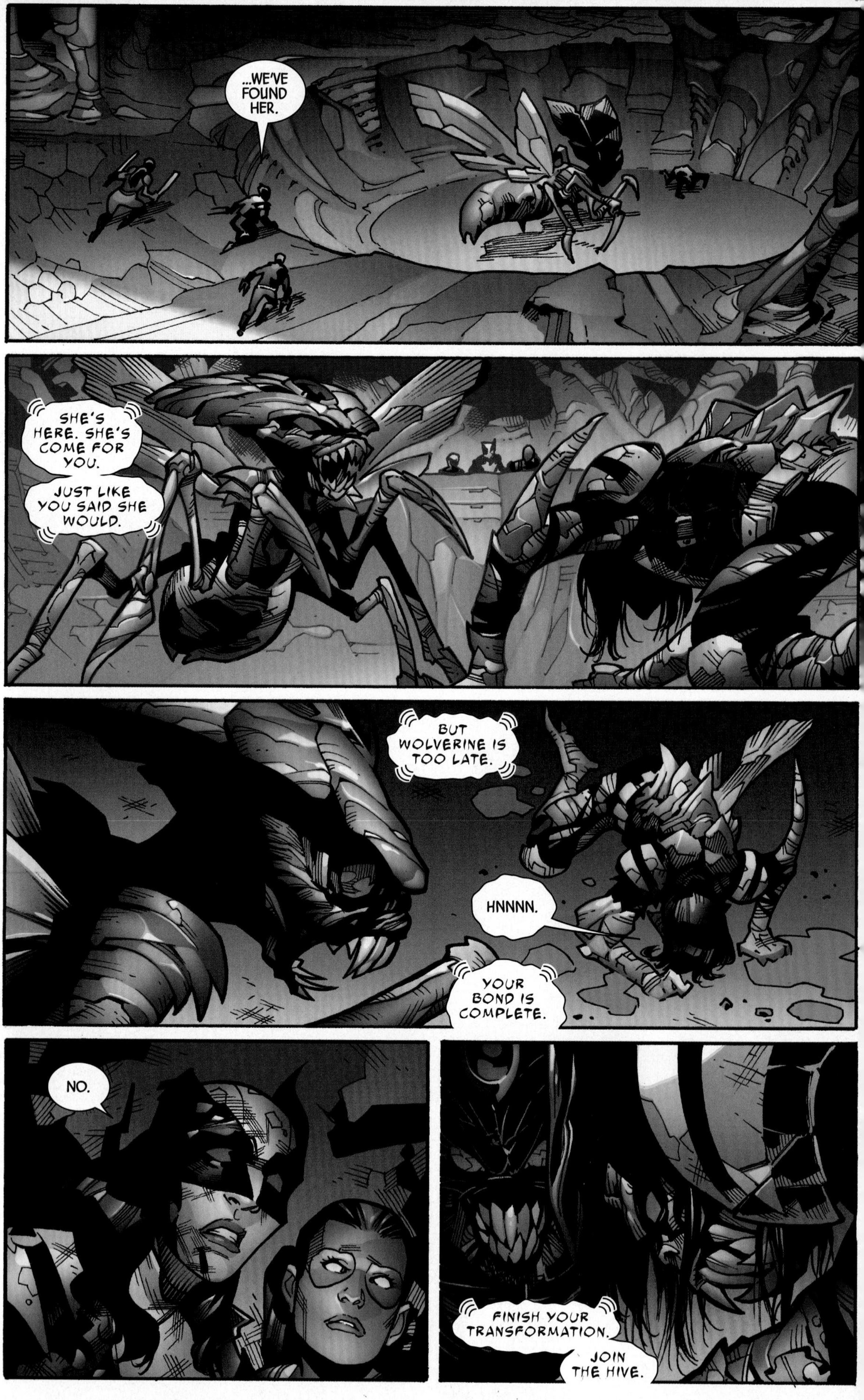
...WE'VE FOUND HER.
SHE'S HERE. SHE'S COME FOR YOU.
JUST LIKE YOU SAID SHE WOULD.
BUT WOLVERINE IS TOO LATE.
HNNNN.
YOUR BOND IS COMPLETE.
NO.
FINISH YOUR TRANSFORMATION.
JOIN THE HIVE.

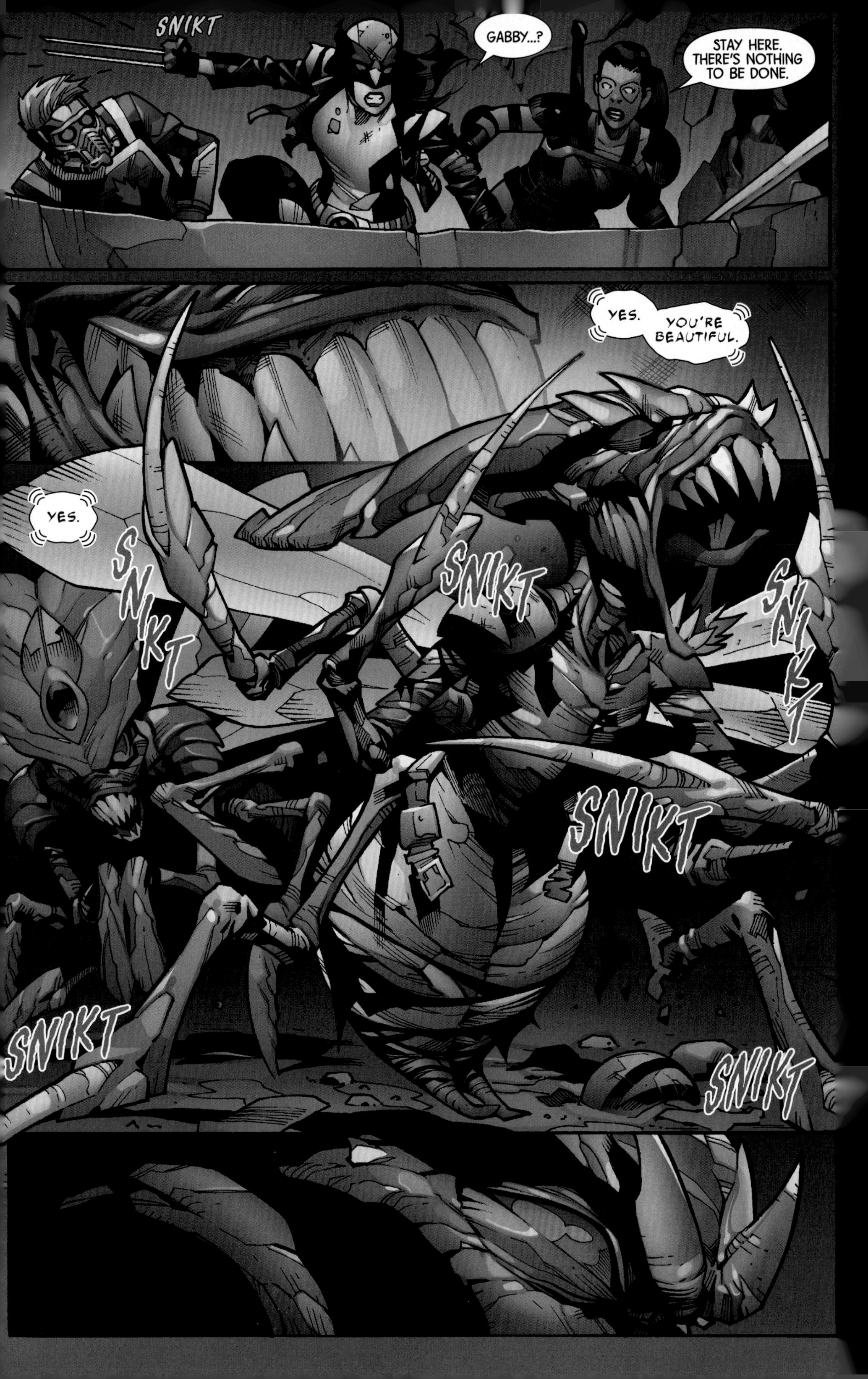
SNIKT
GABBY...?
STAY HERE. THERE'S NOTHING TO BE DONE.
YES.
YOU'RE BEAUTIFUL.
YES.
SNIKT
SNIKT
SNIKT
SNIKT
SNIKT
SNIKT

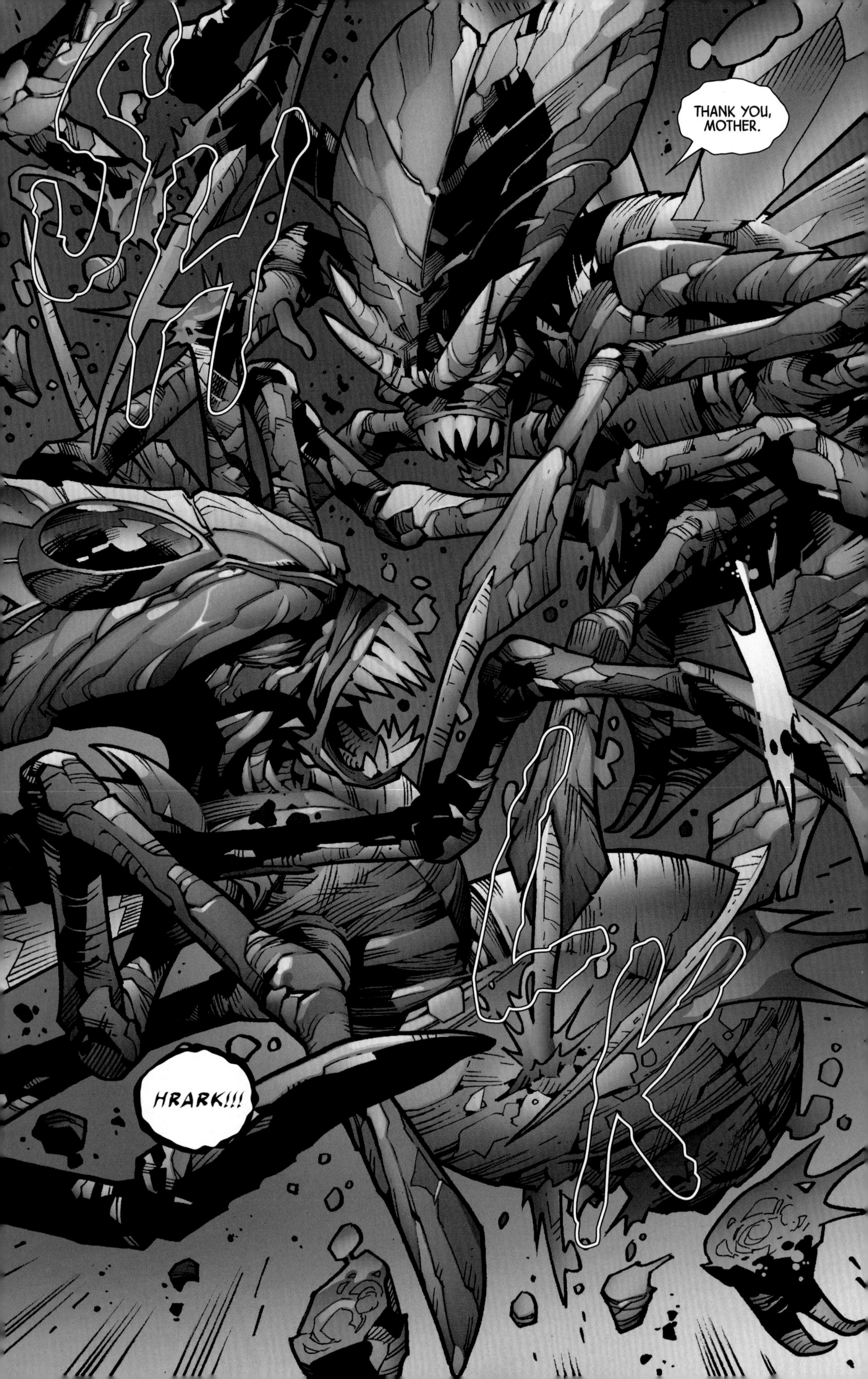
THANK YOU, MOTHER.
HRARK!!!

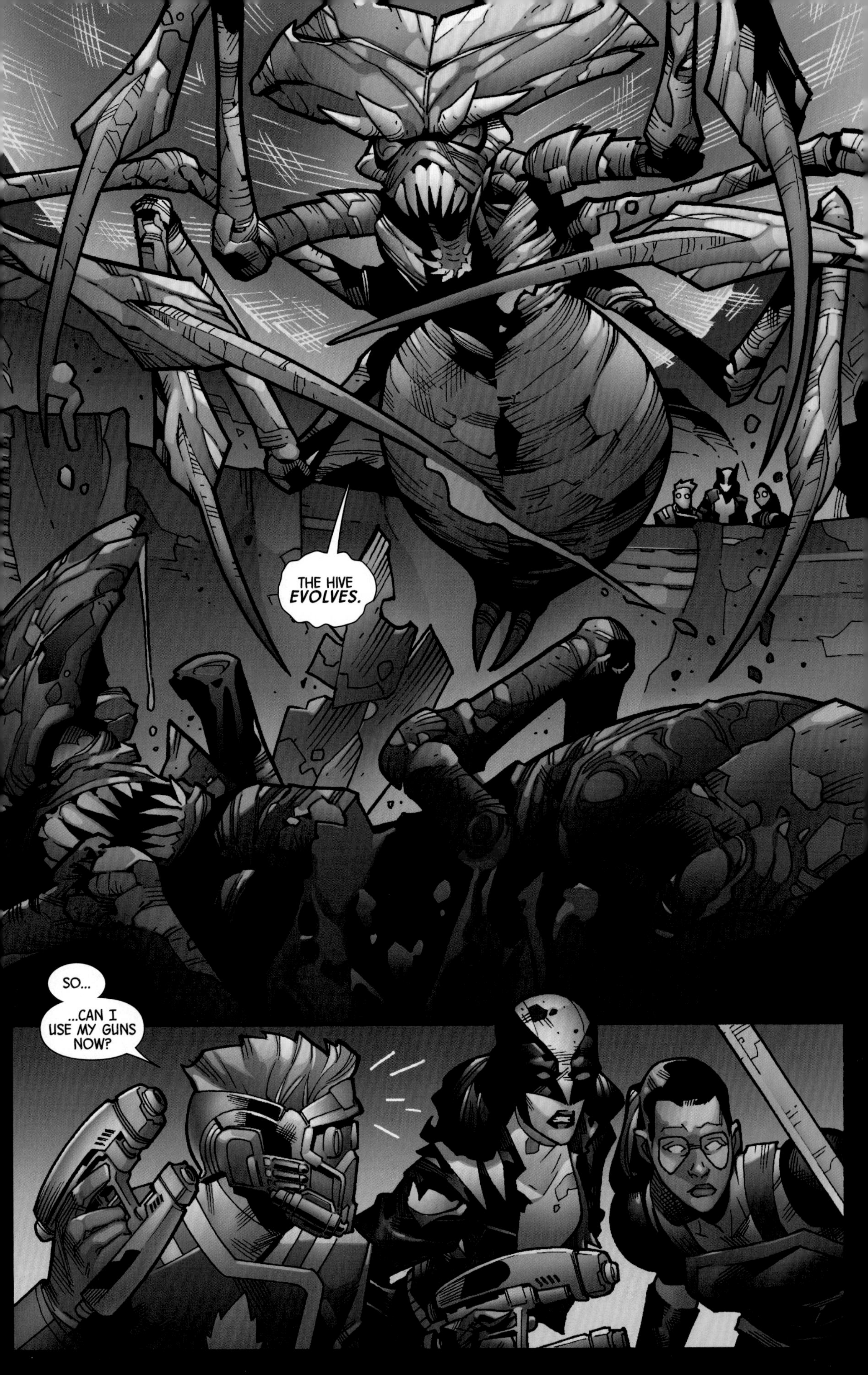
THE HIVE EVOLVES.
SO...
...CAN I USE MY GUNS NOW?

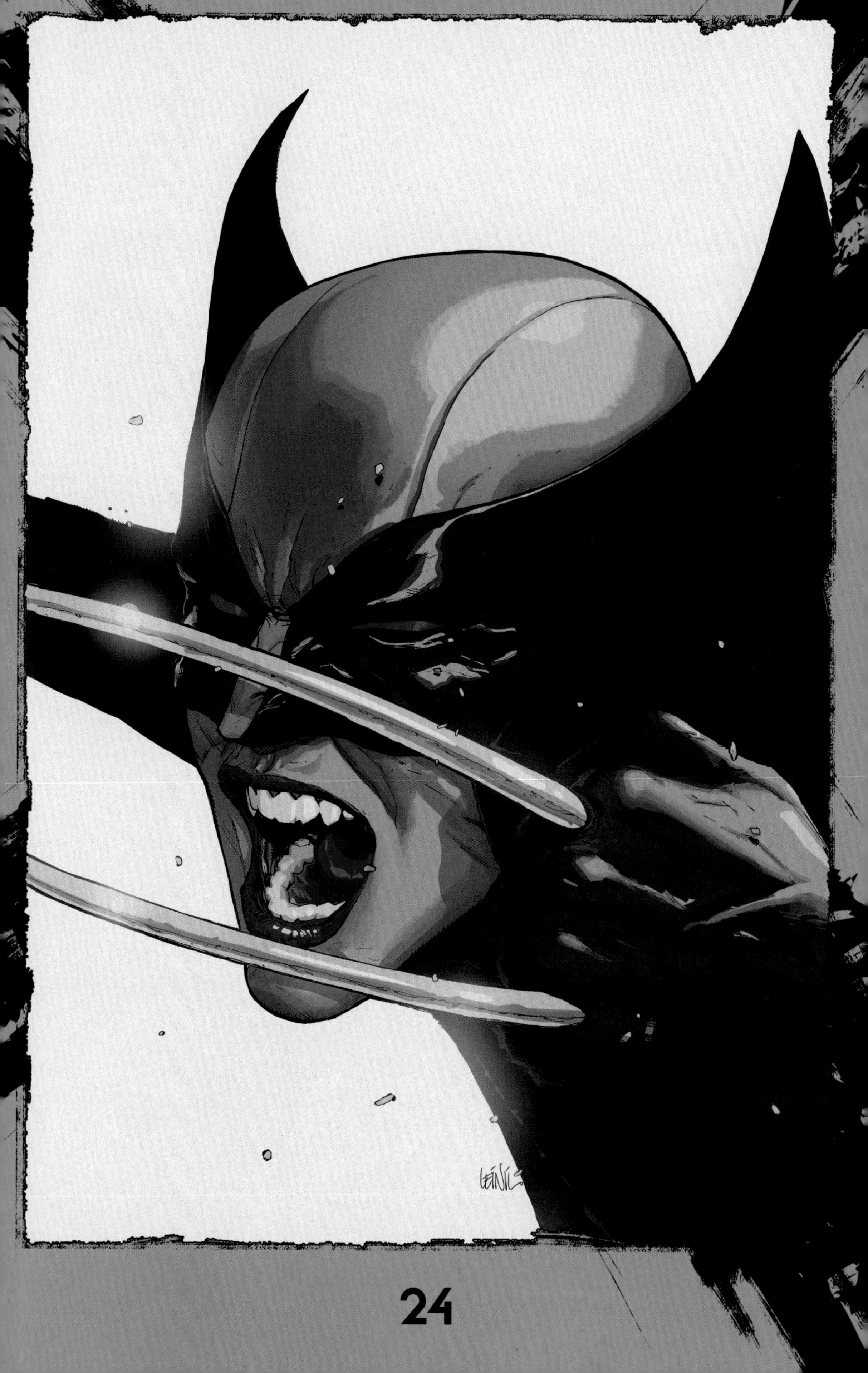

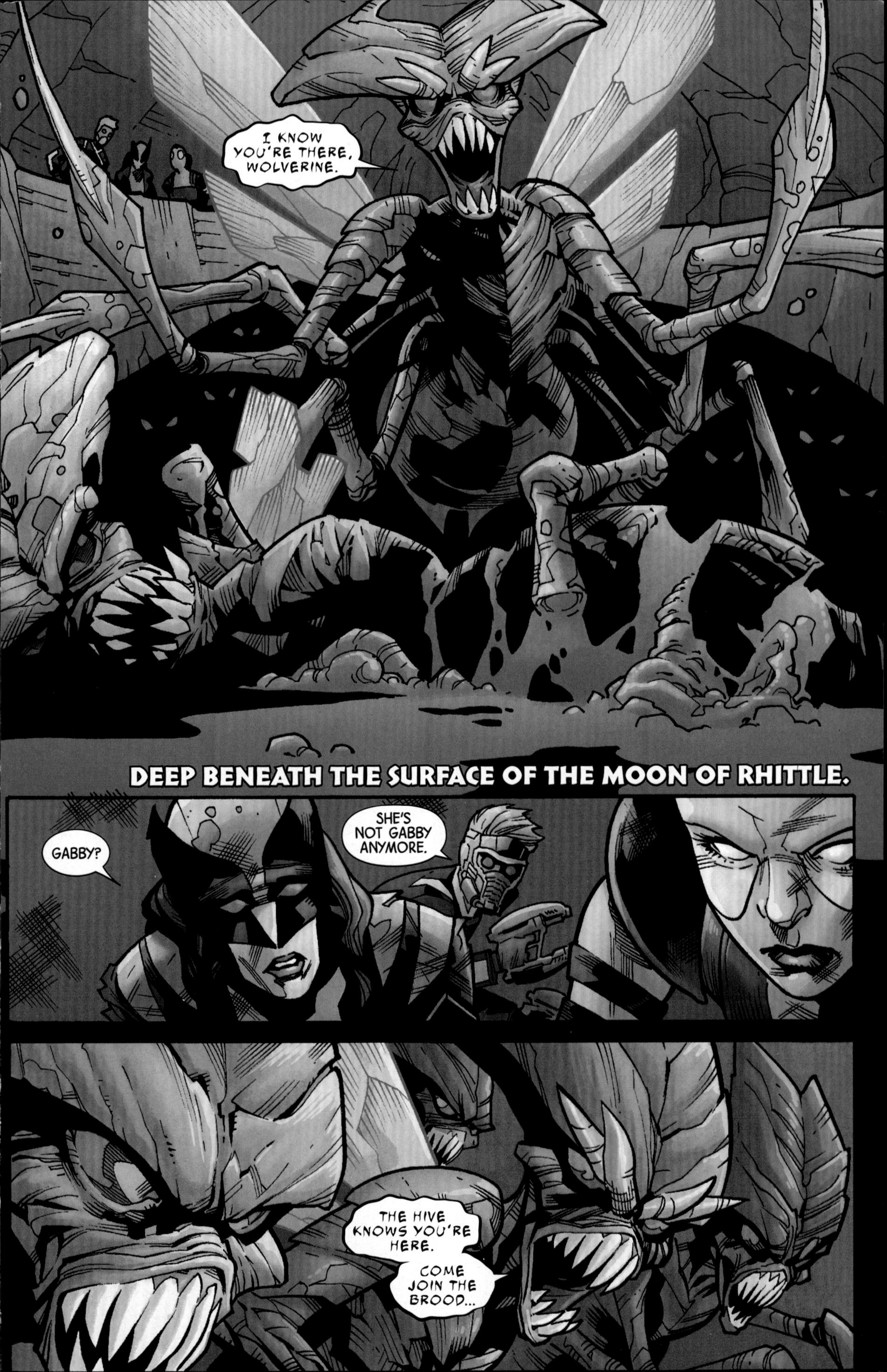
I KNOW YOU'RE THERE, WOLVERINE.
DEEP BENEATH THE SURFACE OF THE MOON OF RHITTLE.
GABBY?
SHE'S NOT GABBY ANYMORE.
THE HIVE KNOWS YOU'RE HERE.
COME JOIN THE BROOD...

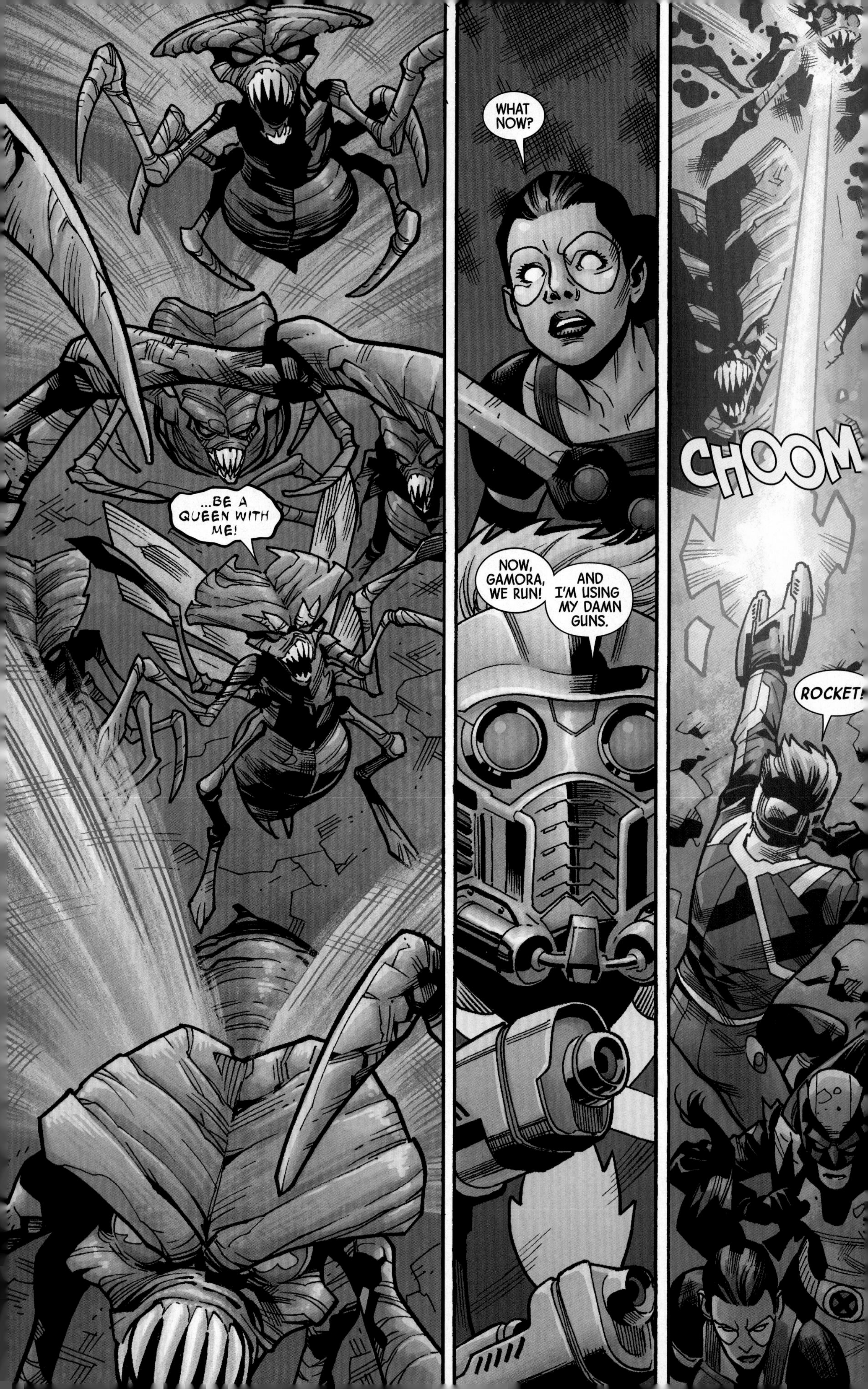
...BE A QUEEN WITH ME!
WHAT NOW?
NOW, GAMORA, WE RUN!
AND I'M USING MY DAMN GUNS.
CHOOM
ROCKET!

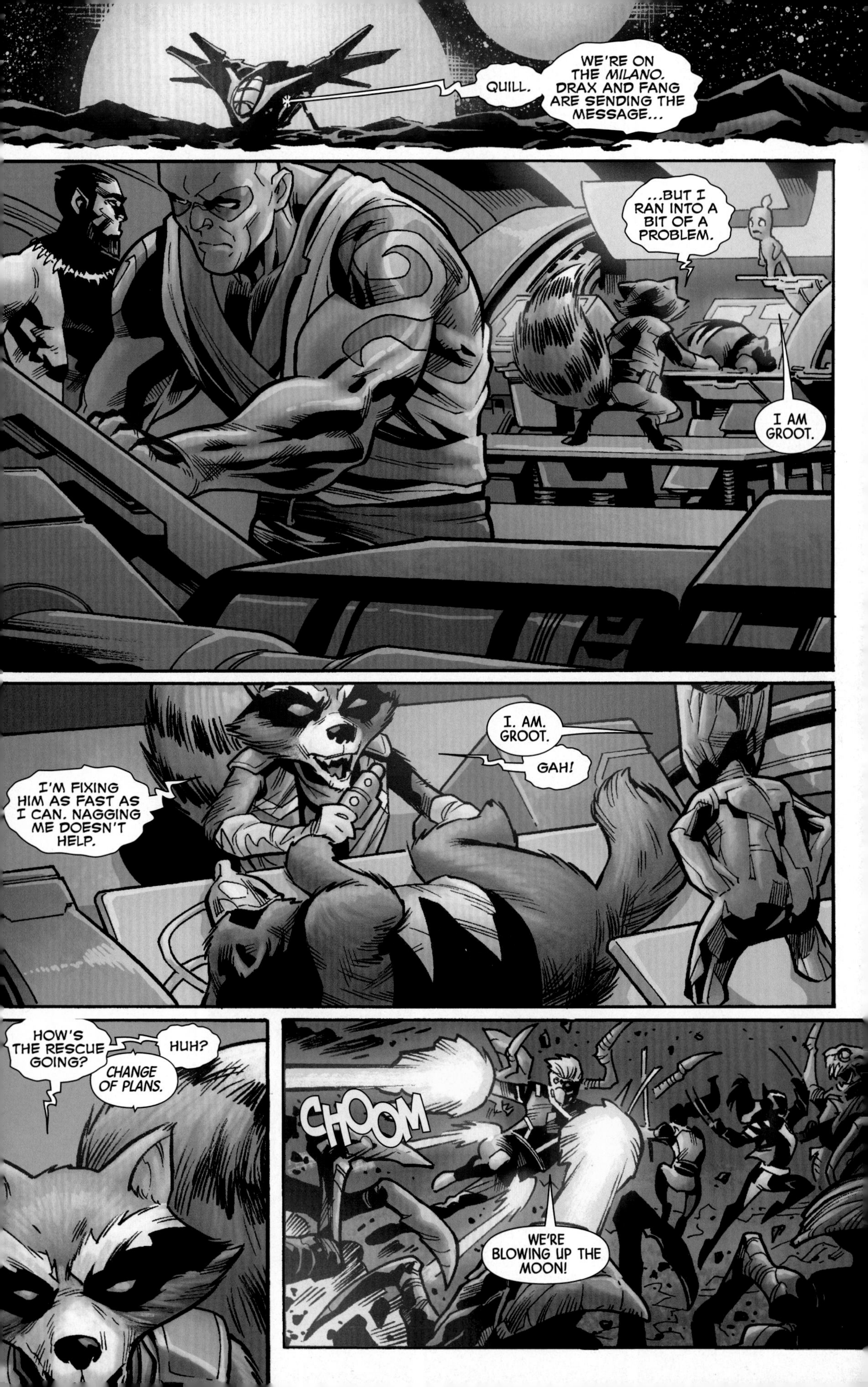
QUILL.
WE'RE ON THE MILANO. DRAX AND FANG ARE SENDING THE MESSAGE...
...BUT I RAN INTO A BIT OF A PROBLEM.
I AM GROOT.
I. AM. GROOT.
GAH!
I'M FIXING HIM AS FAST AS I CAN. NAGGING ME DOESN'T HELP.
HOW'S THE RESCUE GOING?
HUH?
CHANGE OF PLANS.
CHOOM
WE'RE BLOWING UP THE MOON!

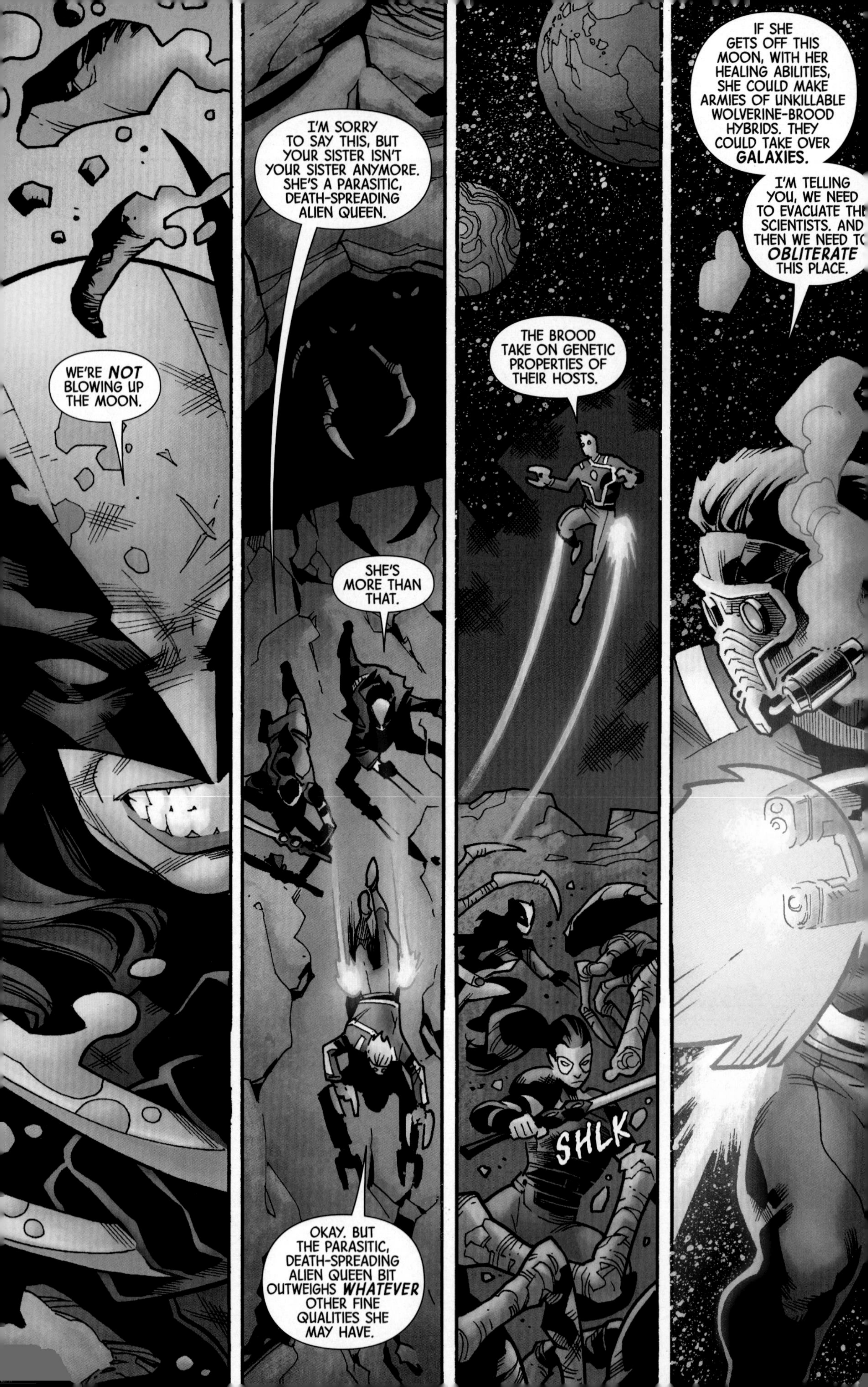
WE'RE *NOT* BLOWING UP THE MOON.
I'M SORRY TO SAY THIS, BUT YOUR SISTER ISN'T YOUR SISTER ANYMORE. SHE'S A PARASITIC, DEATH-SPREADING ALIEN QUEEN.
SHE'S MORE THAN THAT.
OKAY. BUT THE PARASITIC, DEATH-SPREADING ALIEN QUEEN BIT OUTWEIGHS *WHATEVER* OTHER FINE QUALITIES SHE MAY HAVE.
THE BROOD TAKE ON GENETIC PROPERTIES OF THEIR HOSTS.
SHLK
IF SHE GETS OFF THIS MOON, WITH HER HEALING ABILITIES, SHE COULD MAKE ARMIES OF UNKILLABLE WOLVERINE-BROOD HYBRIDS. THEY COULD TAKE OVER **GALAXIES.**
I'M TELLING YOU, WE NEED TO EVACUATE THE SCIENTISTS. AND THEN WE NEED TO ***OBLITERATE*** THIS PLACE.

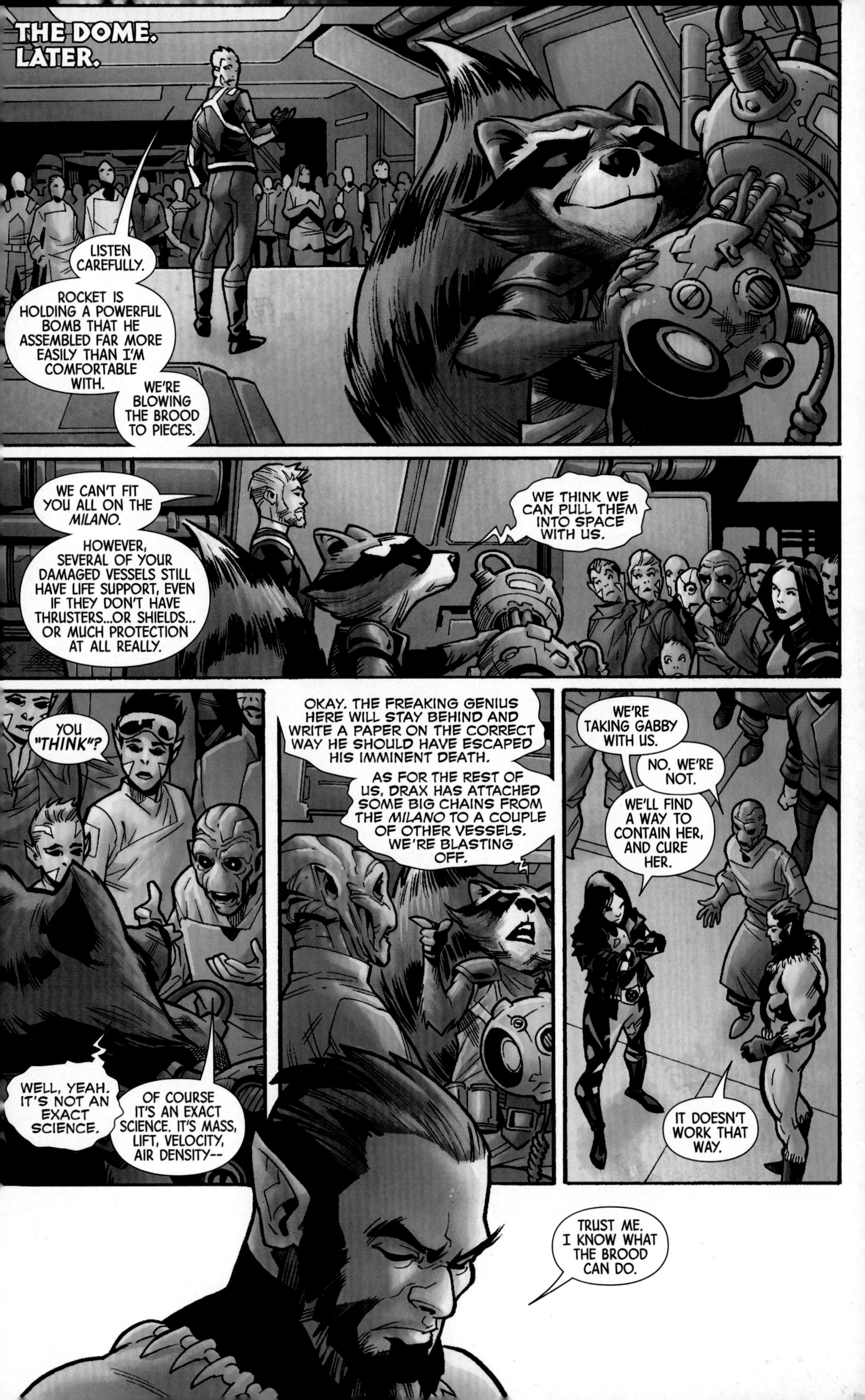
THE DOME. LATER.
LISTEN CAREFULLY.
ROCKET IS HOLDING A POWERFUL BOMB THAT HE ASSEMBLED FAR MORE EASILY THAN I'M COMFORTABLE WITH.
WE'RE BLOWING THE BROOD TO PIECES.
WE CAN'T FIT YOU ALL ON THE *MILANO.*
HOWEVER, SEVERAL OF YOUR DAMAGED VESSELS STILL HAVE LIFE SUPPORT, EVEN IF THEY DON'T HAVE THRUSTERS...OR SHIELDS... OR MUCH PROTECTION AT ALL REALLY.
WE THINK WE CAN PULL THEM INTO SPACE WITH US.
YOU "*THINK*"?
WELL, YEAH. IT'S NOT AN EXACT SCIENCE.
OF COURSE IT'S AN EXACT SCIENCE. IT'S MASS, LIFT, VELOCITY, AIR DENSITY--
OKAY. THE FREAKING GENIUS HERE WILL **STAY** BEHIND AND WRITE A PAPER ON THE CORRECT WAY HE SHOULD HAVE ESCAPED HIS IMMINENT DEATH.
AS FOR THE REST OF US, DRAX HAS ATTACHED SOME BIG CHAINS FROM THE *MILANO* TO A COUPLE OF OTHER VESSELS. WE'RE BLASTING OFF.
WE'RE TAKING GABBY WITH US.
NO. WE'RE NOT.
WE'LL FIND A WAY TO CONTAIN HER, AND CURE HER.
IT DOESN'T WORK THAT WAY.
TRUST ME. I KNOW WHAT THE BROOD CAN DO.

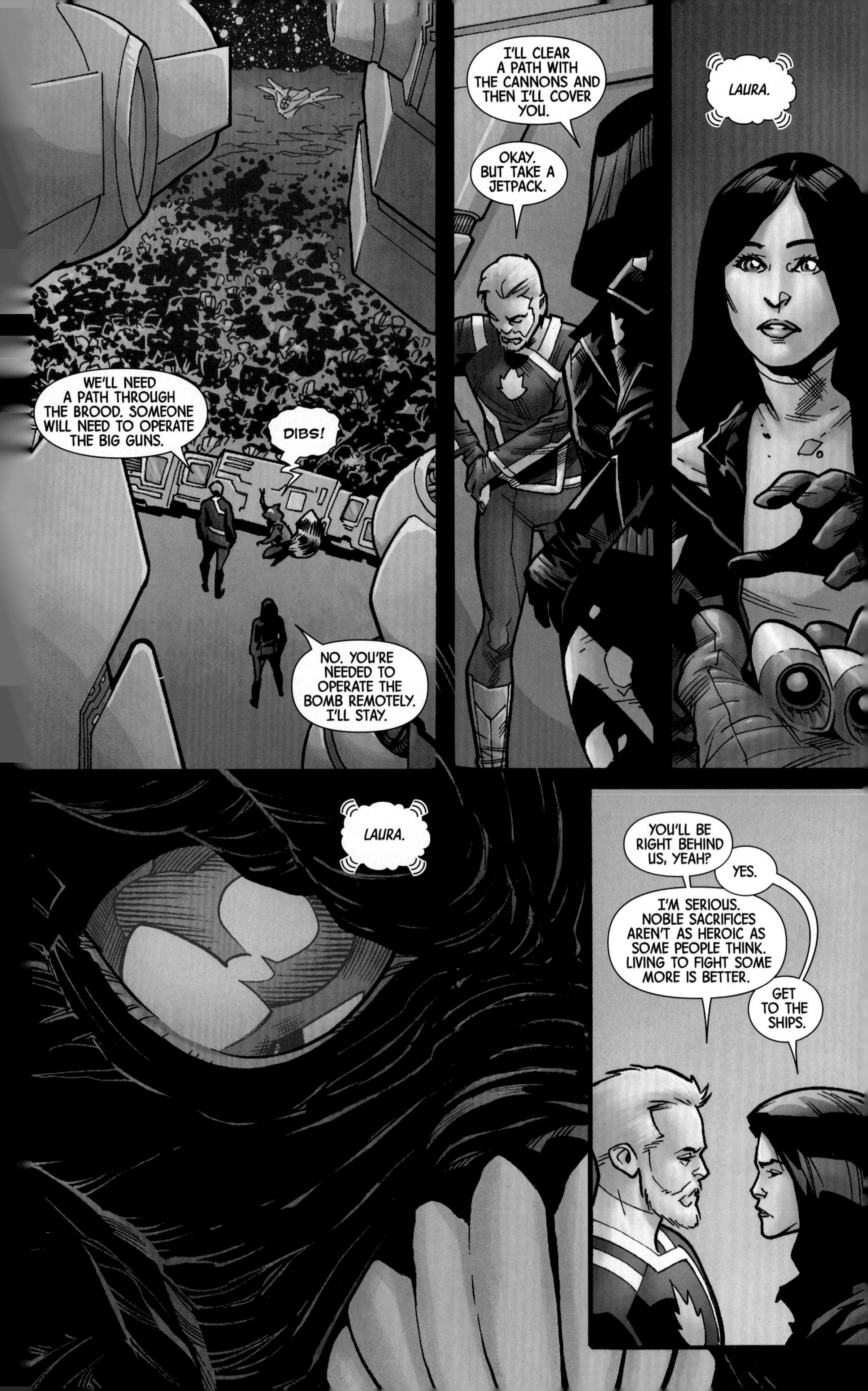
WE'LL NEED A PATH THROUGH THE BROOD. SOMEONE WILL NEED TO OPERATE THE BIG GUNS.
DIBS!
NO. YOU'RE NEEDED TO OPERATE THE BOMB REMOTELY. I'LL STAY.
I'LL CLEAR A PATH WITH THE CANNONS AND THEN I'LL COVER YOU.
OKAY. BUT TAKE A JETPACK.
LAURA.
LAURA.
YOU'LL BE RIGHT BEHIND US, YEAH?
YES.
I'M SERIOUS. NOBLE SACRIFICES AREN'T AS HEROIC AS SOME PEOPLE THINK. LIVING TO FIGHT SOME MORE IS BETTER.
GET TO THE SHIPS.

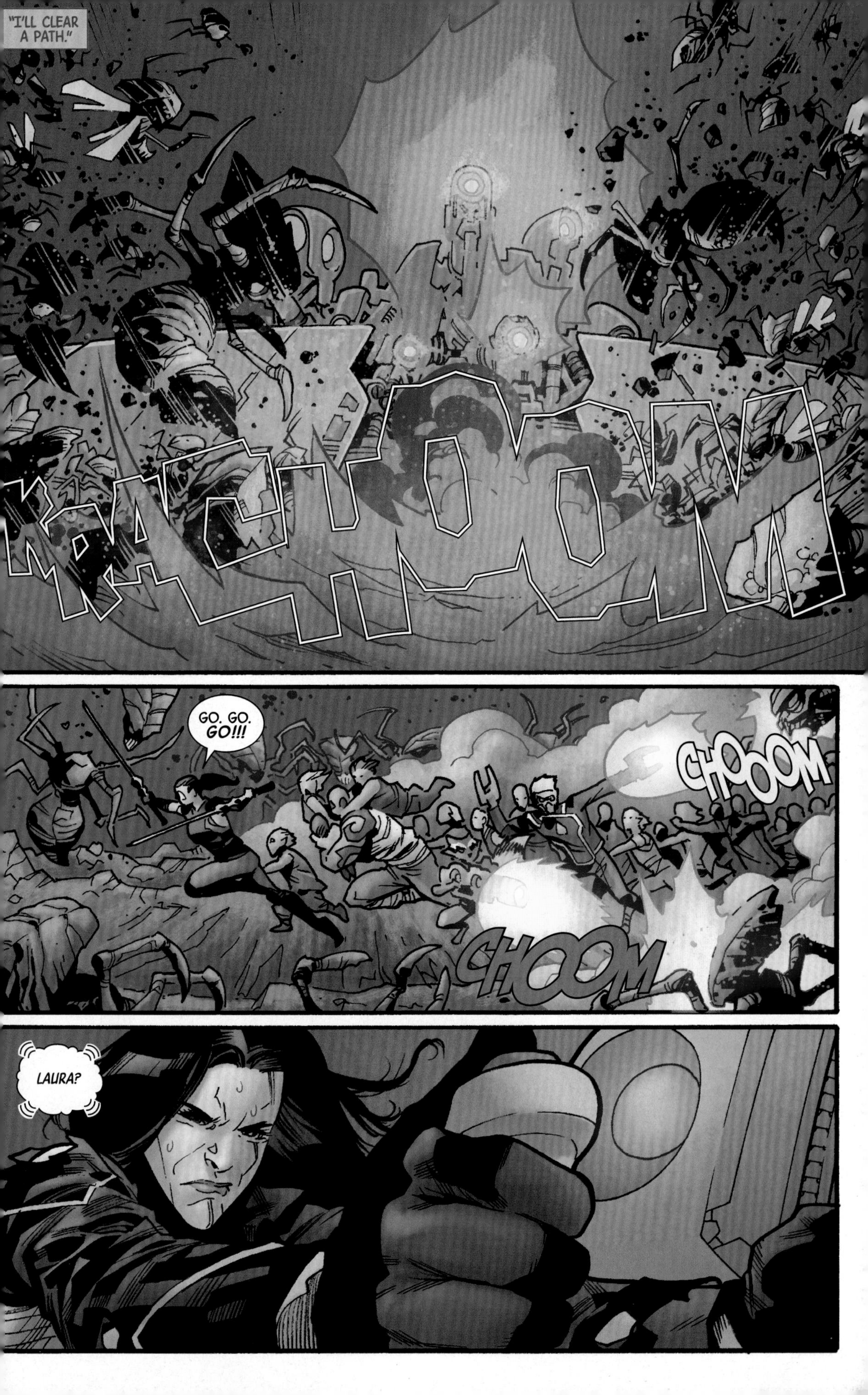
"I'LL CLEAR A PATH."
KRACHOOOM
GO. GO. GO!!!
CHOOOM
CHOOOM
LAURA?

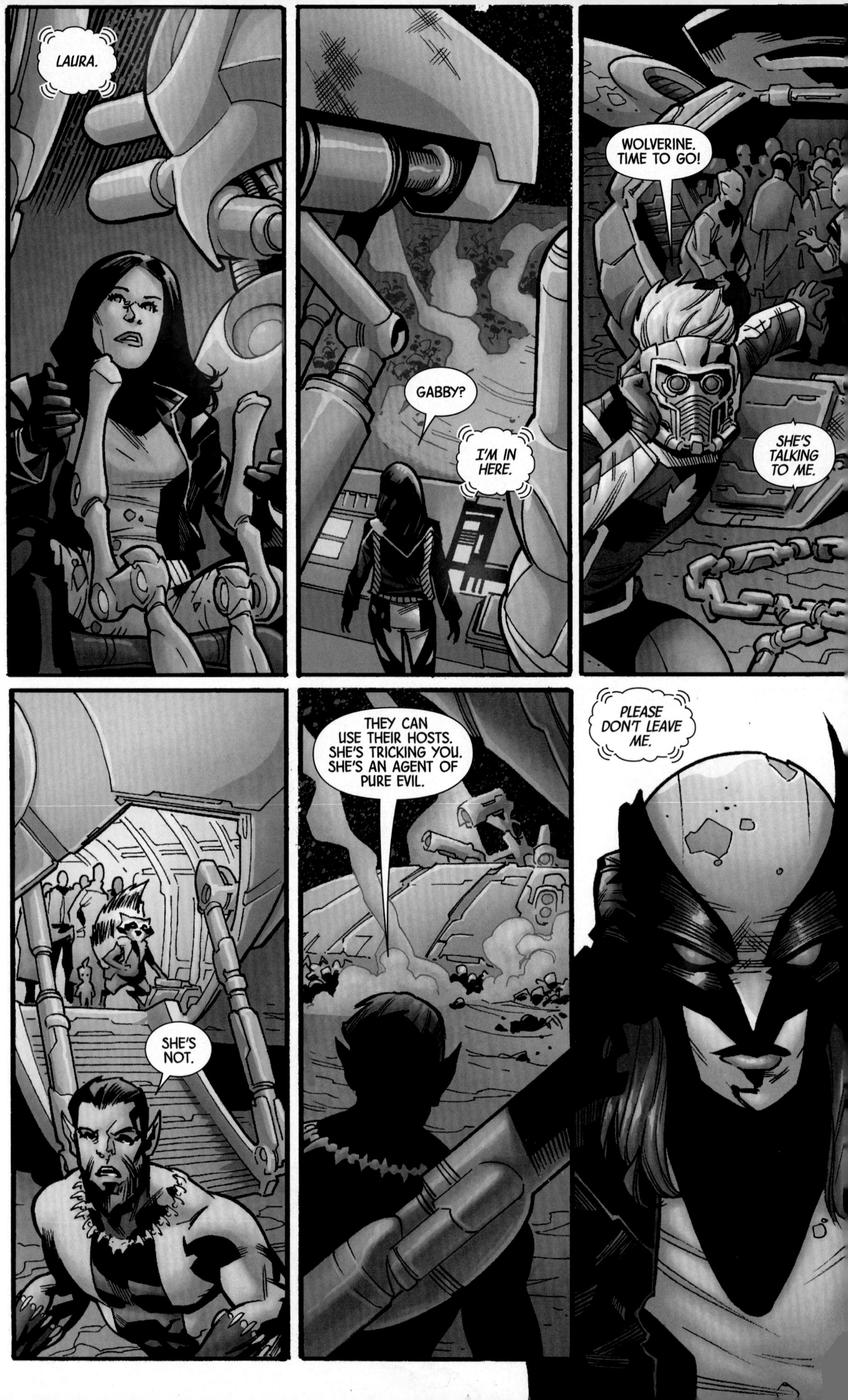
LAURA.
GABBY?
I'M IN HERE.
WOLVERINE. TIME TO GO!
SHE'S TALKING TO ME.
SHE'S NOT.
THEY CAN USE THEIR HOSTS. SHE'S TRICKING YOU. SHE'S AN AGENT OF PURE EVIL.
PLEASE DON'T LEAVE ME.

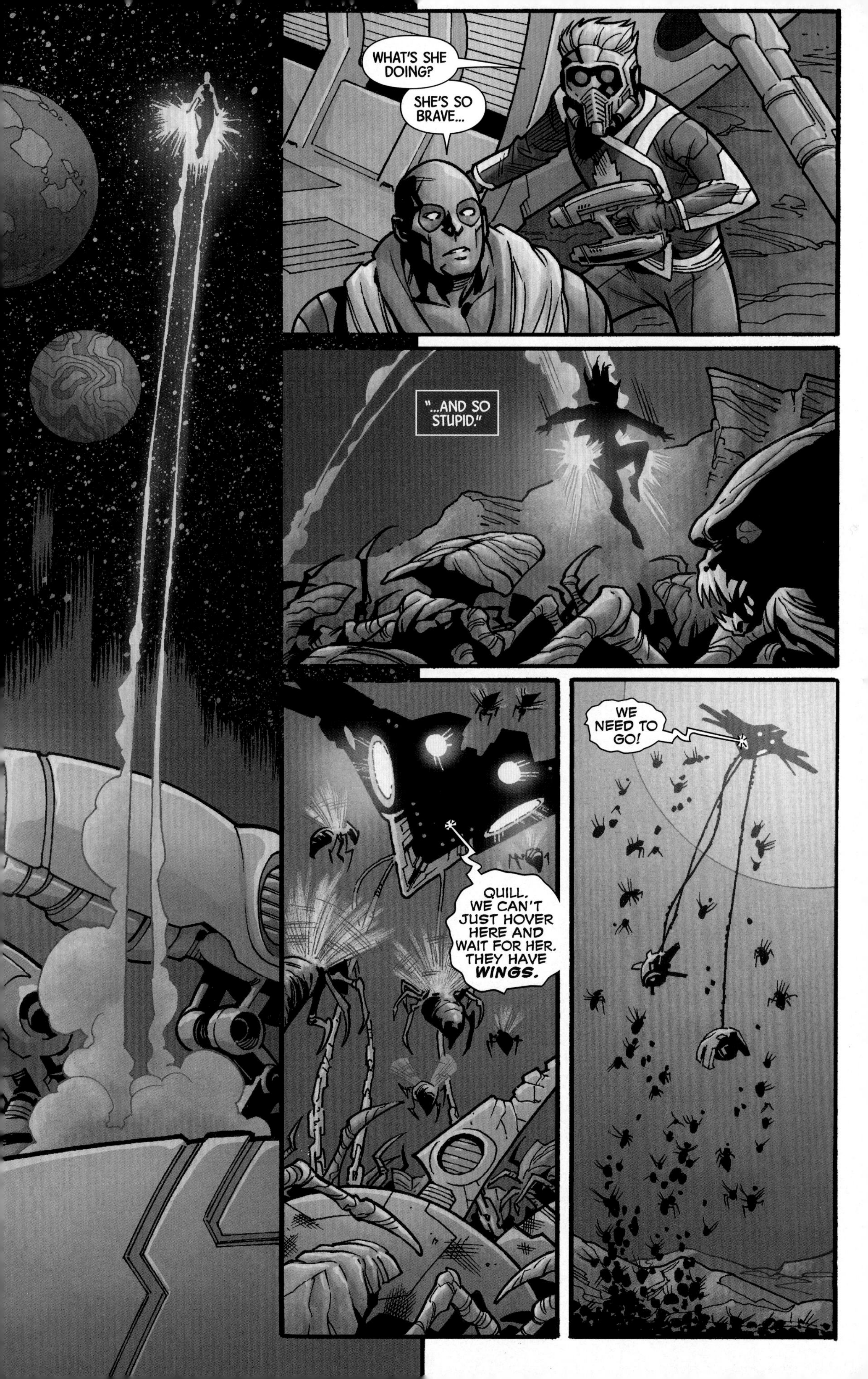
WHAT'S SHE DOING?
SHE'S SO BRAVE...
"...AND SO STUPID."
QUILL. WE CAN'T JUST HOVER HERE AND WAIT FOR HER. THEY HAVE WINGS.
WE NEED TO GO!

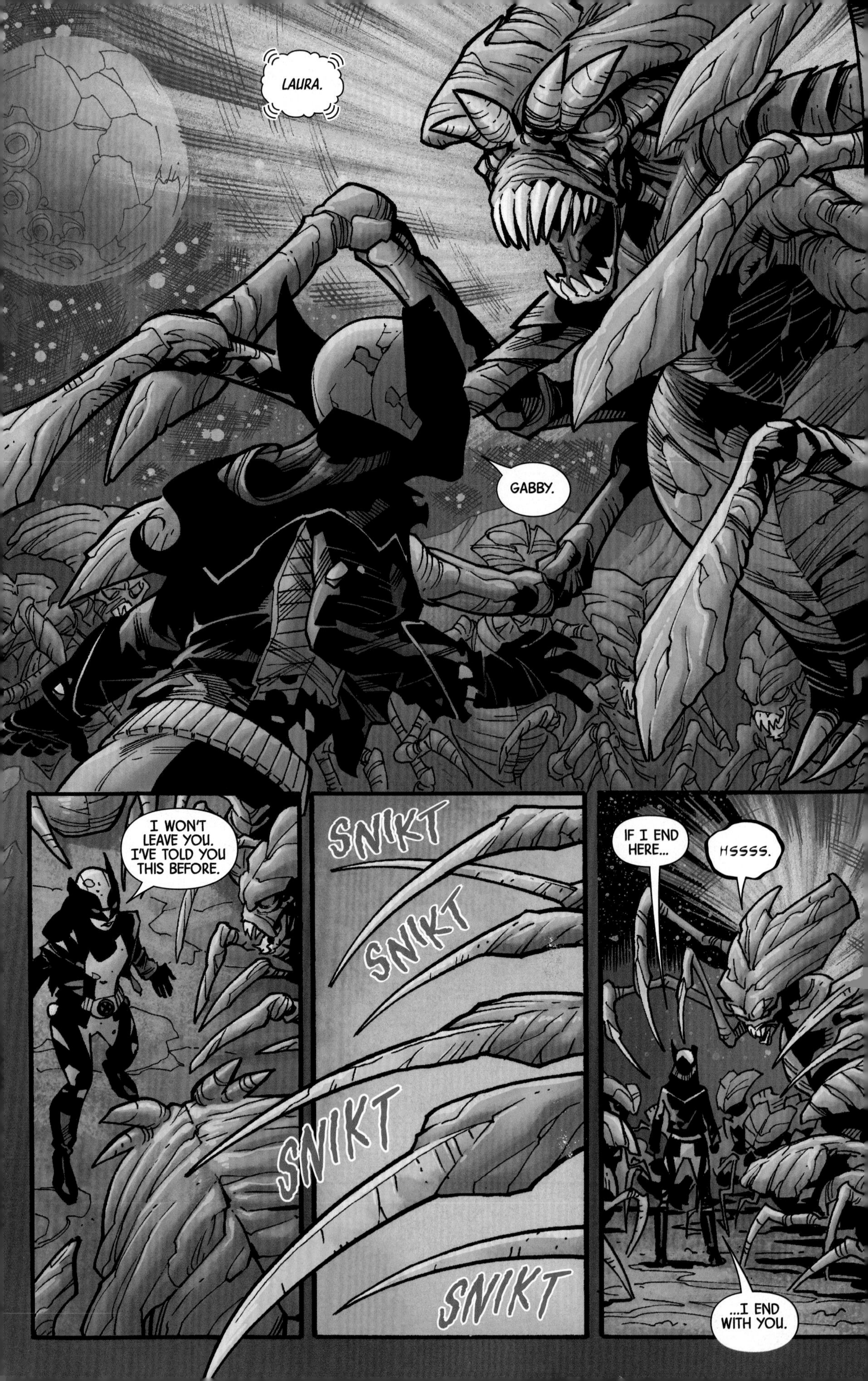
LAURA.
GABBY.
I WON'T LEAVE YOU. I'VE TOLD YOU THIS BEFORE.
SNIKT
SNIKT
SNIKT
SNIKT
SNIKT
IF I END HERE...
HSSSS.
...I END WITH YOU.

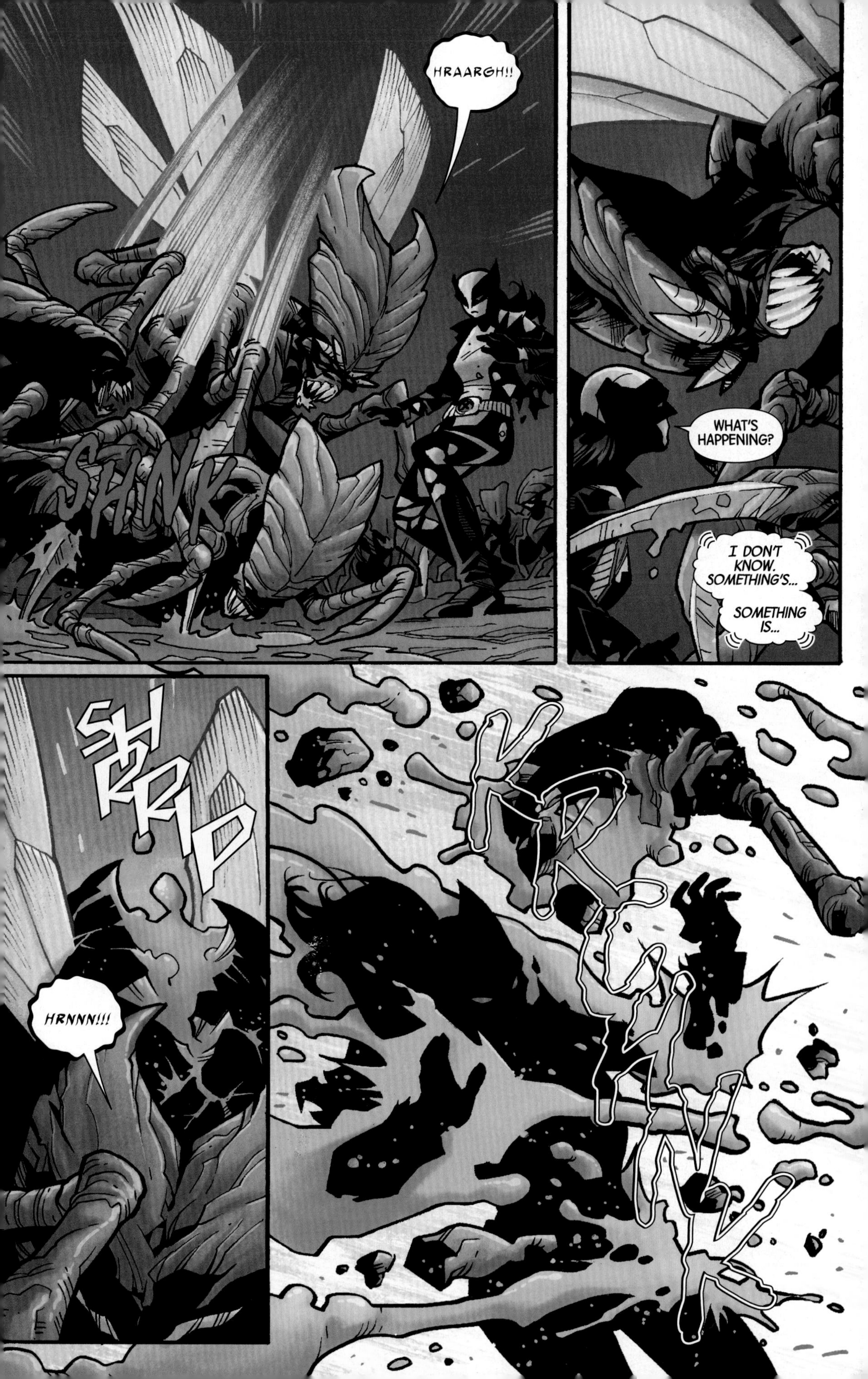
HRAARGH!!
SHINK
WHAT'S HAPPENING?
I DON'T KNOW. SOMETHING'S...
SOMETHING IS...
SHRRIP
HRNNN!!!
KRUNK

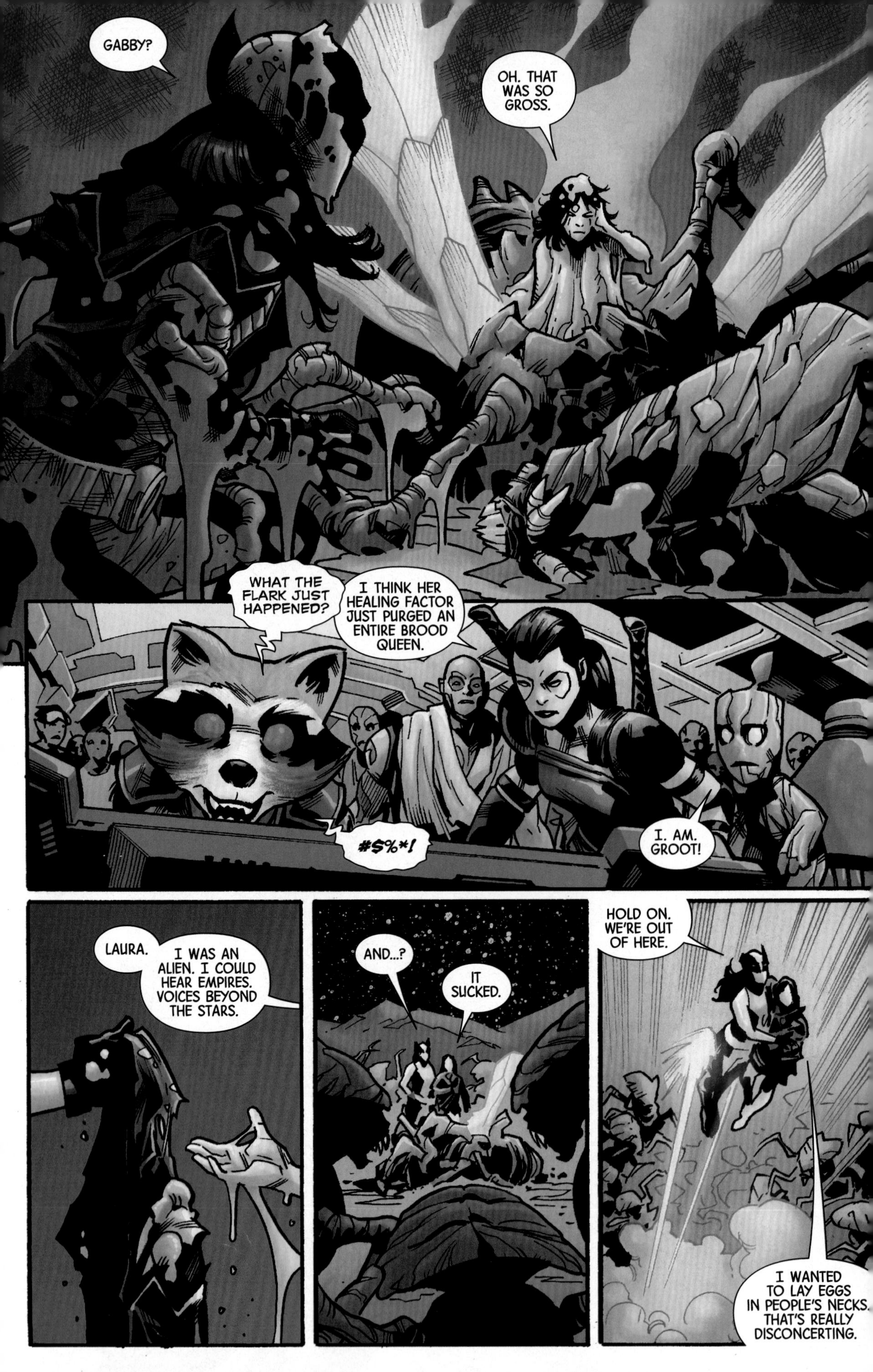
GABBY?
OH. THAT WAS SO GROSS.
WHAT THE FLARK JUST HAPPENED?
I THINK HER HEALING FACTOR JUST PURGED AN ENTIRE BROOD QUEEN.
#$%*!
I. AM. GROOT!
LAURA.
I WAS AN ALIEN. I COULD HEAR EMPIRES. VOICES BEYOND THE STARS.
AND...?
IT SUCKED.
HOLD ON. WE'RE OUT OF HERE.
I WANTED TO LAY EGGS IN PEOPLE'S NECKS. THAT'S REALLY DISCONCERTING.

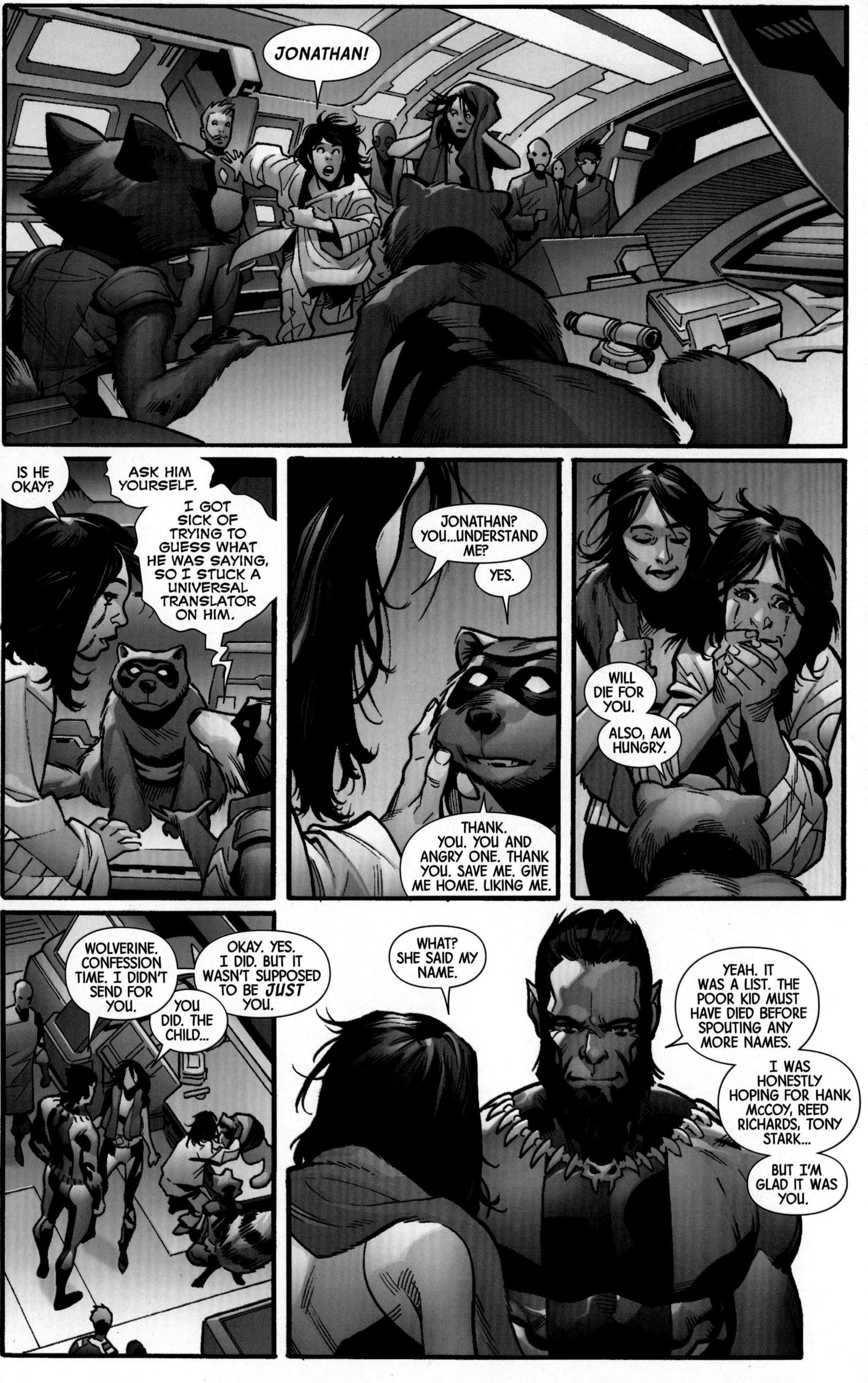
JONATHAN!
IS HE OKAY?
ASK HIM YOURSELF.
I GOT SICK OF TRYING TO GUESS WHAT HE WAS SAYING, SO I STUCK A UNIVERSAL TRANSLATOR ON HIM.
JONATHAN? YOU...UNDERSTAND ME?
YES.
THANK. YOU. YOU AND ANGRY ONE. THANK YOU. SAVE ME. GIVE ME HOME. LIKING ME.
WILL DIE FOR YOU.
ALSO, AM HUNGRY.
WOLVERINE. CONFESSION TIME. I DIDN'T SEND FOR YOU.
YOU DID. THE CHILD...
OKAY. YES. I DID. BUT IT WASN'T SUPPOSED TO BE JUST YOU.
WHAT? SHE SAID MY NAME.
YEAH. IT WAS A LIST. THE POOR KID MUST HAVE DIED BEFORE SPOUTING ANY MORE NAMES.
I WAS HONESTLY HOPING FOR HANK McCOY, REED RICHARDS, TONY STARK...
BUT I'M GLAD IT WAS YOU.

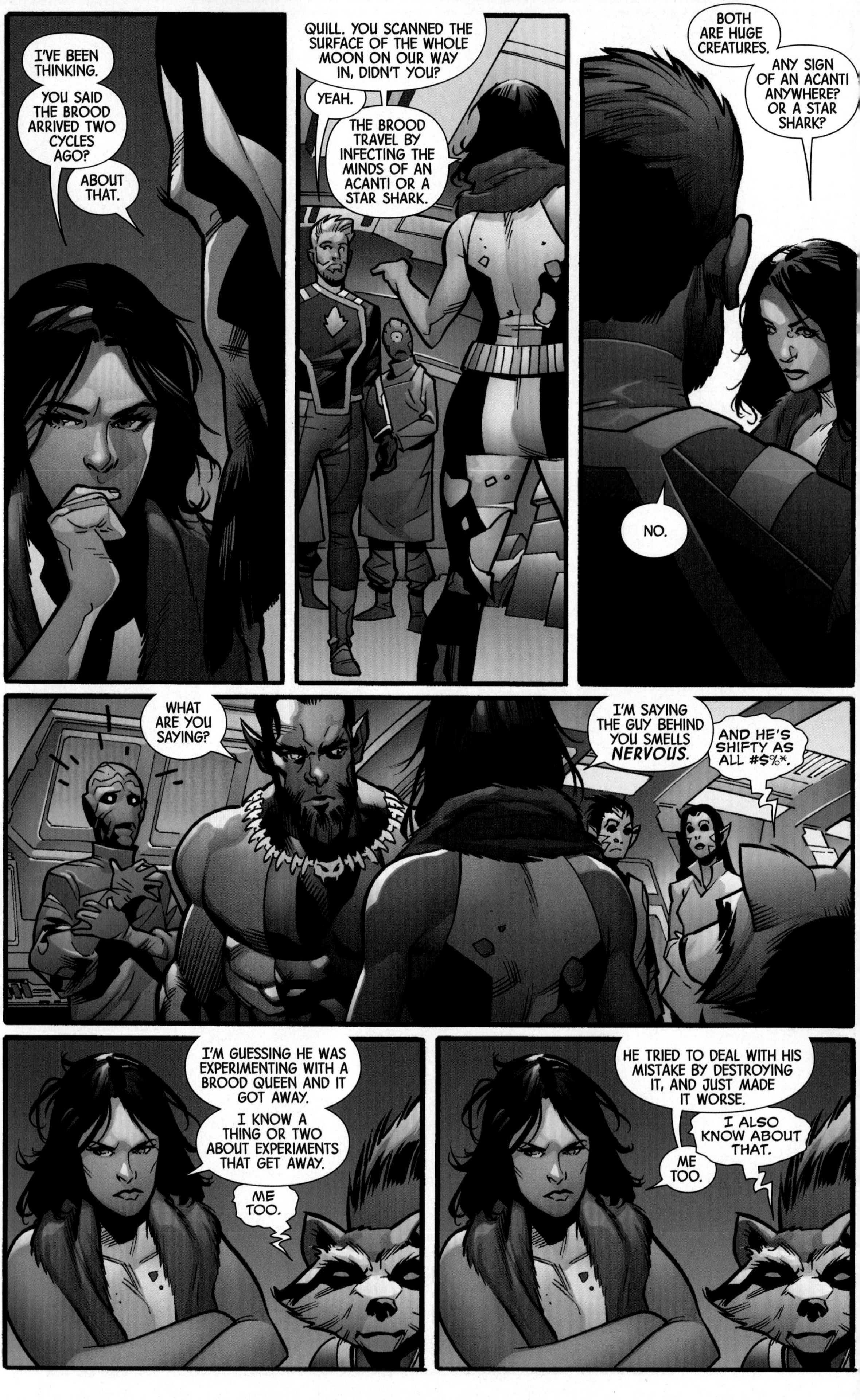
I'VE BEEN THINKING.
YOU SAID THE BROOD ARRIVED TWO CYCLES AGO?
ABOUT THAT.
QUILL. YOU SCANNED THE SURFACE OF THE WHOLE MOON ON OUR WAY IN, DIDN'T YOU?
YEAH.
THE BROOD TRAVEL BY INFECTING THE MINDS OF AN ACANTI OR A STAR SHARK.
BOTH ARE HUGE CREATURES.
ANY SIGN OF AN ACANTI ANYWHERE? OR A STAR SHARK?
NO.
WHAT ARE YOU SAYING?
I'M SAYING THE GUY BEHIND YOU SMELLS NERVOUS.
AND HE'S SHIFTY AS ALL #$%*.
I'M GUESSING HE WAS EXPERIMENTING WITH A BROOD QUEEN AND IT GOT AWAY.
I KNOW A THING OR TWO ABOUT EXPERIMENTS THAT GET AWAY.
ME TOO.
HE TRIED TO DEAL WITH HIS MISTAKE BY DESTROYING IT, AND JUST MADE IT WORSE.
ME TOO.
I ALSO KNOW ABOUT THAT.

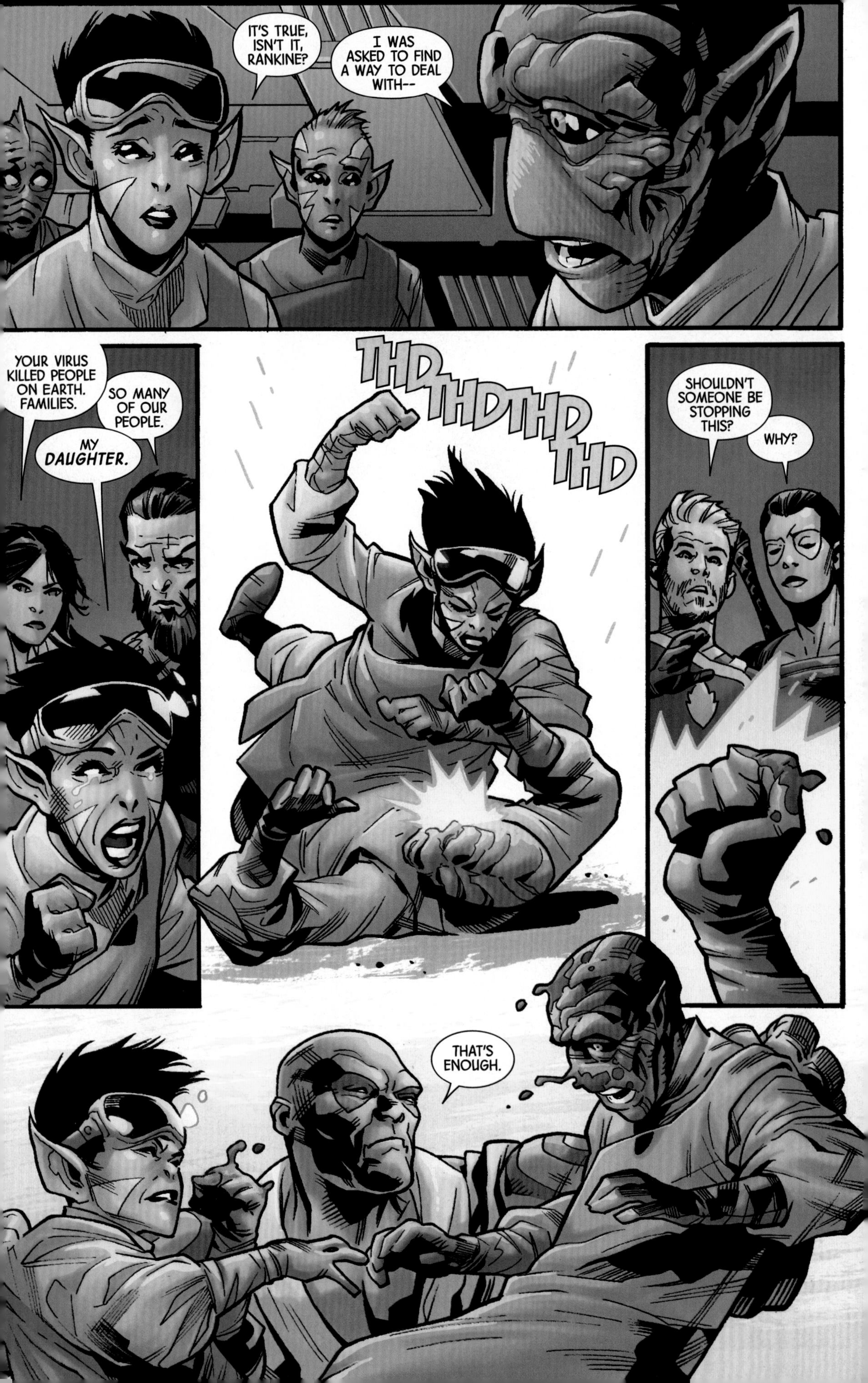
IT'S TRUE, ISN'T IT, RANKINE?
I WAS ASKED TO FIND A WAY TO DEAL WITH--
YOUR VIRUS KILLED PEOPLE ON EARTH. FAMILIES.
SO MANY OF OUR PEOPLE.
MY *DAUGHTER.*
THDTHDTHDTHDTHD
SHOULDN'T SOMEONE BE STOPPING THIS?
WHY?
THAT'S ENOUGH.

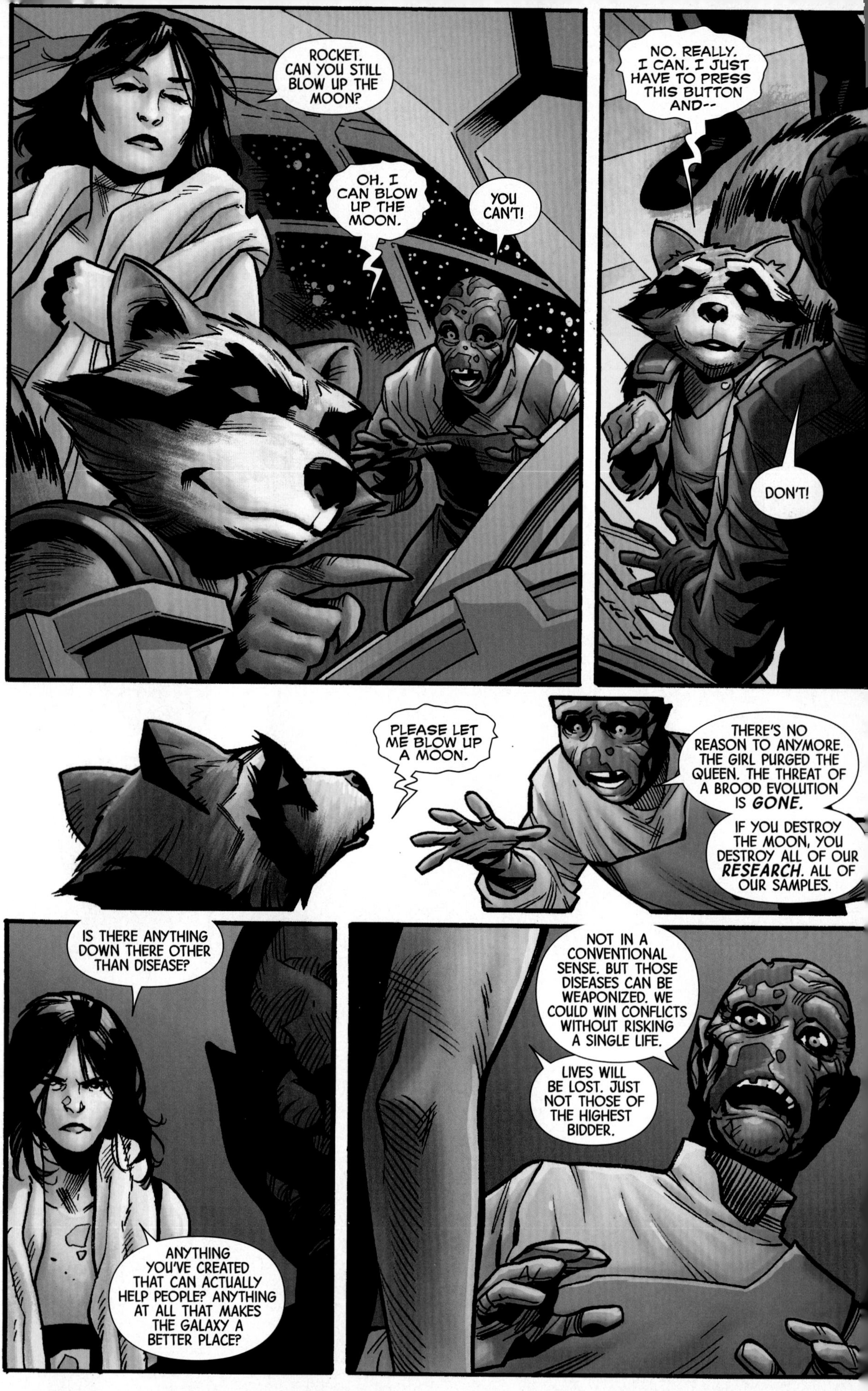
ROCKET. CAN YOU STILL BLOW UP THE MOON?
OH. I CAN BLOW UP THE MOON.
YOU CAN'T!
NO. REALLY. I CAN. I JUST HAVE TO PRESS THIS BUTTON AND--
DON'T!
PLEASE LET ME BLOW UP A MOON.
THERE'S NO REASON TO ANYMORE. THE GIRL PURGED THE QUEEN. THE THREAT OF A BROOD EVOLUTION IS *GONE.*
IF YOU DESTROY THE MOON, YOU DESTROY ALL OF OUR *RESEARCH.* ALL OF OUR SAMPLES.
IS THERE ANYTHING DOWN THERE OTHER THAN DISEASE?
ANYTHING YOU'VE CREATED THAT CAN ACTUALLY HELP PEOPLE? ANYTHING AT ALL THAT MAKES THE GALAXY A BETTER PLACE?
NOT IN A CONVENTIONAL SENSE. BUT THOSE DISEASES CAN BE WEAPONIZED. WE COULD WIN CONFLICTS WITHOUT RISKING A SINGLE LIFE.
LIVES WILL BE LOST. JUST NOT THOSE OF THE HIGHEST BIDDER.

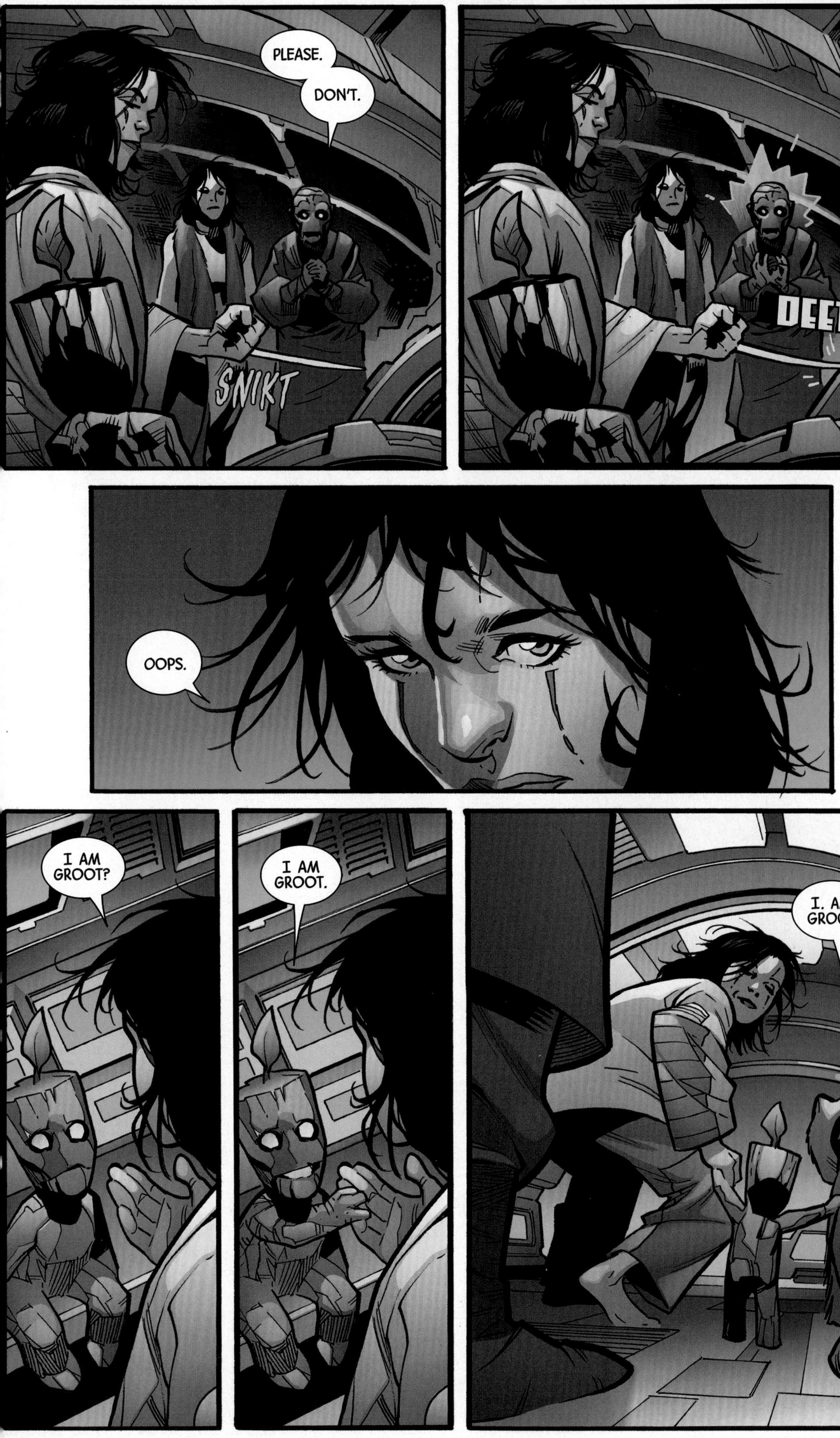
PLEASE.
DON'T.
SNIKT
DEET
OOPS.
I AM GROOT?
I AM GROOT.
I. AM. GROOT.

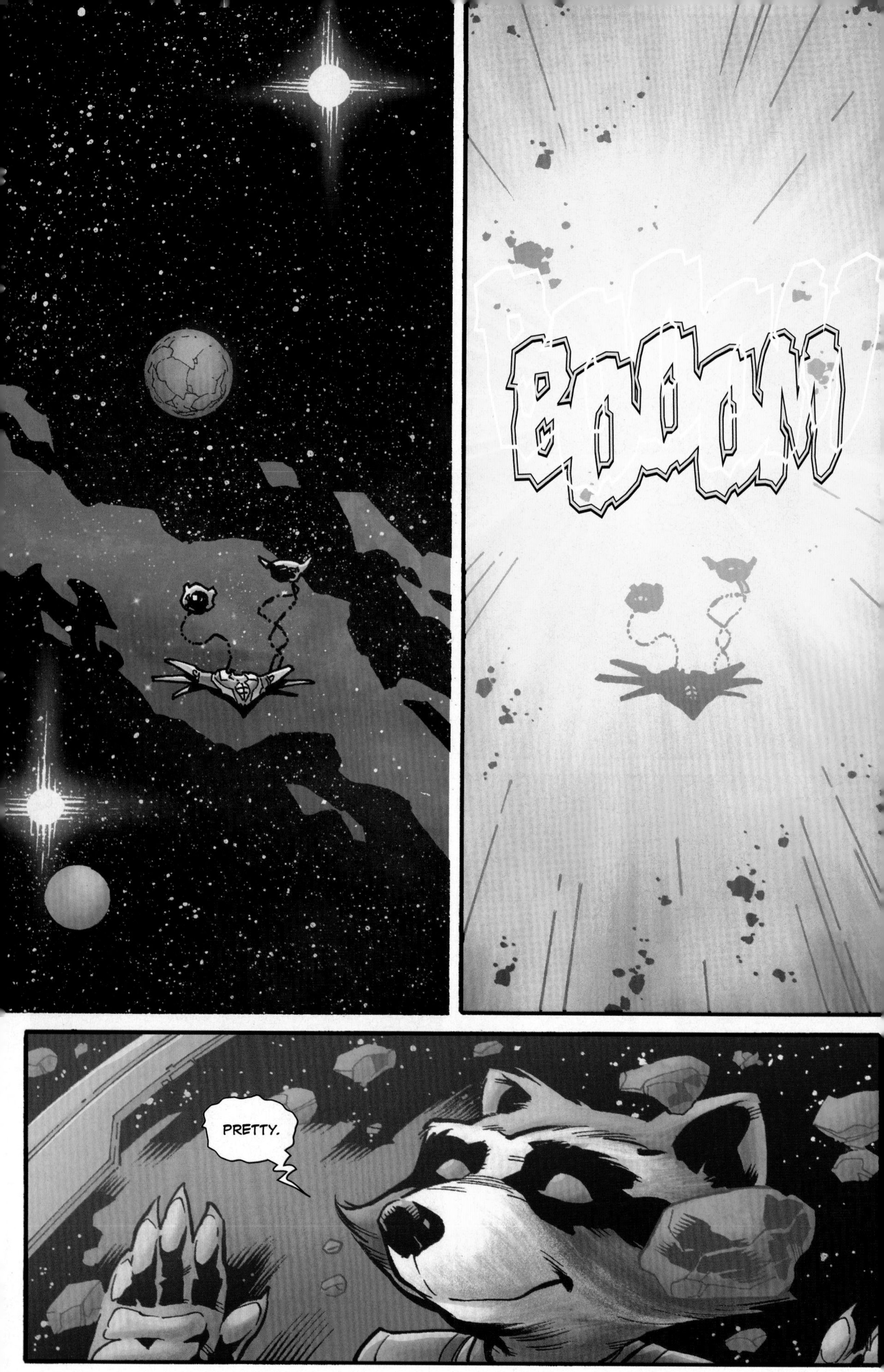
BOOOOM
PRETTY.

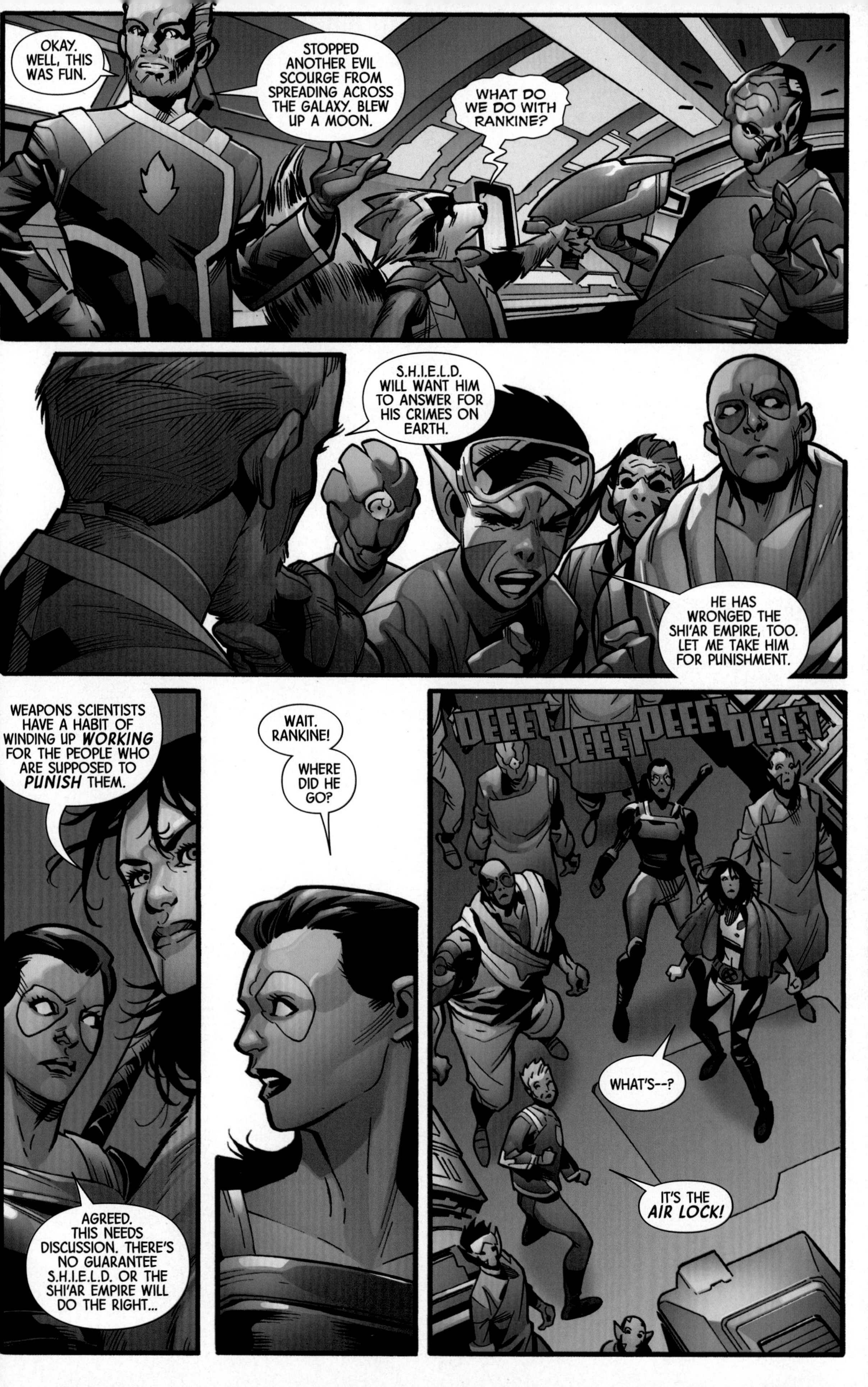
OKAY. WELL, THIS WAS FUN.
STOPPED ANOTHER EVIL SCOURGE FROM SPREADING ACROSS THE GALAXY. BLEW UP A MOON.
WHAT DO WE DO WITH RANKINE?
S.H.I.E.L.D. WILL WANT HIM TO ANSWER FOR HIS CRIMES ON EARTH.
HE HAS WRONGED THE SHI'AR EMPIRE, TOO. LET ME TAKE HIM FOR PUNISHMENT.
WEAPONS SCIENTISTS HAVE A HABIT OF WINDING UP WORKING FOR THE PEOPLE WHO ARE SUPPOSED TO PUNISH THEM.
AGREED. THIS NEEDS DISCUSSION. THERE'S NO GUARANTEE S.H.I.E.L.D. OR THE SHI'AR EMPIRE WILL DO THE RIGHT...
WAIT. RANKINE!
WHERE DID HE GO?
DEEET DEEET DEEET DEEET
WHAT'S--?
IT'S THE AIR LOCK!

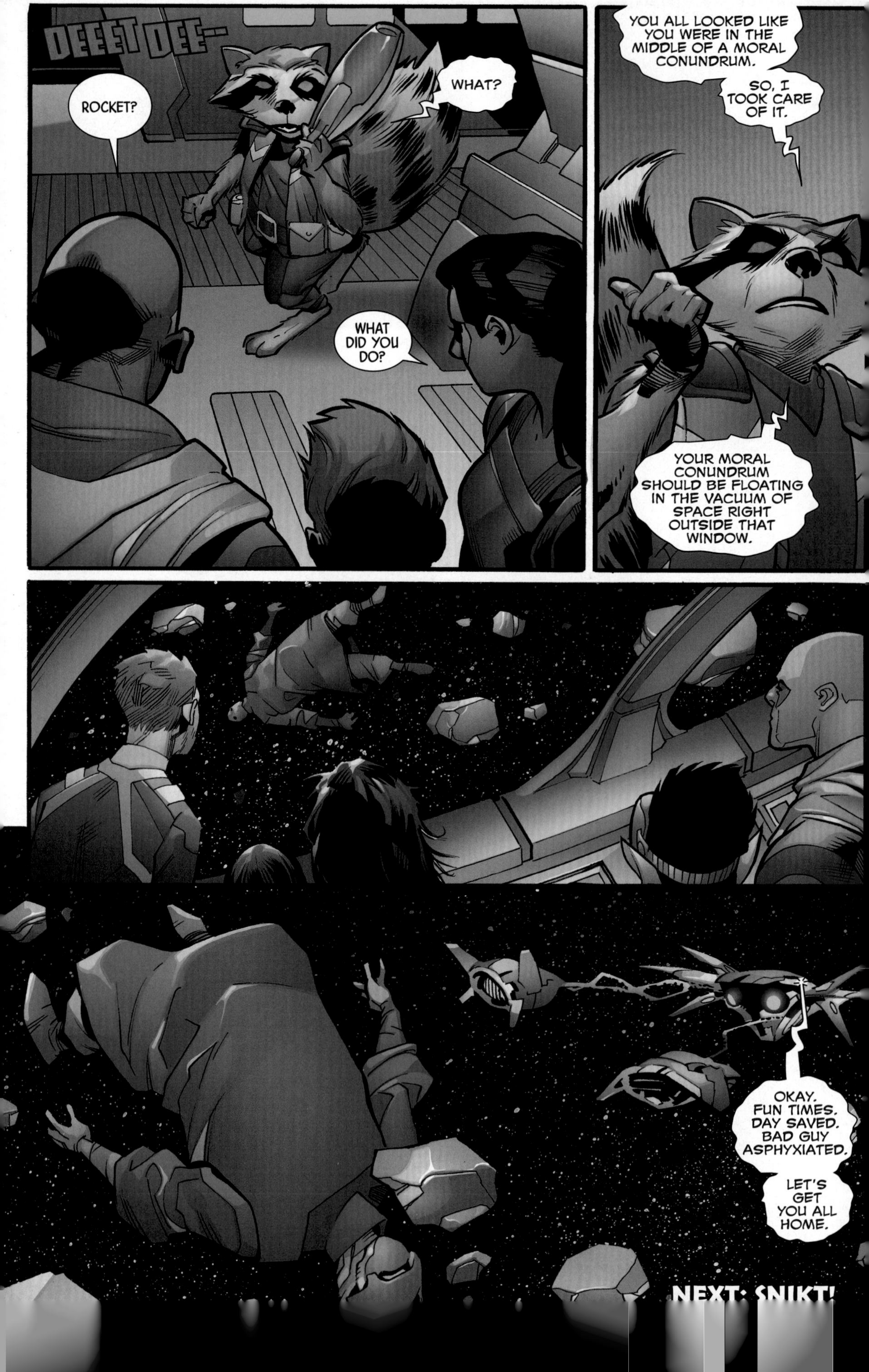
DEEET DEE--
ROCKET?
WHAT?
WHAT DID YOU DO?
YOU ALL LOOKED LIKE YOU WERE IN THE MIDDLE OF A MORAL CONUNDRUM.
SO, I TOOK CARE OF IT.
YOUR MORAL CONUNDRUM SHOULD BE FLOATING IN THE VACUUM OF SPACE RIGHT OUTSIDE THAT WINDOW.
OKAY. FUN TIMES. DAY SAVED. BAD GUY ASPHYXIATED.
LET'S GET YOU ALL HOME.
NEXT: SNIKT!

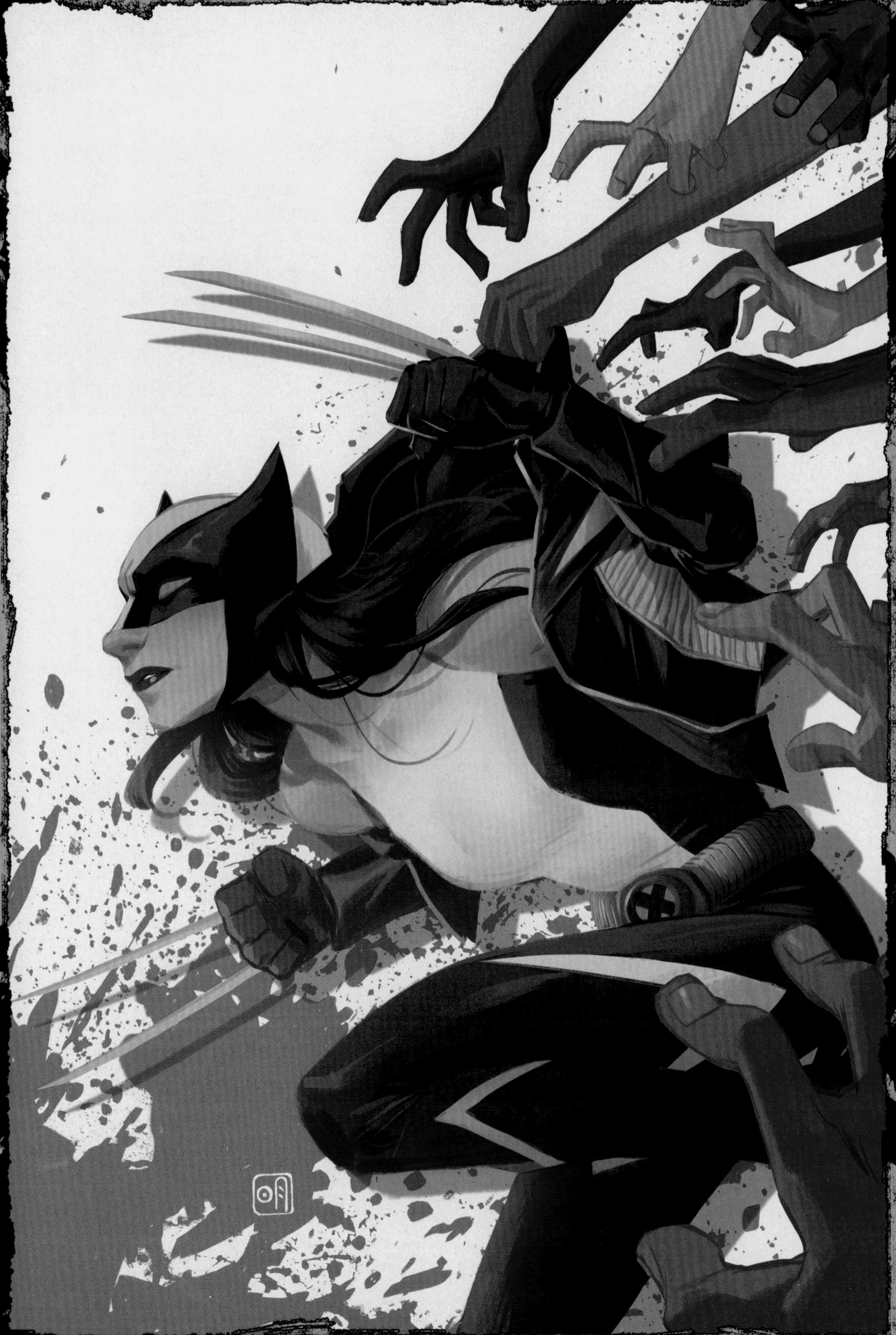

#20 variant by
HELEN CHEN

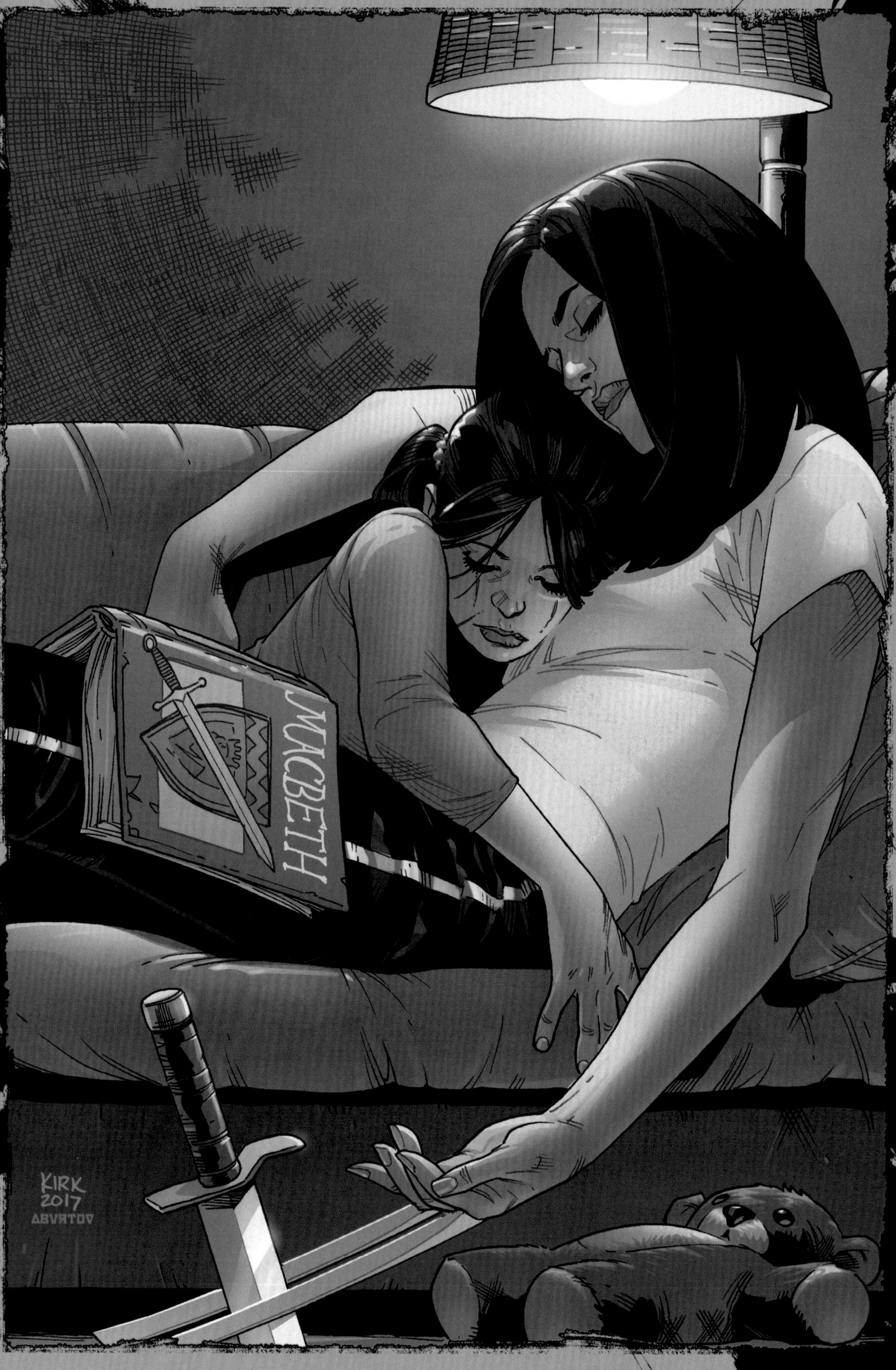
MACBETH
KIRK
2017
ABURTOV

#20 variant by
LEONARD KIRK & **JESUS ABURTOV**

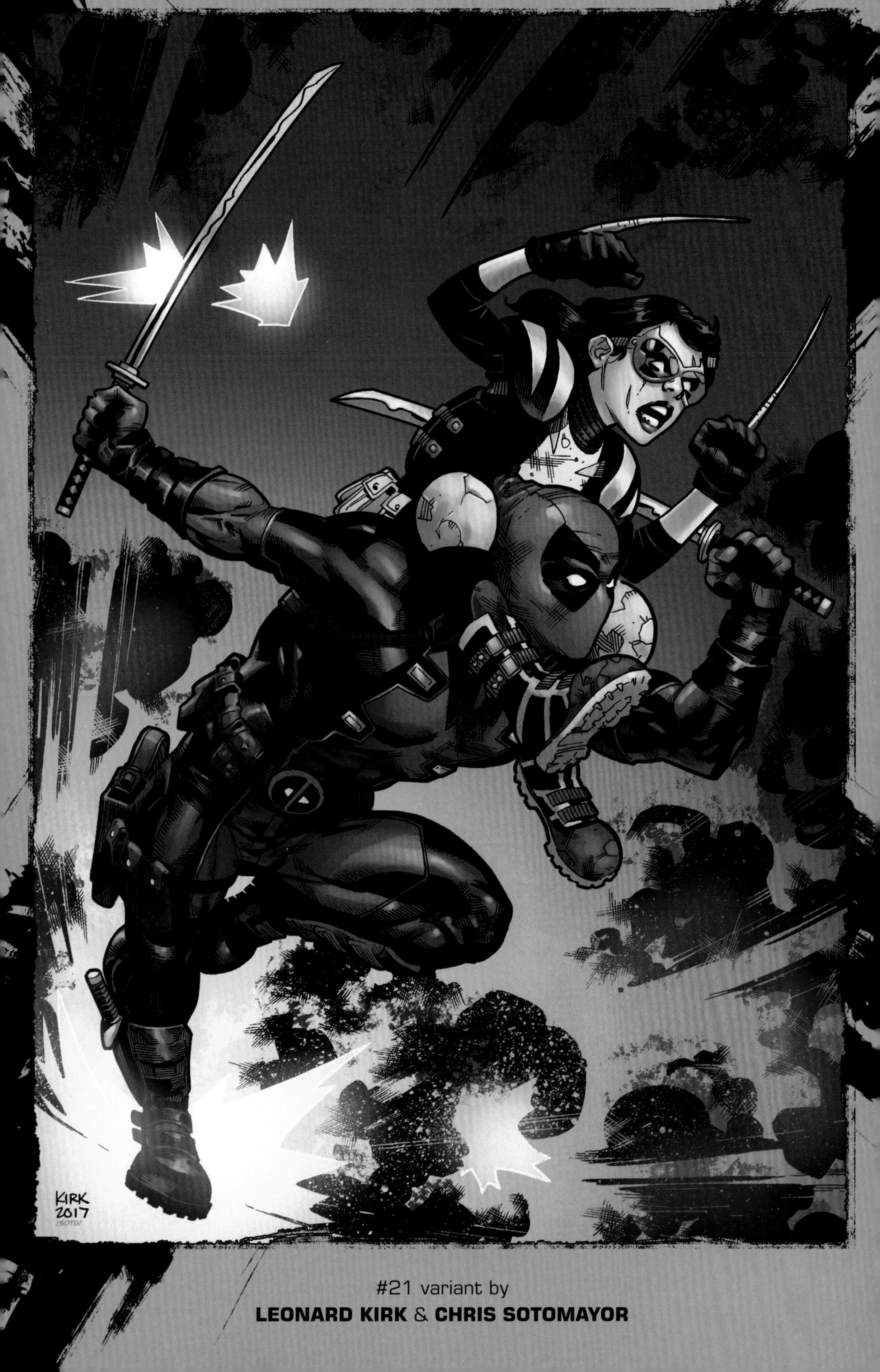
KIRK
2017
¡SOTO!

#21 variant by
LEONARD KIRK & **CHRIS SOTOMAYOR**

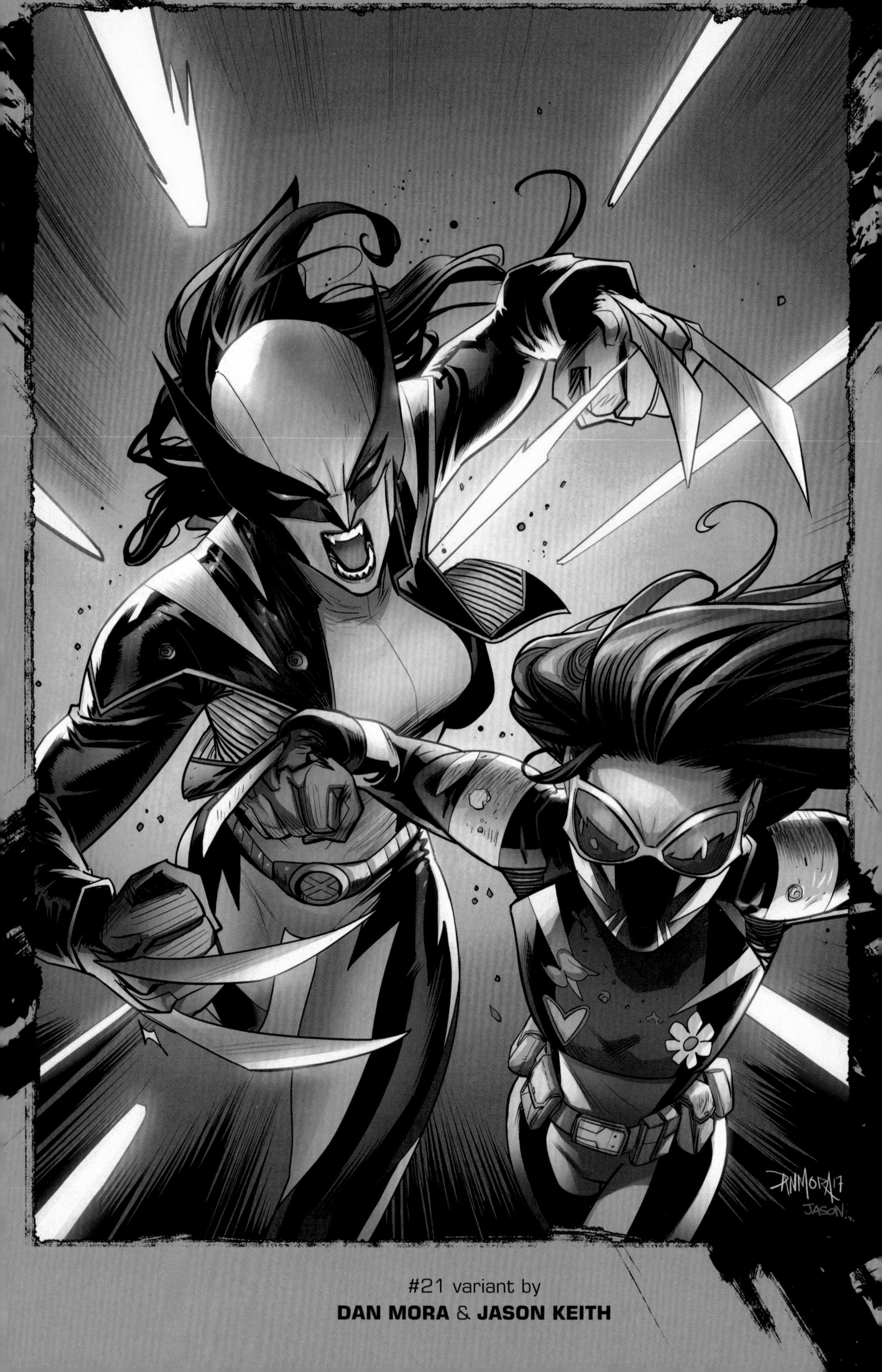

DNMORA'17
JASON

#21 variant by
DAN MORA & **JASON KEITH**

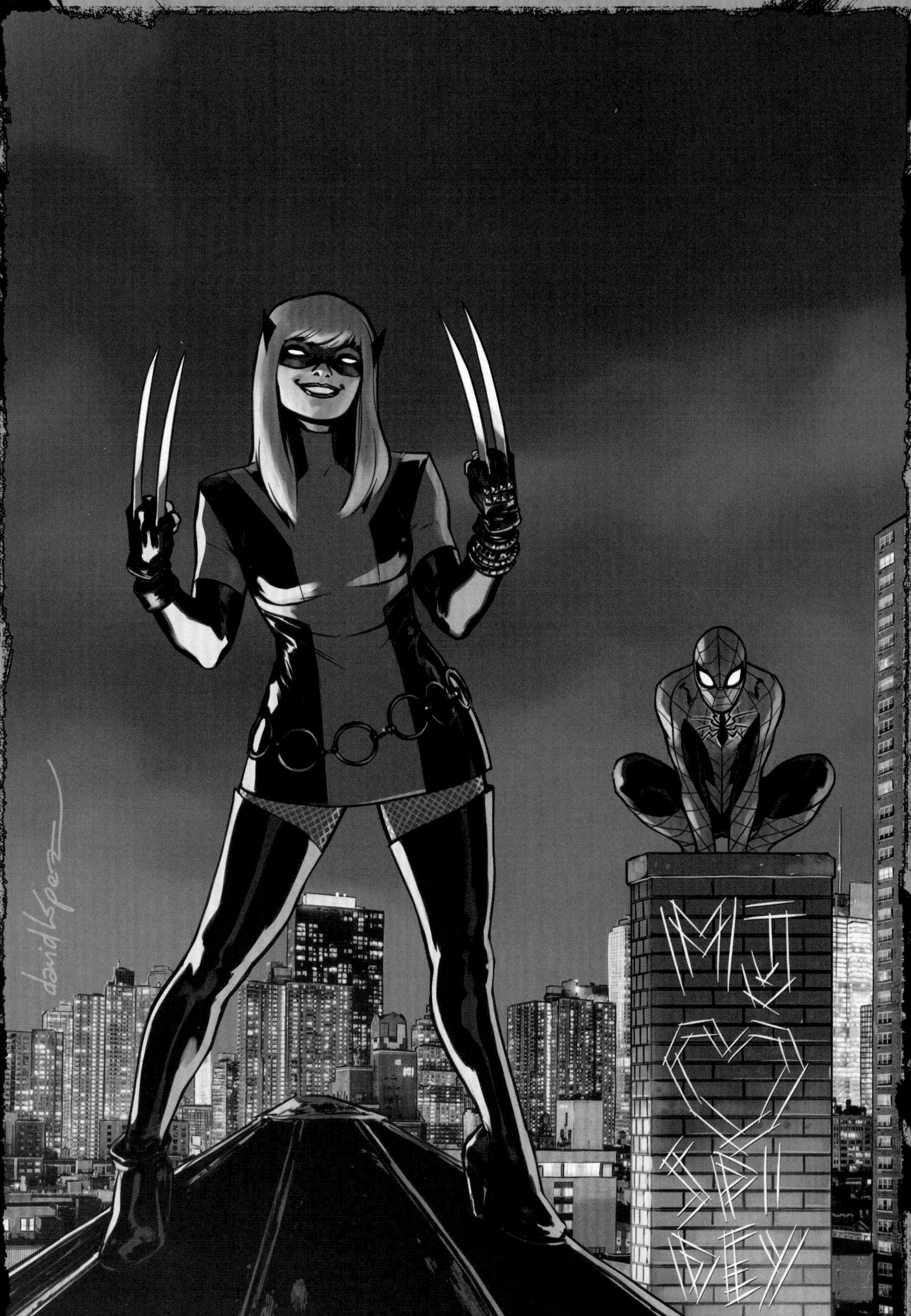
MJ
SPI
DEY

#21 Mary Jane variant by
DAVID LOPEZ

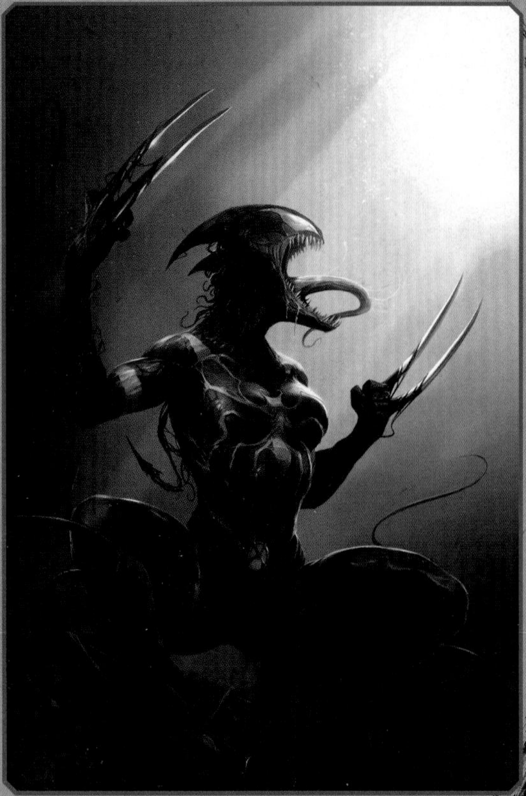

#19 Venomized variant by
FRANCESCO MATTINA

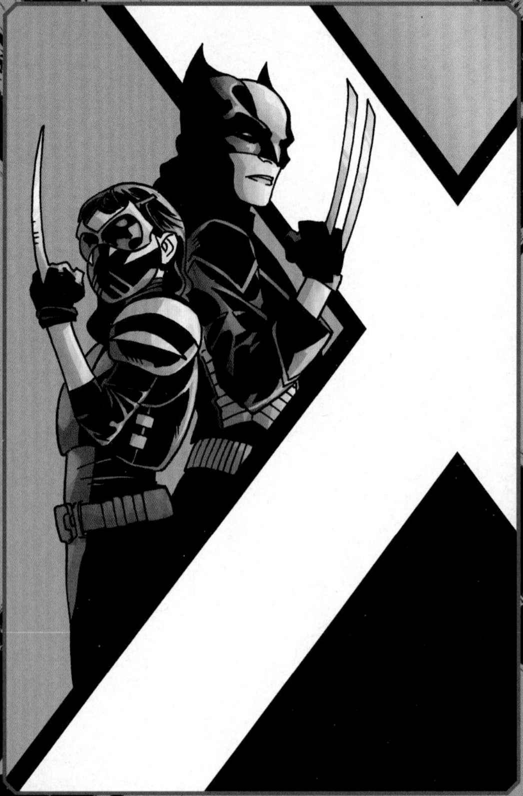

#19 corner box variant by
LEONARD KIRK &
MICHAEL GARLAND

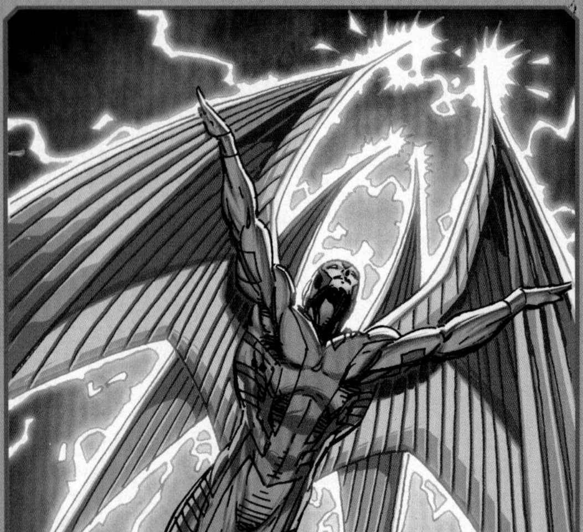
JIMLEE

#22 X-Men variant by
JIM LEE & **ISRAEL SILVA**
with **MICHAEL KELLEHER**

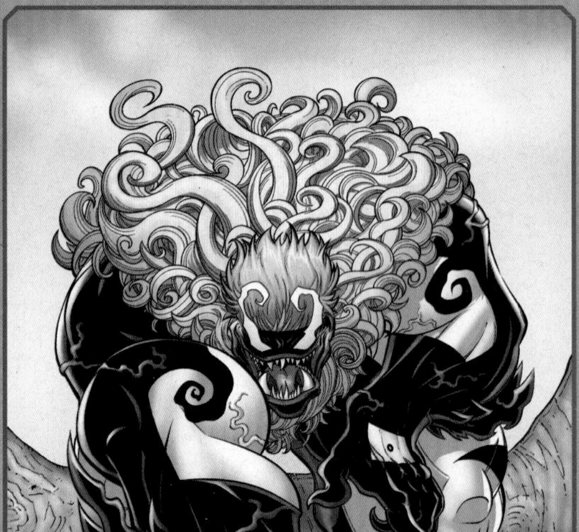

#24 Venomized villians variant by
WILL ROBSON, WALDEN WONG
& **EDGAR DELGADO**